# HOTEL ORGANISATION AND MANAGEMENT – A CRITICAL APPROACH

# HOTEL ORGANISATION AND MANAGEMENT – A CRITICAL APPROACH

M. C. METTI

ANMOL PUBLICATIONS PVT. LTD.
NEW DELHI - 110 002 (INDIA)

**ANMOL PUBLICATIONS PVT. LTD.**

*H.O.:* 4374/4B, Ansari Road, Darya Ganj,
New Delhi-110 002 (India)
Ph.: 23278000, 23261597

*B.O.:* No. 1015, Ist Main Road, BSK IIIrd Stage
IIIrd Phase, IIIrd Block
Bangalore - 560 085 (India)
Visit us at: www.anmolpublications.com

*Hotel Organisation and Management – A Critical Approach*

ISBN 978-81-261-3236-2

PRINTED IN INDIA

Printed at Mehra Offset Press, Delhi.

# Contents

## Contents

# Preface

The guest-focused approach to hospitality management, and other progressive hospitality organizations, is a whole new way of managing. This book blends an explanation of this approach to hospitality management with relevant research findings about managing hospitality organizations.

Hospitality organizations managed their businesses from the customer's or guest's point of view. The way they ran their businesses was not a mere modification of the traditional management principles long taught in business schools. They were using principles, practices, and methods that were part of the emerging services literature plus much that was based largely on their acquired knowledge—gained through hard experience—of the differences between the service industry and smokestack industries.

The material has been detailed by practicing executives in many successful hospitality organizations. A proven principle of hospitality management keys each chapter of this book. Leading hospitality organizations have found these principles to be important, workable, and useful.

They represent the key points to keep in mind when putting the book's material into practice. They can guide hospitality organizations and their managers as they seek to reach the levels of excellence achieved by the benchmark organizations.

Author

Chapter 1

# A Critical Hotel Management Approach

## REWARD MANAGEMENT

The pricing in hotels evinced a lot of interest with the top-end hotels in India justifying the rise in prices at a time when there is a severe shortage of rooms. It is time that Indian hotel rates match up to international standards since there is a rise in demand of five per cent matched with minimal or no supply. When compared with other international cities like New York, the service standards in India are better.

Taking steps towards the right direction, the property to increase entry-level salaries in order to reduce the high turnover. From the hotel point of view, staff retention has become vital. Hotels also need to tell the hotel management institutes about the hard facts of the industry so that students don't find themselves on a wrong footing when they become professionals. About 20 per cent of those leaving jobs in hotels are essentially doing so for higher salaries and position.

There is need to bring in an innovative approach and thinking out-of-the-box to achieve success in every parametre of business. Technology is definitely the way to go, and with its help hotels must try and give their guests control of how they want their experience to be.

The interest in reward management has been given added impetus by the rewriting of the UK Institute of Personnel and

Development (IPD) professional education syllabus, which now contains a dedicated set of units under the generic title 'Employee Reward' and a specific textbook for the subject. Prior to this, matters concerning payment systems fell under two separate headings-employee relations (which dealt with pay bargaining and legislation affecting pay) and employee resourcing (which dealt with matters such as pay structures, job evaluation and benefits such as sick pay and pensions). The new IPD syllabus therefore gives a higher profile to the remuneration aspects of personnel management practice (although collective bargaining over pay is still located within the employee relations syllabus).

This more holistic approach to pay and benefits matters has not, to date, been reflected in the academic literature, where there remains a strong dichotomy between the 'macro-economic' literature of the labour economists and the human resource management literature. The former is primarily concerned with the effect of pay determination upon the wider economy and, in particular, the impact upon employment, productivity and inflation.

The latter, in contrast, draws both upon the industrial relations preoccupation with the regulation of the employment relationship and also on the organisational behaviour literature, with its emphasis upon motivation and equity theory. In recent years, the occupational psychology literature has been of increasing importance, but of course the determination of pay continues to be of interest to industrial sociologists too. Increasingly, however, there is a need for a more integrated approach to the study of remuneration and the reward management paradigm might provide a useful vehicle for this to develop.

The existing reward management textbooks, largely practitioner oriented, concentrate heavily on techniques rather than theory, and neglect the role which collective bargaining, and employee voice, continues to play in many UK organisations. Armstrong's key IPD text has only a one-page reference to collective bargaining and does not mention the fact that around a third of establishments (and indeed many of the larger employers) still negotiate about pay with trade unions and that over two-fifths of employees have their pay determined in this way.

The parallel employee relations text by Gennard and Judge also has little to say about pay bargaining systems. Most importantly, the impact of power relations within the workplace and their influence upon reward management policies and practice are glossed over in the essentially managerialist IPD texts-the IPD Core Personnel and Development text by Marchington and Wilkinson being an honourable exception to this approach.

**A Critical Approach**

This book attempts to provide an integrated approach to reward management, drawing on the analytical traditions of industrial relations and the insights provided by specialist writers. It brings together the work of a number of contributors from a range of disciplines within the generic field of 'reward management'. Some are academics and some are consultants. The book is not intended to provide prescriptions for managers handling current problems; there are other texts that already do this job.

Rather, it is intended as a guide through some of the themes and issues that are of current concern to employers, employees and government. The subtitle is a 'critical text', an important signal that this book seeks to provide a more theoretical and discursive approach to the subject than is normally found in practitioner texts. Each not only summarises recent research on a particular aspect of reward management but also provides a critique of that research. This enables the student of reward management, be it at undergraduate or postgraduate level, IPD syllabus focused or not, a range of views about key aspects of managing payment systems.

The overall thrust of this challenges the unitary or normative approaches taken in many other texts. It seeks to present a dispassionate analysis of trends and patterns and will hopefully provide students of both reward management and employee relations with some stimulating reading which will supplement the traditional material found on the human resources management (HRM) syllabus. It will also, hopefully, be of interest to the 'reflective practitioner' seeking new and independent thinking about reward systems.

As indicated above, reward management has attracted increased attention in recent years. Pay structures and systems of pay determination are socially determined and are influenced by the context and culture in which they are implemented. Most importantly, they reflect power relations in the workplace between employers and employees. Inevitably this means that they have changed significantly over time and must be understood in historical context.

The renewal of interest in this field is part of a wider concern about changes in work and employment. For this reason we look first at the historical background, considering changes in work organisation and labour markets over the last twenty years. We consider the significance of innovation in work processes and technologies. Second, we look at the political framework for discussions and consider the ways in which it has affected the context for reward management.

Third, we point to the associated changes in management theory and fashion-to the growth in human resource management and the ideological impetus towards 'individualisation' of the employment contract. We then relate the book to the themes identified. In the Coda to this book we provide a conclusion and discuss the impact of 'New Labour' on reward systems.

### *Work Organisation and Processes*

Although pay systems have been of recurrent interest during the twentieth century, there has been little agreement about their potential or actual role. Whilst the concept of a job is founded on a two-way commitment-the promise of pay in return for work performed, there are diverse views about the significance and composition of pay. The globalisation of business, moreover, raises questions about management across frontiers. To what extent does national culture affect the design of pay systems? How do multinational corporations tackle questions of international employment and reward?

Pay structures and the dispersion of pay reflect fundamental social values. Should there be a minimum level of reward for work below which no one should fall? If so, how should it be set and who should decide the level? Narrow pay differentials suggest a society with more egalitarian values, whilst a yawning gulf between the highest earners and the lowest paid points to wide social distinctions between these social groups. A widening of differentials may be taken as a proxy for increasing social inequality.

Pay systems are an arena for conflict, wherein norms may be established and questions of equity are raised. There are questions about the responsibilities that business organisations may have to the wider community. To what extent should employers carry social costs for their employees-for example, for sickness, medical care, or old age? Will such arrangements disadvantage those who are outside of the labour market, or will they permit the state to provide more amply for this group? To what extent should the state ensure that social benefits are standardised at least at a minimum level and what impact will state benefits have on labour market participation?

There are questions too about the meaning that pay may have for the individual recipient and the extent to which it can be regarded as a means to improving performance. Questions of motivation have been explored but not resolved, and such issues are best understood within their particular social and historical context since questions of culture, class and gender are relevant to our understanding. How important are pay and benefits as motivational tools when compared with the satisfaction of doing a particular job and doing it well? Money rewards are often perceived to be only a part of the real benefit derived from work.

Theories of motivation point to the higher satisfaction that can derive from a job well done, but this seems to be a consideration that is applied more frequently to women's work in the caring professions than to the senior male executive in corporate life.

A discussion of reward management in practice must necessarily be located in the context of wider economic and social change. There is no easy or automatic correlation between forms of production and payment systems but some broad trends are evident. The legacy of (the overwhelmingly male) craft-based payment systems of the nineteenth century was challenged towards the end of the century by management theories and practices that sharpened the division of labour between the planning and organisation of tasks and their execution. The 'scientific management' theories of Frederick Winslow Taylor epitomised these developments. He asserted the principles of direct control through which management aggregates to itself the knowledge base that was previously the prerogative of the workforce.

Through this process an organisational 'brain' is created, responsible for planning and work organisation. This was compounded by assembly-line production with management activities increasingly conducted separately from the shop-floor, where workers were to be spurred on to high performance by the use of incentive payments. The distinction between management and production processes that became more marked from the end of the nineteenth century was paralleled by a division within the workforce, with differential treatment in terms of pay and conditions for management, professional and administrative staff on the one hand and production workers on the other.

Although time-based payment remained at the core of the employment relationship, payment was defined for employees associated with the management of the enterprise in terms of annual and monthly payments (salaries), whilst for production workers, calculations were often based on the notion of an hourly rate of pay, with associated incentive payments.

From the end of the First World War mass production came to be associated with standardized pay arrangements, often negotiated at industry level, through multi-employer bargaining. Pay was set on the basis of a 'rate for the job' and each job was a 'precisely defined aggregate of well-specified tasks and seniority'. As Mahoney comments, 'the concept of job was the unifying concept in the Scientific Management approach to organisation and management'.

Moreover, the development of such systems led to 'the development and application of a concept of job ownership expressed in the labour movement and collective bargaining'. Trade union representation was based around particular skills or grades, and trade unions were engaged in a struggle to defend the interests and to improve the circumstances of those sections of workers-most often men-whose interests they represented.

Time rates of pay, often determined through multi-employer collective bargaining, were often supplemented at establishment level with incentive payments which, together with shift and overtime pay, contributed significantly to total earnings for manual workers. Arrangements for administrative, professional and managerial staff were less standardised than those for craft or production workers in the private sector, but the principles of equity and public accountability that operated in the public sector encouraged a formalisation and standardisation on the basis of a recognised rate for the job.

Working women were at a significant disadvantage because social values emphasised women's domestic role and, outside of specific sectors of employment, such as the textile and garment industries, the social definition of 'skill' tended to exclude them from higher-paid work. Yet their growing labour market participation, coupled with changes in the law, encouraged women to challenge traditional patterns of discrimination. The notion of 'fair' employment standards that attached to the internal labour market provided a context for women to claim equality of treatment in terms of employment opportunity and pay-as Sue Hastings demonstrates.

Over recent decades there have been fundamental changes in the nature of work and in the management of the employment relationship. There has been a significant shift in the pattern of employment, a reduction in organisational size and a change in workforce composition, which have together redefined the context for reward practices. The reduction in manufacturing employment and the rise in unemployment during the 1980s were accompanied by a growth in the service sector that continued steadily during the 1990s.

Employment in the heavily unionised areas of manufacturing and heavy industry in the UK-in engineering, mining, shipbuilding and steel-diminished whilst employment in the retail industry, in hospitality, the leisure industry, finance and business services increased. As full-time male employment dwindled, so part-time and predominantly female employment became more significant. The number of temporary workers and of temporary agency workers increased too.

The decline in male, manufacturing activity called into question pay structures that had been associated with 'blue-collar' employment. The application of information and communication technologies (ICTs) blurred some of the distinctions between 'blue-collar' and 'white-collar' workers. Changes in work organisation through lean production (fewer workers) have been associated with changes in job content and in status-generating conflicting pressures-both for upskilling and for deskilling and creating the potential for new forms of control in the employment relationship within and across these groups.

For many years it seemed that the concentration and centralisation of capital would inevitably be associated with a growth in organisational size as technology advanced and economies developed. Yet larger corporations now emphasise the benefits of decentralisation and business units have distinctive identities within complex corporate portfolios. Smaller, accountable units can more easily be bought and sold and work can be relocated from one country or region to another. Larger firms have downsized whilst public sector organisations have been subject to compulsory competitive tendering and contracting out. Since the Bolton Committee's report in the early 1970s, small and medium sized enterprises have been seen as the engine of economic growth in the UK. Establishment size is, in general, smaller than in the past and may be small even within global corporations.

Firm and establishment size is critical to reward management for a number of reasons. Larger establishments are more likely to employ personnel or compensation specialists and to be unionised. They are more likely to use job evaluation and to have recognised grading structures. They are more likely to offer the benefits of continuous employment too, with a possibility of career progression within a salary structure of some kind.

Smaller businesses with simpler, flatter structures-particularly those that are not subsidiaries of larger parent companies-are more likely to be associated with direct forms of management and communication and simpler payment structures. There is clear evidence that the lowest-paid workers, often associated with small businesses, have fairly simple payment systems with few additions to the basic rate of pay.

Collective bargaining arrangements have been undermined and the scope of bargaining has diminished under the impact of these changes. Increased product market pressures and the drive for improved performance have encouraged employers to break with employers' associations and to seek to determine pay and conditions in relation to the needs and the performance of the individual business. Changes in work organisation and a growing employer interest in flexibility have encouraged the process of decentralisation.

Managerial discretion at enterprise and establishment level was enhanced where multi-employer collective agreements were dismantled-in the docks, engineering, banking and television. Pay determination through industry-level bargaining was ended in at least sixteen industries covering more than one million employees in the late 1980s. Even where unions continue to be recognised, they are now less likely to be involved in pay bargaining. By 1998 only 41 per cent of the workforce was covered by collective bargaining and only 14 per cent by multi-employer collective bargaining.

At the individual level, the process of downsizing and the widespread experience of redundancy in the 1980s and 1990s undermined established notions of employment security and career progression-at least for the groups that had been previous beneficiaries, notably white-collar employees who had expectations of a 'career'. Leaner and flatter organisations have more limited scope for upward mobility, although those with key skills in the new technologies may have choices about movement within and between organisations.

Paradoxically, the diminished opportunities for progression within internal labour markets have been accompanied by increased emphasis on human resources as key assets and on growing concern to reward individual development and performance in ways that do not necessarily imply promotion. Performance-related pay and competence-based payment systems have supported such developments. It is a process that challenges the traditions of job evaluation and the 'rate for the job-including equal pay for work of equal value-which have been so important to notions of internal equity in the past.

Changing technologies and new forms of work organisation play an important part in defining the framework for employment too. Information and communication technologies (ICTs) have eroded traditional skills and grading structures associated with apprenticeship training for (mostly) male entrants. Employers now seek new or enhanced skills that facilitate the rapid pace of ICT innovation. The reconfiguration of work processes and the demands of knowledge-based technologies mean that employees must adapt rapidly and use their skills and their discretion in the way that tasks are performed. Effective business performance relies on individual performance and seems to give further support to the notion of payment for the person, rather than payment for the job. It may be associated with forms of skill-based payments, with reward for the acquisition of skill or payment intended to mould behaviour and encourage greater responsiveness to change.

These changes in organisational structures and processes have not taken place in a vacuum. The political and economic context is also key to understanding the changes in pay which have taken place in Britain over the last twenty years.

### *The Eeconomic Context*

The election of Margaret Thatcher's Conservative government in 1979 heralded a period of major change in British politics. Elected on a radical right-wing manifesto, which sought to break the mould of existing consensus policies on employment and industrial relations matters, the years of Conservative governments between 1979 and 1997 saw a gradual erosion of existing labour market institutions. This was to be achieved through legislation designed to free business from government regulation on the one hand and to limit the freedom of trade unions to regulate employers' behaviour on the other. There was also some diminution in individual employment rights, although this was tempered by increasing European regulatory measures.

This is not the place to discuss in detail the ideological basis of the post-1979 Conservative government and its effects upon the employment relationship. This is covered elsewhere. Suffice to say that the Conservatives borrowed heavily, at least in their rhetoric, from the neo-classical economists of the New Right in both the USA and Britain. The government therefore rejected the post-war consensus belief in a planned economy and a regulated labour market in favour of neo-classical theories of supply and demand and the 'unseen hand of the market'.

Attempts to control economic growth (and hence prices, wages and employment) through statutory (or indeed voluntary) prices and incomes policies were rejected and unemployment rose to post-war record levels. Unemployment never fell below 1.5 million in the 1980s and 1990s whilst it never exceeded 1.5 million in the 1960s and 1970s. The growth in unemployment was seen by the Conservatives as a necessary discipline to curb trade union pay demands and high inflation, the latter seen as a direct result of trade union intervention in the labour market.

In the private sector rising joblessness acted as a sharp brake upon earnings growth; consequently pay settlement levels fell rapidly in the early 1980s. At the same time new trade union legislation and the introduction of compulsory competitive tendering in the public sector weakened the power of trade unions in both the private and public sectors. The collapse of many traditional manufacturing industries in the early 1980s, coupled to the growth of new service sector companies, however, was to be a more important element in reducing the coverage of collective bargaining.

There was also a dramatic shift in the balance between the private and public sectors within the economy, with a considerable decline in the size of the public sector. Large parts of publicly owned industry and the public utilities were sold to the private sector and the remaining public services were opened up to private competition in the delivery of services to the public.

Privatisation of the nationalised industries was to lead to major changes in pay arrangements for those employed in them, not least a substantial pay increase for senior managers. Compulsory competitive tendering for public services had significant effects upon the pay and conditions of staff working in these services, both those employed by the private contractors and those employed directly.

### The Rhetoric and Reality

If we seek to discover the views of the Conservative governments from 1979 to 1997 on pay matters, we must look in two places. First, we must consider their general rhetoric and stated objectives and specific legislative changes. Second, we must consider how they managed the pay and conditions of their own employees in the state sector.

In terms of the former, the government adopted a policy that encouraged employers to abandon various aspects of traditional pay determination. The political agenda on pay was set out by Kenneth Clarke, then Minister of State at the Department of Employment, in a speech to the City University Business School in February 1987. He stated that: 'We must move towards a system more clearly based on market forces, on demand and supply, on competition and on ability to pay'. He went on to call for the ending of the national pay round, the going rate, comparability, job evaluation and national pay bargaining. He stated:

If we can move to a system where pay increases are primarily based on performance, merit, company profitability and demand and supply in the local labour market, we will dethrone once and for all the annual pay round and the belief that pay increases do not have to be earned. Ten years later, in 1996, the President of the Board of Trade, Ian Lang, would argue that:

Payment systems in Britain have been transformed over the last decade. The era when most workers were paid the same 'rate for the job' with little or no regard to their performance-or to business and local labour market conditions-is at an end.

In terms of the legislative programme, there was little in the way of new law specifically about pay, as opposed to the large amount of trade union legislation throughout the period. The major legislative changes were as follows:

- The repeal in 1980 of Schedule 11 of the Employment Protection Act, which had allowed claims to the Central Arbitration Committee that an employer was not observing industry-recognised terms and conditions, or was paying less than the 'general level' in industries without collective bargaining.
- The ending in 1983 of the Fair Wages Resolution, which had first been introduced in 1891 and which allowed the government to lay down minimum terms and conditions for those employed on government contracts.
- The Social Security Act 1983 which transferred the responsibility for state sickness benefit from the government to employers with the introduction of Statutory Sick Pay (SSP).
- The Wages Act 1986, which repealed the Truck Acts and introduced the right of employers to pay employees by credit transfer rather than in cash. This Act also reformed the existing Wages Councils by abolishing some and greatly simplifying the content of the wages orders of those remaining, including the exclusion of young people under the age of 21 from coverage.
- The various Finance Acts encouraging the growth of employee financial participation. The government established the legal framework for share ownership, profit-sharing and profit-related pay.
- The Social Security Act 1986 allowing employees to opt out of SERPS and out of their company occupational pension schemes in favour of private 'money purchase' schemes.
- The final abolition of the remaining twenty-six Wages Councils in Britain under the 1993 Trade Union Reform and Employment Rights Act (although the three agricultural wages boards were to remain).

There were also, of course, changes caused by European employment and health and safety legislation, which tended to strengthen minimum rights in employment. They included the 1983 amendment to the Equal Pay Act, which introduced the concept of 'equal value' in grading systems, and the 1993 Working Time Directive, which set limits to working hours and provided for the first time a minimum statutory enticements to paid holidays. The implementation of the latter was delayed until 1998 in the face of British government hostility.

The government's views on pay impacted directly on public sector workers. The earlier breakdown of the Labour government's approach to voluntary pay restraint-the 'Social Contract' had led to the outbreak of strikes over pay restraint in the public services during the winter of 1978. The establishment of the Standing Commission on Pay Comparability under Professor Hugh Clegg to sort out these various public sector disputes came too late to avoid defeat for Labour.

In contrast to the private sector, where the Conservatives saw no need for direct intervention on pay, in the public sector strict pay limits were continued (these had been initiated by the previous Labour government in 1976). The Conservatives, however, honoured the commitments of the Clegg Commission, leading to substantial 'catching up' awards in public sector pay. The 'pay provision figures' of the early 1980s were followed by less stringent controls during the Lawson boom years between 1986 and 1991 until strict limits were again imposed from 1992.

Within the remaining public services (civil service, NHS and local government), the government made major changes in pay determination arrangements. These included the ending of collective bargaining for nurses and professions allied to medicine in the NHS in 1983 and for school teachers in England and Wales in 1992. New pay review bodies were established for both of these groups.

Moves to relate pay more closely to individual performance were begun in the civil service in the 1980s and spread quickly to other parts of the public sector, although with limited success in the NHS and local government. Individual performance-related pay became the norm for all civil servants but remained patchy in application in the NHS and local government, where it normally only applies to managers. There were also attempts to match pay more closely to market forces, through the use of pay supplements and extra benefits for those with skills in short supply. This was particularly the case in the mid- to late 1980s, when the Lawson boom and deregulation of financial services led to the 'vacuuming' of scarce skills from the public sector into the private sector.

Lastly, the government pursued a long-term objective of introducing decentralised pay determination. This was achieved with the establishment of 'delegated' pay bargaining in the civil service from April 1996 and the introduction of two-tier bargaining arrangements into NHS Trusts from February 1995. While decentralisation in the civil service remains, the NHS arrangements failed and led to a return to national bargaining. A new national pay system is currently under discussion with the NHS unions.

### *The Outcomes of Policy*

The economic outcomes of the Conservatives' policy on pay can be examined under three headings-income distribution, productivity and labour costs. In general, average earnings increased by a greater degree for women than for men between April 1979 and April 1997 (371 per cent for women compared to 303 per cent for men). This reflected some limited desegregation of women's work and the growth in employment in areas of better paid, female non-manual work. It also reflected the growing impact of equal pay laws, but women's weekly earnings remained at 73 per cent of men's in 1997. Taking into account inflation, however, both men and women saw a real increase in pay.

Throughout the 1980s pay increases in the UK continued to outstrip inflation and indeed were greater than most of the UK's competitors. As Kessler and Bayliss (1998) comment, this fact is intriguing, given the very high unemployment throughout the period and the decline of trade union power. Earnings growth slowed in the early 1990s, following the major recession at the start of the decade, and has remained flat since, although earnings growth continues to outstrip inflation and is still high in comparison to competitor countries.

There were also changes in the distribution of earnings. Non-manual workers' pay increased much faster than that for manual workers and the earnings distribution widened considerably. While earnings continued to grow moderately for the lower paid, increases were much greater for the higher paid. The growing divide between the bottom decile of earners and the top was to be a major feature of the Conservative years. The relative wealth of the highest earners, moreover, was enhanced further by reductions in taxation which meant that they kept much more of their income.

This widening of the earnings distribution was only exceeded by the USA. The growing inequality in the UK has also been stronger than elsewhere. Looking at national sources, only New Zealand in the second half of the 1980s had inequality growing as rapidly as in the UK. In comparison, in many OECD countries the earnings distribution remained stable in the 1980s and in the case of Germany, France and Italy it actually narrowed. This contrary trend continued into the 1990s with the UK differing from the other countries in experiencing a widening earnings distribution.

It was senior management pay that was driving wage inflation during the 1980s, rather than trade union pressures. The growth of senior management and board members' pay was to become an increasingly difficult political issue for the Conservatives, especially when the newly appointed executives of the privatised public utilities were seen to have been given excessively large pay increases to bring them up to the level of other private sector managers.

There was also a profusion of generous share option schemes which added to the total pay package. Given the government's rhetoric both about workers needing to demonstrate pay restraint and about the importance of linking pay to performance, the fact that many senior managers were being granted extremely generous increases, even when their companies had experienced poor performance, produced some hostile public and press reaction. Investors also began to show concern about how pay decisions were taken for such managers.

As a result, three attempts at 'self-regulation' by employers were tried-the Cadbury Report in 1993, the Greenbury Report in 1995 and the Hampel Report in 1998. These recommended various degrees of voluntary regulation through introducing more independent and transparent pay determination mechanisms but 'Top Pay' remains a political issue for the current government. There is still a threat that statutory regulation may be necessary.

According to R. Dickens, in addition to these clear rises in wage differentials between the highest and lowest earners, there has also been an equally important rise in within-group pay dispersion. There are two possible reasons for this. The first is that it reflects a growing demand for skilled and educated workers and greater discrimination by employers in evaluating employee performance. The second reason is the changing role of labour market institutions. Gosling and Machin estimate that 20 per cent of the growing inequality can be attributed to the decline in unionization. Similarly Bell and Pitt find that 20 per cent of the rise in variation in earnings is explained by declining union density.

In terms of productivity, there was a decline at the beginning of the 1980s but thereafter there were substantial improvements, especially in manufacturing. Between 1980 and 1996 output per person increased by 38.8 per cent within the whole economy and by 95 per cent within manufacturing. According to Metcalf (1989), the improvement in productivity was due to three factors: the shock effects of the recession in the early 1980s; more competitive product markets; and the reduction in union power.

However, the view that Conservative policies were an unmitigated success has been challenged Certainly the 'success' of the 1980s was not followed in the 1990s. If we compare labour productivity in various OECD countries in the period 1979 to 1995, UK growth was ahead of the USA and Germany but the same or less than many other OECD countries. UK growth was exceeded by both France and Italy. Clearly, productivity was to some extent improved through increased pay flexibility but continued improvements relate more to such issues as capital investment and research and development, both of which remain low in the UK compared to competitor countries.

Labour costs per unit of output decreased from 1981 until 1986 but there was then a rapid increase until the recession of the early 1990s, when labour costs fell sharply. Over the period 1980-96 unit labour costs rose much less in manufacturing than in the whole economy. Increases in labour costs in the late 1990s have been low.

The political and economic agenda of successive Conservative governments had a profound effect on pay. Income distribution widened sharply, reflecting the declining role of trade unions in pay setting; inequality increased but productivity improved. Labour costs fell significantly. The question is whether this change reflects a transformation in reward management at the organisational level. In the next we review the impact of human resource management upon pay practices.

This explores some implications for reward strategy of the increasing globalisation of business organisations. A neglected area of research is the problem of how organisations take account of national characteristics and contexts in the design of reward systems. In considering pay design within an international context, we have to engage the debate about convergence and divergence in the rewards field. There are pressures to alter the level at which pay determination takes place, and there is an attack on the collective process in Japan and sector-wide agreements operated in Germany. Many tensions, however, are faced by organisations as they attempt to harmonise reward packages, notably the influence of national culture on pay systems.

Rather than focus attention on the management of expatriate compensation and benefits, which has been a traditional focus in the international IHRM literature, this analyses the factors that international organisations should consider when they make decisions about how to manage their rewards systems across national boundaries. A number of psychological factors, such as national value orientations, distributional justice, the concept of socially healthy pay, and the role of pay as a motivator, are considered.

The issue of international convergence in rewards systems has taken centre-stage. Depending on the level of analysis adopted, different conclusions may be drawn about the desire for and actual level of convergence in rewards systems. Certainly at the level of HR philosophy, the convergence argument can find some support. Even at the beginning of the 1990s, organisations (especially MNCs, but also large domestic organisations) around the world could be seen to be converging managerial attention around the need to improve the link between pay and performance.

Analysis of data from the Towers Perrin/IBM study of 1991 for twelve countries showed that the issue of individual performance-related pay was one of the philosophies that all HR managers saw as being central to the achievement of competitive advantage. It was anticipated that it should be reflected in actual practice. However, depending on the level at which we analyse rewards systems, the evidence of international convergence around best practice has to be tempered by an increasingly sophisticated awareness of the distinctive nature of rewards policies and behaviour across countries.

This notes a range of cross-national factors that influence reward practices in organisations, but gives particular attention to the role of national culture. Why is a consideration of national culture so important? Naisbitt and Aburdene (1990) point out that whilst the lifestyles of managers around the world are becoming more homogeneous, the faster the pace at which this happens, the more steadfastly they shall cling to and cherish the traditions that spring from within.

We might expect that deeper values will predict responses to new reward initiatives. Although ultimately the forces for convergence might prevail, the harder organisations push for convergence in rewards practice, the bumpier their ride to convergence will become. What pressures then are making our worlds more similar, perhaps at a pace too fast for some?

### *Pay Flexibility*

Rewards systems in Germany, Japan and China are facing radical change. There are also high levels of reward failure in the US and UK, where a shift from jobs-based to people-based systems is currently taking place. The pursuit of flexibility in human resource management (HRM) has led to calls for more pay flexibility. The drive towards flexibility requires more ease with which employees' or managers' pay can be adjusted, especially to reflect the correlation between:

- Pay level and the organisation's success (or otherwise)
- Pay focus and general strategic policy objectives
- Risk-sharing between the organisation and the employee
- Pay level and the individual effort.

Flexibility is intended to deliver greater differentiation between individuals, teams or units within an organisation and requires greater market sensitivity of rewards.

### *The German Kostenkrise Debate*

Europe has seen calls for more wage flexibility. The Kostenkrise in Germany has become the centre of much attention. The Bundesverband der Deutschen Industries (BDI) argues that German enterprise is blighted by high tax, wages and welfare costs and there is pressure to break up the 42,000 'tarifvertrag'. These are the conventional contracts that cover not just wages rates, bonuses and sick pay, but also training, part-time work, and sometimes longer hours in return for job security. They regulate German pay and compensation negotiations.

Until recently firms operating outside the system actually ended up paying wages at least as high, if not higher, than those within the system. This is now changing. The number of individual contracts with unions has increased from 2,500 in 1990 to 5,000 by 1997: for example, the IG Chemie trade union in Germany agreed in June 1997 to allow Hoechst, Bayer and BASF to cut wages by up to 10 per cent in difficult economic periods; while in Eastern Germany twenty firms have official permission to pay below the 'Tarif' whilst many employers shun the system and negotiate on-site with workers.

Although productivity has increased in Germany by 8.5 per cent and unit labour costs have fallen by 10 per cent, it is argued that high labour productivity (partly the result of a highly skilled and functionally flexible workforce and harmonious plant-or company-level industrial relations) is not sufficient to compensate for the labour cost disadvantage.

The accumulated unit labour cost (ULC) disadvantage for Germany from the period 1989-96 amounted to 18 per cent. Of this disadvantage, 33 per cent can be attributed to internal (non-currency value) labour cost factors, and of this, non wage labour costs (which amount to 80 per cent of direct wages in Germany) have accounted for much of the increase. Social security contributions, paid for jointly by the employer and employee, have raised from 26.5 per cent of gross wages in 1970 to 36 per cent in 1989, and now stand at 42 per cent.

Germany is actually at the mid-point in terms of social costs. Social costs (as a percentage of gross average pay adjusted to reflect purchasing power relative to the US) range from as low as 22 per cent in the US, to 26 per cent in the UK, 83 per cent in Germany, 122 per cent in Sweden, 127 per cent in Switzerland and 128 per cent in Japan. Table given below shows that the cost and burden factors in Germany compare unfavourably to other major OECD countries in the 1990s.

It is argued that the result of this is an exodus of capital in a globalising market and that this will force domestic organisations to reform wage systems. Certainly, German outward foreign direct investment (FDI) did increase substantially during the 1990s.

**Table: Comparison of Selected Location Cost Factors in Manufacturing Sector**

| | *WG* | *EG* | *USA* | *J* | *UK* | *F* | *NL* | *B* |
|---|---|---|---|---|---|---|---|---|
| Labour costs on DM basis, 1996, WG=100 | 100 | 66 | 55 | 69 | 47 | 65 | 74 | 75 |
| Labour productivity, 1996, WG=100 | 100 | 59 | 76 | 85 | 58 | 98 | 109 | 99 |
| Labour unit cost change, 1989-96, national currencies, % | 20.1 | – | 11.4 | 6.8 | 24.3 | 7.5 | 2.8 | 16.2 |
| Annual working time, 1996, WG=100 | 100 | 105 | 121 | 117 | 112 | 112 | 109 | 110 |
| Effective marginal tax burden of joint stock companies, 1996, WG=100 | 100 | 76 | 51 | 111 | 36 | 73 | 44 | 53 |

*Key:*
WG=Western Germany, EG=Eastern Germany, USA=United States, J=Japan, UK=United Kingdom, F=France, NL=The Netherlands, B=Belgium

*Source:* After Tüsselmann (1999). His calculations based on data from: Institute der deutschen Wirtschaft, IW Trends-Quartalshefte zur

Empirischen; Wirtschafts-
forschung, no. 2, 1997 and
no. 3, 1997; Bundesministerium
fur Wirtschaft, Wirtschaft in
Zahmen, September 1997.

Outflows increased by 120 per cent from 1983-89 to 1990-96, with inflows amounting to just 20 per cent of outflows in the latter period. However, it is too narrow a perspective to attribute increases in outflows solely to cost factors. In addition to labour costs and corporate taxation, qualitative factors such as the skills level of the workforce, density and tightness of regulatory frameworks, market demand, geo-political location and national culture all play a role in multinational location and investment decisions. Indeed, 80 per cent of German FDI has gone to western industrialised countries, not low-wage locations. Only a small proportion of total FDI has been driven by wage and related rewards/benefits factors, despite the popular press attention.

Rewards are notoriously difficult to compare across countries for many reasons. Flexibility deals that surround pay conditions can mask inflated or deflated pay levels and simple comparisons of unit labour costs and hourly manufacturing wage rates hide many complexities. For example, in Germany, wage rates aver-aged DM48 an hour in manufacturing in 1996, higher than any of the other fifty-two countries surveyed by the World Economic Forum.

However, the number of hours actually worked also varies markedly. Data from the International Institute for Management Development show that the annual hours worked by full-time employees in the United States is 1,920 compared to 1,840 in the UK, 1,830 in Sweden, 1,810 in Japan, 1,750 in France, but only 1,700 in Germany. Moves to a shorter working week and early retirement increase the proportion of gross wages that must be used to cover social costs. Given the ageing workforce, the Federation of German Industry estimates that social security costs will amount to 55 per cent of gross wages by 2040.

Today's 20-year-olds can expect zero returns on half of their lifetime contributions, whereas today's 60-year-olds receive three times what they have paid in. This said, the younger generation benefits from and can expect about three times as much inherited wealth in terms of savings and property than their grandparents had. The Kostenkrise will lead to some rewards system reform, but the business rhetoric often ignores the subtle ways in which national systems can balance out rewards and benefits across societal groups.

### *Therisutora Process in Japan*

Japan has also changed from being a role model for HRM policies and practices, to becoming a major target for those who argue for the break-up of national business systems. The restructuring process associated with the revitalisation of its post-bubble economy is called risutora. Within the HRM arena, attention has focused on:

- The introduction of performance-based career and compensation standards;
- Open feedback systems regarding performance evaluation;
- Even more differentiated employment tracks between core, specialist and flexible employment groups;
- Externalisation of much corporate welfare; and non-discriminatory hiring practices.

In order swiftly to lower or alleviate labour costs, in the short term Japanese firms have reduced the level of overtime payments, and transferred employees between companies. The social contract, based on lifetime employment and seniority-based pay, is slowly breaking down as forces of internationalisation, global competition, demography, slowed economic growth and the collapse of investment banks begin to bite.

In practice, the substantial bonus proportion of annual wages and the introduction of job ability-based grading schemes have simply been added on to existing seniority-dominated practices, in that most firms linked bonus pay and ability-related remuneration largely to the age of employees and the length of employment with the firm.

Some of the rewards problems facing Japanese organisations reflect structural issues, such as demographic pressures. Salaries and earnings in Japan peak at age 50-54 (compared to 45-49 in the UK), but by the year 2000 a quarter of the Japanese workforce will be aged 55 or older, creating high fixed cost. The chairman of the Japan Federation of Employers Association urged pay restraint in wage and bonus demands, stating that Japanese companies employ 1.2 million excess workers.

Deregulation is expected to lead to 10 per cent job losses in the finance, public administration and construction sectors. Despite apparent collectivist preferences, employees in Japan have regularly been found to be dissatisfied with the opaqueness of work and performance evaluation systems and the highly centralised nature of decision-making.

Flexibility in rewards is an issue in Japan, but although wage increases are flexible, the annual wage bargaining ritual known as 'shunto' (or spring labour offensive) in practice means that wages increase uniformly across sectors, as awards have been made irrespective of productivity. There was some divergence from the uniform agreements in 1997, when profitable firms like Toyota offered well above the average, whilst Nissan and Honda fell behind.

The seniority-based wage system has also come under threat within organisations. Honda and Sony introduced pay systems placing greater emphasis on performance; Mitsubishi Corporation allowed the pay of managers of the same age to vary by plus or minus 10 per cent; and many firms are introducing what on the surface resembles western-style, performance-related pay schemes. Matsushita introduced the first tiered wage system in Japan, which differentiates between those following a lifetime employment 'contract', newcomers who want to bring forward and forgo the substantial retirement benefits, and those with specialist skills in demand, who wish to contract-out of most age- and service-related benefits.

Several commentators now argue that more dramatic changes are needed if 'risutora' is to prove viable in the long run, such as regrouping and reclassifying employees into different employment tracks (core groups, specialists and flexible labour reserves) in order to make the introduction of standardised norms and performance criteria, customised training programmes, incentive schemes, and strategically motivated cost externalisation programmes more manageable. Basic wages in Japan make up about 70 per cent of total compensation.

Although nominal wage rises in Japan have been relatively low, bonuses and overtime can still offset wage moderation. The move to a 40-hour working week in 1997 was accompanied by a 10.5 per cent increase in overtime work. Although employees are not taxed in Japan until earnings amount to $38,000 (compared to $28,000 in Germany, $20,000 in the US, and $8,000 in the UK), 70 per cent of all tax revenue still comes from direct taxes on earnings in Japan, so the incentive impact of salaries is diminished, and the top individual tax rate at 65 per cent (53 per cent in Germany) is one of the highest in advanced economies.

However, a loss of loyalty to the employer is being observed as Japanese employees realise that they have limited opportunity to express grievances over unfair evaluations, and feel that neither the evaluation criteria nor the results are being communicated to them (Japan Productivity Centre for Socio-Economic Development 1997). There are concerns that these restructuring strategies, in aiming at the introduction of standardised evaluation schemes and individualised remuneration systems, are potentially counter-productive:

These two trends are fraught with considerable misunderstandings and even contradictions...many Japanese firms are thus embarking on a perilous road leading to two clearly undesirable effects simultaneously: the unravelling of a corporate culture based on team work orientation and labour organisation flexibility on the one hand, the systematic destruction of individual motivation and personal loyalty on the other.

### *Glorious Rich in China*

Nowhere is wide-scale transition more apparent than in China. Until recently Chinese employment arrangements centred around 'the administrative allocation of life-time jobs by the state, the virtual non-existence of unemployment, redundancy or retrenchment, and a strict separation maintained between urban and rural labour'.

In addition to divisions between 'the new glorious rich' and those working in the state sector, sharp divisions also exist in the state-owned sector between labcurers and cadres based upon the level of completed education and job assignment. The two groups represent different labour markets and are administered by different organisations or bureaux: the Ministry of Labour and Ministry of Personnel.

Historically, employment planning was fairly basic, politically influenced and constrained by a shortage of trained personnel. The labour-management relation system was unsophisticated, although a number of practices had been institutionalised. Morale and material rewards were subjugated to ideology. Selection and appraisal were based on group norms, and human resource development was conducted within a narrow framework.

This system showed the fallacy of viewing rewards simply in western terms, i.e. focusing attention on direct financial benefits and areas of organisational autonomy, since in the People's Republic of China (PRC) factories had to strive to establish and maintain a health-care system, schools, meal services, entertainment facilities, a guest house, and a car pool and also try to find employment for the offspring of employees and fund the pensions of retired workers. It organises sports teams and cultural events.

The labour market has been portrayed as the 'iron rice-bowl', a system with built-in rigidities, but one that offered cheap housing, free health and welfare benefits and jobs-for-life for those (albeit a minority) in the state-owned enterprises (SOEs). Such traditions still resonate today. None the less, a long process of reform has attempted to create floating wage systems that link individual wages to enterprise or individual performance. The range of wage fluctuation is usually half or less of total income. Wage-fixing powers for more of the structural elements of the wage system-such as basic pay, job-related pay, seniority pay (based on the length of service) and bonuses-were handed down to enterprises in 1987.

Four major working factors were emphasised in 1992-the knowledge and skills required, responsibility assumed, work intensity (load) and working conditions in order to make it easier to quantify a worker's performance and link it to pay. A survey of 440 Chinese organisations (104 state-owned enterprises; forty-five collectively owned enterprises; sixteen privately owned enterprises; and fifty-three foreign-invested enterprises) found that pay has become more linked to individual performance and an important incentive to Chinese employees.

As in Japan, demographic factors are playing an important role, and there is an increasing drain on resources from an ageing population. Many enterprises are now imposing an early retirement age of 45 for women and 50 for men, five years before the retirement age set by the state.

This situation is only expected to get worse as dramatic changes continue to take place within the Chinese business structure, and it continues to move towards a labour contract system whereby employers assume total responsibility for all welfare programmes, subsidies and pensions during one to five year contracts. In 1997 President Jiang Zemin announced acceleration in this transition, consolidating the previous pattern of reform. Such transitions are altering the social contract.

**Factors**

The scope for national differences in rewards systems is broad and the presence of any specific attitude towards rewards or compensation practices reflects a range of determinants. Simple recourse to 'culture' as an explanation of the behaviour or presence of the practice is very often misleading.

To what extent do the changes discussed above in Germany, Japan and China signal deep shifts that determine the future frame of reference for rewards behaviour within organisations? Questions are being raised about the assumptions that underlie much reward behaviour, and the implications of perceived changes in trust, motivation and commitment. It is important to understand what pay means to people in different cultures.

Psychological analysis of rewards behaviour suggests that there is a generic cross-cultural process of pay satisfaction and the subsequent influence that this has on work behaviour. Pay tends to have four meanings. It carries motivational properties. People differ in the extent to which they see pay as a good means of achieving important objectives. Pay signals relative position, both in terms of achievement of tasks or goals, and in relation to performance in comparison with others.

Pay carries meaning in relation to the relative level of control an individual has, through the different composition of the pay package and perceived ability to influence others and create autonomy over reward. Finally, pay carries meaning in terms of the utility it creates, the ease or difficulty with which it can be spent. The structure of a pay system (elements of pay, form of payment, and climate factors such as level of secrecy or participation) can determine the meaning that individuals derive from it and, as we have seen, the structure of pay systems varies markedly across societies.

So too does the extent to which a pay policy is integrated into the strategic context of the firm, and is tailored to the goals of other HRM policies such as selection, evaluation and management development. Of these four meanings, 'relative position' seems to be the most powerful influence on motivation. Relative deprivation models of pay satisfaction suggest that pay satisfaction falls when there is:

- A discrepancy between desired and received pay;
- A discrepancy between received pay and other comparable referents;
- A discrepancy between received pay and historical parity (in terms of inflationary factors and grading systems);
- A low future expectation of more pay.

The pay motivation process has been assumed to be generic across societies, even though the content (i.e. what motivates people) has long been known to differ across countries. Should we assume that even the pay motivation process is generic? National culture should influence many of the causal dynamics between perceived meaning of pay and actual satisfaction.

### *Rewards-related Preferences*

National culture influences the efficiency of various pay formulae and techniques. Unravelling the complex set of influences that culture can have on rewards behaviour has become a focus of recent research. When the individual behaviour of a broad set of people is considered (behaviour of non-managerial workforces, and the external labour pool from which and to which pay policies are applied), then evidence of convergence in rewards behaviour is not as marked.

A number of important mechanisms must be considered. White et al. note that international comparisons of pay systems focus on four aspects. If we overlay our knowledge of national culture on to these, we can see that each of these factors can have a cultural cause:

1. The locus of decision-taking (reflecting the emphasis on centralisation and hierarchical authority, attitudes to worker participation)

2. Management criteria for pay determination decisions (reflecting the different mindsets, perceived causal factors, and cognitive schemata that managers use to interpret differentially what might be a common idea)
3. The effect of particular reward strategies on employees' behaviour (reflecting the role of values and the attitudes and actual behaviour that these values will generate)
4. The content and practice of the actual rewards packages in various countries (acting as an amalgam of the above three factors).

***The Cultural Value Orientations***

The analysis of values has formed the basis of much comparative work on rewards. Why? Principally because they have been found to be less malleable and more stable than attitudes about pay. They also influence an employee's activity indirectly by shaping their attitudes and goals, The theoretical process through which cultural factors, including values, account for differences in the effectiveness of many management interventions and tools has been examined by Erez and Earley (1993). In this process, values become important because they reflect:

- Enduring beliefs that a specific mode of conduct is personally or socially preferable
- An objective state of mind, relationship or material condition that people seek to attain
- Normative standards that are used to judge and choose among alternative modes of behaviour
- Conceptions of the desirable that guide the way that leaders, policy-makers and individuals select actions, evaluate events and explain their actions.

Unlike attitudes to pay (which may be negative or positive), values have to reflect a positive position-a conscious judgement in favour of something. They clearly mediate the four meanings of pay outlined above. Values might also enable better prediction of employee response to new pay policies. If the objection to a particular pay policy tool or technique is due to the cultural values held by individual employees, then international HRM managers have a real problem.

Values are more predictive of behaviour than specific attitudes, and if the policy is counter cultural, it will either simply be rejected locally, or will be modified in a way that the organisation did not intend, or even worse will apparently be adopted but will actually be operated on a totally different set of behavioural and decision rules. The international HRM manager needs to know which HRM policies are values-free and which are values-linked.

A recent analysis by Schuler and Rogovsky (1998) has begun to address this question. They examined data from three international HRM surveys: the IBM/ Towers Perrin world-wide study of HR practices; the International Social Survey Programme (ISSP); and the Price Waterhouse/Cranfield project. Under the ISSP programme, data have been gathered for eleven countries covering the US and Europe. Standardised stratified survey data for over 6,600 employees have allowed for sophisticated statistical analysis of work value and orientation data covering such components as high income, job security and interesting work.

By controlling for the effects of occupational grouping and demographic variables of age and sex, it was found that both line of country, and the cultural value orientation prescribed by Hofstede (1980) for that country, were the most significant predictors of work values. Those compensation practices that were based on status were linked to national culture. Countries with a high level of 'uncertainty avoidance' (such as Greece, Portugal, Italy and Japan) were more in favour of compensation being based on either seniority or level of competence and skill; they were less inclined to favour a focus on individual performance or on employee ownership plans, but favoured benefits such as provision of workplace childcare and career break schemes.

Countries with a strong individualistic culture (such as the United States, Britain, Australia, and The Netherlands) understandably preferred pay for performance, a focus on individual performance, employee stock options and commission paid to clerical and manual staff. Countries with feminine cultures that do not respect aggressive goal-orientated behaviour (such as Norway and Sweden) favoured flexible benefits, workplace childcare schemes, and career break and maternity break schemes for all levels of staff. Countries with high-power distance (such as France, Greece, Brazil, India or Far Eastern countries) were set against employee share options or share ownership for manual, clerical or technical employees.

Given the comments made about the role of German non-wage costs, it is important also to consider the impact that national culture has on employee benefits plans. The need to understand and to co-ordinate global benefits plans is evidenced by the alliances and mergers that occurred between US benefits consulting firms and overseas consulting firms throughout the 1990s. National culture helps determine how easy it is to meld workers into the desired corporate culture-an important point given that a significant motive behind many benefits programmes is a desire to facilitate or reflect changes in corporate culture.

Benefits lie at the heart of the employment relationship. Indeed, the lifetime employment system that Japan once held was seen as a cornerstone benefit within their employment relationship. As with the Schuler and Rogovsky analysis, Hempel (1999) relates various Hofstede cultural dimensions to rewards and benefits policies, such as levels of pension income, and job and income protection schemes. For example, power distance scores for Belgium (65), Japan (54) and Norway (31) are negatively linked to the level of redistribution of income achieved through social pension income replacement ratios.

In high-power distance societies, retirees below or above national average earnings levels all receive a smaller level of income replacement. In low-power distance societies those below average earnings receive a far higher level of income replacement than those with above-average earnings. Similarly, high-uncertainty avoidance scores are associated with greater levels of job protection and income protection.

More feminine societies, where quality of life considerations are typically important, tend to prefer income protection rather than job protection benefits programmes. In designing culturally acceptable pension schemes, Hempel argues that multinational organisations should provide separate plans for different employee groups in high-power distance countries, and provide defined benefits plans and highly formalised low-risk pension systems in high-uncertainty avoidance societies.

These two analyses link national data on cultural values post hoc to national rewards policies or attitude data. Some studies have examined the operation of specific processes that can be involved in decisions that influence reward. For example, will employees from different cultures apply upwards appraisal assessments in the same way? If not, multinational organisations have to think carefully about applying many advanced performance management systems. Adsit et al. (1997) examined attitude survey data from 6,400 employees making upwards appraisal ratings of 751 managers in a multinational electronics and consumer products firm headquartered in Europe.

Data were analysed for employees from France, Germany, Poland, the US, Mexico, Brazil, Singapore, Malaysia, Hong Kong and Thailand. Items were linked to those that formed part of Hofstede's four cultural scales. Countries differed in the extent to which their employees rated managers across various items, so that in Germany employees had high expectations for managerial performance, especially compared to Poland, Mexico and Brazil. In France managers were rated particularly highly on under-standing customer responsiveness.

Managers from Thailand and Poland were perceived by their subordinates as placing more emphasis on clarifying goals and giving feedback about performance. Brazilian managers were perceived as being poor at this. What is impossible to tease out from such data is whether the managers from the respective countries were better truly at the noted characteristics, or whether national culture values tempt employees towards more leniency or strictness in making upwards assessments. Similar patterns might be expected in downwards assessments. For multinationals, it is important to know what the answer is before converging international rewards around performance-related pay or competency-based pay systems that will rely on such assessment processes.

These types of analysis move us towards a better understanding of the relative importance of national culture. But just how important a variable is national culture? In the Schuler and Rogovsky (1998) analysis, aggregated data on Hofstede's values accounted for about 7 per cent of the cross-national variance in the importance accorded to the work value for high income. However, do such culture-rewards attitude relationships hold at the individual level?

Sparrow and Wu (1998) examined the relationship between individual orientations across four of Kluckhohn and Strodtbeck's (1961) value orientations: human nature (good-bad, changeable-immutable); human position towards nature (subjugation-mastery-harmony); activity (being-doing-thinking); and relational (collective-individual-hierarchical). They similarly found that national value orientations accounted for around 10 per cent of HRM preference when examined at the individual level, but also found that many HRM choices appear to be values-free, i.e. bear no relationship to the underlying national value orientations held by the individual.

Starting from the most values-free HRM functions, they found that 50 per cent of compensation choices, 44 per cent of staffing choices, 44 per cent of performance appraisal choices, 36 per cent of planning choices, but only 29 per cent of training and development choices fall into this category. In relation to compensation, individual preferences for market-based (as opposed to internal-equity based) pay rates, linkage of compensation to functional flexibility, separation of fringe benefits from wages, rewards of a financial rather than non-monetary nature, and rewards based on individual needs and individual choice were all values-free.

As an international HRM manager operating in Taiwan, the message was that whilst many HRM policies were clearly not seen as appropriate, dependent on the individual's national value orientations, at least the above list of rewards policies would not offend the basic value orientations of local employees.

### *Distributional Justice*

Another cultural factor that the design of comparative rewards systems has to account for is distributional justice. Studies of distributional justice concern them-selves with the rules and standards by which decisions about the allocation of resources (financial or non-financial) are both made and perceived to be fair. Exploring the nature of these decisions and the motives that surround them is seen as one way in which researchers can gain insight into the social systems that surround rewards behaviour.

Allocation problems are resolved by resorting to a series of decision rules that determine the entitlement of recipients. In practice, these rules reflect the familiar, normative rules of a society that concern issues of social and industrial justice. They are also seen to embody decision logics and the value position of individuals and their motives. These logics and value positions are linked to national culture: 'the particular cognitive and behavioural manifestations of justice, as they take place in the resolution of allocation problems, may be conditioned by the culture at large within which the organisation is embedded'.

When there is a pot of 'reward' to be shared out, what is the fairest way to do it? Several rule-sets have been identified.

The two most potent rule-sets distinguish between principles of meritocracy and egalitarianism. They are based on principles of:

- 'Equity' – whereby entitlements are based on relative contributions and differential reward is legitimate as long as it is based on an equitable way of differentiating performance. These are felt to be dominant in the US and related national cultures such as the UK, Australia and Canada
- 'Parity' or 'Equality' – in which allocation solutions are insensitive to input differences and call for resources to be distributed equally to all, regardless of relative productivity. These are felt to be applicable in collectivist cultures such as China and Japan. The decision rule is clearly bounded, in that collectivists make a clear distinction between in-group and out-group members and do not apply equality rules to out-group members. Where teams operate as in-groups, incentives and bonuses should only be given to the group, not to individuals.

There is evidence however, especially in the special economic zones of China, that a radically altered institutional and social environment can change previously deep-seated psychological determinants of rewards behaviour, such as distributive justice. The 'new glorious rich' in China's free market challenge the underlying value of equality-based rather than equity-based justice held by the many. Meindl, Cheng and Jun (1990) analysed justice rules amongst a small sample of eighty-six Chinese managers and ninety-six US managers. The analysis showed that the Chinese managers were more equity-driven than might be expected.

They were also more unsophisticated in their allocation rules. US managers were prepared to override equity rules in situations where there was high work interdependence and where values of solidarity (low conflict) were present. The Chinese managers pushed equity-based solutions in all contexts. This might reflect low levels of experience of actually making these decisions and so a lack of sophistication. It might also reflect a process of 'going native' in that, knowing that foreign systems are being vaunted as worthy of emulation, respondents conform to the new rhetoric somewhat unthinkingly.

A similar picture emerged in another cross-cultural study into distributive justice, which compared 277 employees in three state-owned enterprises and 205 employees in two US companies. In-basket role plays were used to establish preferences for reward type, allocation rules and goal priorities.

Chinese employees emphasised economic organisational goals over the US humanistic goals and a differential logic for the allocation of both material and socio-emotional rewards. The study revealed a complex pattern of continuity and change. Confucian values were still evidenced in the continued emphasis on the social hierarchy, with a higher ranking for differential rewards according to rank and seniority in the Chinese sample.

However, performance and job needs outranked seniority and rank as a differential allocation rule. This new emphasis of Chinese employees towards an economic logic and rejection of equality-based rules was felt to be more a product of recent environmental pressure and institutional practice than any shift in underlying cultural values. Such research suggests that some individuals can make a transition in deep-seated drivers of rewards behaviour, whilst others may not, and some can do it intelligently, whilst others may apply new rule-sets rather uncritically.

### *Healthy pay and Pay Differentials*

A final concept, related to the justice rules above, is that of 'socially healthy pay'. Within societies there are boundaries placed around the range of pay differentials or multiples deemed to be legitimate. These are generally measured by metrics such as the ratio between the highest and average, or highest and lowest paid. In the US high multiples are both legitimate and expected. In continental Europe much narrower multiples are felt to be appropriate.

If differentials move beyond accepted limits, then social reaction can be marked. Research on pay differentials has shown that the gap between the remuneration of workers and the most senior managers in organisations has increased markedly in recent years across the world. For example, the pay differential ratio between the average worker and the CEO in the US has increased from 41 in 1960, to 79 in 1970, 157 in 1992, 152 in 1993, 209 in 1996 and 326 in 1997. When the pay differential between the average worker and the highest paid executive is considered, by 1997 the differential was a ratio of 8,130.

In the United States there has, however, been a groundswell against salary imbalances between those at the top and the average employee. Research by the United Auto Workers Union suggests that in 1965 US CEOs were paid forty-five times the average wage, rising to 187 times average wage by 1995. O'Reilly and Pollock tracked 120 large public companies over five years and found that employee turnover levels were higher than average in the firms that paid CEOs above the industry norm.

The power of market competition to overcome norms about socially healthy pay and to alter rules of distributional justice should not be ignored. Research that has examined employee preferences and motivational factors across countries shows that financial factors have high motivational value amongst Chinese employees these days. Survey data from 785 employees of a western-owned hotel group in Shanghai showed that good wages rated as the highest motivational factor.

Comparing this to other national data produced by Silverthorne (1992), it is clear that good wages in China are ranked much higher as a source of pay motivation than in the US (ranked fifth most important out often) or Russia (ranked tenth). In Taiwan good wages are similarly rated as highly motivating (second most important factor).

This issue of increased attention to financial matters in an apparently egalitarian society is also seen in the debate around 'executive pay with Chinese characteristics'. Official guidelines, applied to 70 per cent of the workforce in state-owned enterprises, recommend that directors' pay be tied to company assets and in principle should be no more than three times that of the average worker.

However, consultancy market reports from the region and the financial press indicate that grey income (in the form of benefits, hidden compensation, directorships on subsidiaries and graft) is significant. It is estimated by Chinese government economists to be such that real compensation is at least three times the stated figure. There is no separation between personal and private income at senior levels of the hierarchy in Chinese SOEs.

General managers can ensure that the education of their children, holidays, cars and carpets, are all paid for, and receive free chauffeur-driven sedans, luxurious housing, domestic staff, comprehensive travel expenses at home and abroad, free banquets and unlimited expenses for wining and dining, especially as they near retirement.

If the Chinese tax authorities cannot estimate the true extent of hidden compensations, then academic research into international pay comparability certainly will not. To combat grey income and staunch pay differentials between the state and private sector, the Shanghai authorities introduced a bonus scheme that allowed managers in some SOEs to earn bonuses worth up to three times official pay. Therefore research on grey income is likely to counter many apparent cross-cultural differences in rewards behaviour.

Continued pressure for change is also anticipated in Europe. As US multinationals expand in Europe and pursue strategies built around pan-European structures and teams, the level of competition for talent is forcing change in rewards behaviour. So too will the Euro, which is anticipated to unleash powerful market forces that will transform work practices through the creation of mergers and acquisitions, changes to corporate tax rates, a shift towards an equity culture as shareholders gain more influence over corporate governance, and harmonisation of rewards levels. To close the competitive gap with other peripheral countries in the Euro zone, German wages would have to fall by 2 per cent a year for several years to come.

Many European managers now have from 10 per cent to 50 per cent of their pay tied to the financial performance of the firm, and the trend is for increased compensation at senior levels, though not to US levels. Bonus plans, merit raises and stock options are becoming more commonplace. Daimler-Benz was one of the first German firms to offer a stock option plan-a move challenged in the courts by a German shareholder.

Research on cultural value orientations, distributional justice and pay differentials suggests that MNCs attempting to harmonise rewards systems will face predictable patterns of resistance across different countries. These aspects of national culture are amenable to change, but only amongst highly selected groups. Whilst there may be convergence in pay philosophies across national HR systems, the need to engage the local institutional context means that there should be considerable local autonomy of practice allowed within MNCs, and distinctive practices will remain within domestic organisations.

Institutional differences-legal and economic constraints such as employment law, tax law, and minimum wage legislation-will continue to play a vital role in pay systems because they limit the freedom of action of employers. When considering a converging policy objective such as individual performance-related pay, it is the how of organisational implementation that reveals just how bounded the convergence actually is.

Whilst most managers around the world would now subscribe, for example, to the policy objective of a pay-performance linkage, the cultural interpretation of it differs:

'the difficulty is that they all mean different things by pay and different things by performance'.

The first level at which these different meanings become evident is when we consider the 'drivers' of the policy objective. These differential drivers reflect the fact that whilst managers might have signed up to the same HR policy objective, the local institutional context is different, as are the local labour market concerns. Managers might therefore come to the conclusion that individual performance-related pay is an important and necessary HR policy objective through a very different logic.

More importantly, as far as rewards practitioners are concerned, this different logic means that the 'political' messages that must be communicated in order to 'sell' the convergent policy objective soon become immersed in national culture. A good deal of 'spin doctoring' becomes necessary in the 'selling strategies' adopted by HR managers. They have to find 'engagement points' with the national culture on which they can play to make the audience more receptive to the policy objective.

Consider the following interpretation of White et al.'s analysis of rewards systems in British and Hong Kong banks. Both the British and Hong Kong banks stressed the importance of individual performance-related pay. In the British context, however, the message that was sold stressed the following logic: 'A job for life is no longer possible, nor is much vertical grade movement, so if you want pay progression, linking it to individual contribution makes sense'.

By championing the right of the individual to equitable reward, the point at which local managers engaged with the message was through a set of 'individualistic' values-if I work hard in this uncertain world but my colleague shirks, then I deserve additional reward. In Hong Kong, however, where deferred gratification and a more collective perspective might be expected to work against a performance-related pay objective, the point of engagement was actually another cultural dimension-the 'money ethic' or 'cash mentality'.

Given the desire for financial well-being after high levels of migration from China, considerable importance is given to the role of immediate cash. The point of engagement with the local audience was through the money ethic, not individualism.

From the perspective of an international HRM manager, the future agenda for comparative rewards system research must surely concentrate on understanding how facets of national culture mediate the operation of new pay systems, including initiatives such as broad-banding and competency-based. It must also identify the appropriate 'engagement points' through which policy objectives can be deemed to be in line with underlying values.

Chapter 2

# Industrial Relations and Hotel Management

## NEW INDUSTRIAL RELATIONS

Indian leaders decided to upgrade the EU-India relationship to the level of a Strategic Partnership and to support this partnership through the implementation of a Joint Action Plan. The Joint Action Plan was endorsed at the 2005 Summit held in New Delhi in September 2005 including a range of proposed initiatives in the area of civil aviation aimed at strengthening co-operation between the EU and India in this priority field of activity. In recent years the Indian air traffic market has been among the fastest growing in the world. These developments will boost Indian Hospitality Industries.

In 2005, domestic air passenger traffic in India increased by 22% while international passenger traffic grew by 15%. Since 1990, the number of seats available on scheduled non-stop flights between the EU and India has increased from 2.6 to 5.5 million in 2005 (+116%). Capacity on EU-India routes is expected to grow even faster in the coming few years. With such a rapid development in air traffic, important new challenges and opportunities are emerging.

Market opening and attempts to attract private and foreign capital to the Indian aviation market are seen as part of the measures necessary to develop and modernise India's aviation sector in order to meet increasing demand and consumer expectations. India has therefore in recent years taken decisive steps towards opening up its aviation market. These developments combined with the expansion of the single European aviation market offer both significant new challenges and opportunities to all involved in the aviation sector both in India and within the EU. 'Human resource management' and the 'new industrial relations', like most terms in the field of management and organization, originated in the United States.

Those using the terms were not doing so with a concern for precision; nor were they proposing any tight distinction between them. Rather, they were seeking to convey to a predominantly management audience a sense of innovation and change. There appear to be no compelling reasons why we should therefore seek to impose artificial boundaries of our own. However, 'human resource management' generally conjures up an image of a high technology non-union environment while the use of the term 'industrial relations' inevitably implies that trade unions or some other form of workforce representation are involved. In considering human resource management and the new industrial relations, it is on this absence or presence of a trade union and its consequences for policy, practice, and performance that we will concentrate.

The 1981 Newsweek article which perhaps more than anything else proclaimed ' The New Industrial Relations' in the USA suggested that it had arrived almost unnoticed, and until then unannounced, accelerating the demise of the traditional adversarial industrial relations and its replacement by a new collaborative system. In keeping with the spirit of the times, the article went on to claim that the influences on the new approach came not from Japan or from any European system of codetermination but from a uniquely American tradition with its roots in the work of Mayo, Maslow, and McGregor.

In the kind of system outlined in the Newsweek article, the role of trade unions was rather blurred. The work of Kochan, Katz, and McKersie (1986) presented a positive view of the trade union contribution by focusing on cases where successful union-management collaboration had resulted in significant change. They celebrated the 'new' by entitling their book The Transformation of American Industrial Relations. What they showed was the possibility of bringing about marked improvements through management-union cooperation. What they could not do was indicate if this yielded better performanace than nonunion arrangements.

Alongside the debate on the new industrial relations, human resource management was emerging in the 1980s in the United States as a possible solution to the challenge of an increasingly competitive national and international industrial environment. Although the concept had been around for some time, often as an alternative to the rather jaded image of personnel management, it was given a major boost by the rediscovery of the human side of enterprise in Peters and Waterman (1982) In Search of Excellence. In this book, trade unions scarcely merited a mention; unlike the debate on the new industrial relations, it relegated unions to a minor historical role. Certainly we are left with the impression that they played no significant part in any 'excellent' companies.

As human resource management gained prominence in the United States, it was possible to discern three main strands of work. The first, captured in the work of writers like Tichy, Fombrun, and Devanna (1984), Miles and Snow (1984) and Schuler (1989), was primarily concerned with the relationship between business strategy and human resource management strategy. This implies that the key issue in human resource management is the question of strategic choice and recognition of the importance of considering human resource management issues in terms of their integration with wider business strategy. Driven by business and market considerations, this perspective treats trade unions as irrelevant and they are rarely if ever mentioned.

The second strand of work is captured in what might be termed the Harvard view of human resource management. This is essentially a generic approach which attempts to make the subject area comprehensible and interesting to Harvard MBA students and to general managers who have often been more attracted by the quantitative, financial, and strategic aspects of business. It is therefore an approach which tries to capture and re-present the field of what by tradition had been personnel management. Apart from providing a much more contemporary 'feel',) the resulting analytic and descriptive material does not differ significantly from a number of personnel texts.

Furthermore it explicitly acknowledges the role of trade unions in its conceptual framework by introducing the concept of 'stakeholder interests' as one of the key contingent variables helping to shape policy choices. However, once the more detailed material and the case studies are presented, trade unions are relegated to a very minor role. It was left to Kochan and his colleagues at MIT to present a more comprehensive framework which made explicit both the influences in the wider economic system and the potential role of trade unions.

The third strand, which perhaps links in more directly to Peters and Waterman (1982) as well as to the non-union case studies of Foulkes (1980) and some of the work of academics such as Lawler presents human resource management as an approach which is concerned with the full integration and full utilization of the workforce. This overlaps with the initial new industrial relations interest in the work of people like Maslow and McGregor. Indeed it is captured perhaps best in the writing of Walton and his contrast between the old control philosophy and the preferred new philosophy of high commitment. Both Lawler and Walton acknowledge that in high commitment organizations trade unions could have a role to play, but they tend to pass on quickly to consider non-union environments.

Foulkes is explicitly writing about policies in large non-union companies. This perspective maps out the potentially distinctive features of human resource management which have been developed and presented elsewhere. With its focus on an integrative, unitarist perspective, in which emphasis is placed on commitment to the organization, the role of trade unions is called into question. Indeed, one of the key research questions which emerges is whether it is possible to display commitment to both company and trade union.

This discussion of the emergence of human resource management and the new industrial relations in the United States is relevant partly because, at a key period in the 1980s, the United States was held up as the model to emulate in the UK. This was reflected in the warm relationship between Reagan and Thatcher at a political level and in the interest in monetarist free market economies at a policy level. Another source of interest was the legislative framework for industrial relations which in the United States reflected the dominance given to the operation of the market economy and made it more difficult for the unions to act as a significant economic constraint.

Of course, as Beardwell (1991) has emphasized, there are dangers in taking the comparison too far. The context in the UK in the early 1980s was different in some important respects from the United States; in particular, the trade unions were more powerful and membership was much higher. However, there was a vacuum created by the apparent failure of the pluralist industrial relations strategy to deliver either good industrial relations or an efficient and productive industry. This resulted in a major policy debate about the need for new legislation and about the appropriate role for trade unions. As Beardwell acknowledges, much of the rhetoric of the debate was drawn from America.

What this meant was that the UK became susceptible to American ideas about human resource management and the new industrial relations. Beardwell has drawn a distinction between two approaches to the new industrial relations. He sees one as concerned with the reform of industrial relations, manifested in interest in job control, single union agreements, pendulum arbitration, and the like. The second approach is concerned with the new ideology of human resource management, with its focus on individualism and therefore it's potential to replace the traditional pluralist system.

The typical illustration of the reformist approach is the new Japanese manufacturing site, perhaps Toshiba or Nissan where management appears willing to accept a single union on their own terms. The American high technology firms such as IBM, Hewlett-Packard, Texas Instruments, and DEC represent the stereotype of the second approach.

However, as Garrahan and Stewart have argued in the case of Nissan and McLoughlin has shown in the case of high technology companies, the two approaches overlap, implying that the idea of the two perspectives existing Janus-like is too sharply drawn. Recognition of overlap has also been apparent in some of the debates about industrial relations and human resource management. What this implies is that managements' broad policy choices are not about a reformist industrial relations or human resource management but about options along two dimensions.

The first dimension is concerned with industrial relations. Following the Beardwell analysis, the type of industrial relations sought by management may range from the unreconstructed pluralism still found in some corners of the public sector, through a reformist type of new industrial relations complete with single union deal and pendulum arbitration to an absence of trade unions.

The second dimension is concerned with human resource management. Managers must decide how far they wish to embrace it. If they consider the issue strategically, they may opt to pursue a full-utilization model through policies designed to generate employee commitment, flexibility, and quality; and they may choose to do this for all or part of their staff. Alternatively, they may deliberately set out to pursue a strategy of cost-minimization, seeking high flexibility through short-term contracts and a policy of hire and fire. In such contexts, there is no pretence of seeking workforce commitment to the organization.

Considering the policy choices using these two dimensions takes us away from the conventional debates about the new versus the old or industrial relations and trade unions versus human resource management. Instead it opens up a variety of possible arrangements including trade unions operating alongside a set of human resource management initiatives. Alternatively, management may try to abandon any semblance of either traditional or new industrial relations and at the same time avoid any of the mutual commitments implied by human resource management.

Any consideration of this wider set of choices forces us to look at the key contextual influences in the economy and the market place. It also requires a reconsideration of the ideological framework. The contrast between pluralism and unitarism may need to be replaced by notions of coexistence or complementarity. The possibility that some managers may choose to avoid both trade unions and human resource management opens up the question of the black hole of non-unionism, for too long neglected by researchers.

At present we know too little about the policy choices that managers actually make, about what influences them and about their consequences. In our view the debate about human resource management and the new industrial relations has probably gone on long enough and the best way to take the debate forward is to generate empirical data which can inform it.

The kind of research required must be both sufficiently wide-ranging to detect key trends and developments and sufficiently detailed to explore beneath the surface. Both surveys and case studies are required. We need to know more than whether unions survive; we need to know whether they play an active role or have become an empty shell. We need to know more than whether an organization has introduced single status or quality circles. To explore any comprehensive theory of human resource management we need to understand how these techniques combine to provide some sort of integrated approach.

Researchers have already embarked upon this task. The breadth is provided in the WIRS. WIRS3, carried out in 1990, can find little evidence of major advances in human resource management. Such advances as there have been are more likely to have occurred in unionized workplaces. Non-union workplaces apparently avoid human resource management practices, preferring, it seems, to treat the workforce harshly with consequent costs for both employer and employees.

Such evidence further reinforces scepticism about the value of debates about trade unions or human resource management. Looking at the impact of human resource management, Fernieet al., in their analysis of WIRS3, have shown that those workplaces that adopt single status and employee involvement are more likely to report better performance. However we can only take the debate about human resource management and the new industrial relations forward a little with WIRS3 because the survey omitted large areas of human resource management policy and practice.

McLoughlin and Beardwell, in their research on non-union establishments, have met the research criteria spelt out above by combining survey and case study material to highlight the diversity of practice in the nonunion sector. They explore the question of whether a human resource management strategy reduces the propensity of workers to join a union. The conclusion appears to be that although this may contribute, a range of other factors, centring around the low perceived instrumental value of union membership and lack of encouragement from trade unions, are more important.

Whatever the reasons, only 5 per cent of the establishments in their sample of high technology companies in South-East England recognize a trade union. Useful as it is, their research concentrates on issues of union joining and related management strategy rather than the detailed application and impact of human resource management.

In many respects their work is reinforced and complemented by the findings of the CLIRS2. For example, this survey reports diversity of practice about trade union recognition at new sites. Recognition is more likely where there is centralized pay bargaining and less likely in companies which, strategically, can be classified as financial controllers. Perhaps predictably, the decision about whether or not to recognize a trade union at a new establishment is usually taken centrally. This survey also finds that only a few companies practice what can be described as 'sophisticated' human resource management, reflected in eight indicators, but those that do are more likely to recognize a trade union.

These major surveys, together with a certain amount of detailed case study work, help to shed some light on the relationship between aspects of the new industrial relations and human resource management. However, they are unable to explore in sufficient detail the issue of the impact of trade unions on human resource management policy, practice, and performance. If we take the range of practices associated with human resource management, are there any which are more likely to be found in union or non-union workplaces? Are unions inhibitors or facilitators of human resource management initiatives and, keeping an eye on the new industrial relations, does it matter whether the presence of a union is based on traditional UK multi-unionism or a single union deal? The aim of the remainder of this is to report research which helps to answer these questions.

In seeking to answer the question of whether human resource management is compatible with trade-unionism, we will operationalize the two dimensions described above. Along the dimension concerned with industrial relations policy and the union role we group establishments into four categories according to whether they recognize no union, recognize a single union in the context of a single union deal, recognize a single union but without any special deal, and whether they recognize multiple unions.

On the human resource management dimension, we identify four categories acccording to whether they have an explicit human resource management strategy and the extent to which they make use of a range of human resource management practices. This provides us with a classification which we have initially applied to non-union establishments but which can equally well be applied to any workplace.

Those with an explicit human resource strategy and a high use of human resource practices we label the Good. They adopt an approach close to the kind of 'high involvement' management espoused by Lawler. At the other extreme, those with no human resource strategy and a low adoption of human resource practices we label the Bad. This could be construed as cautious pragmatism, but it is more likely to be poor, ill-thought through management. Those with an explicit strategy but one which results in a low take-up of human resource practices we label the Ugly.

By implication, since they claim to have a strategy, they have thought through how they wish to manage their human resources and decided not to adopt a 'full utilization' approach. They fit the pattern outlined by Millward of bleak environments and limited rights. The Good and the Ugly have some parallels with the 'soft' and 'hard' versions of human resource management identified among others by Keenoy and Storey. Finally, those with no human resource strategy but a high use of human resource practices we label the Lucky. They are lucky in that they have stumbled on a set of practices, perhaps through outside guidance, perhaps through emulation or perhaps by following fads.

The potential value of a classification of this sort is that it explicitly takes into account the issue of strategic integration, emphasized by many writers on human resource management. Good human resource management should be based on a strategy and on extensive rather than narrowly focused application of human resource management practices. The research can explore the association between the two dimensions.

The second central research question is whether the trade unions act as a drag or a spur to performance. To explore this we will again use the same classification but add data on outcomes. Three types of outcome will be explored since they are the most central to the debates on the new industrial relations, the role of the unions, and the efficacy of human resource management. These outcomes are those predicted as first level outcomes by human resource management theory such as levels of commitment, staff quality, and flexibility. The second are employee relations outcomes such as industrial conflict, labour turnover, and absence. The third are performance outcomes including resilience in the face of recession and benchmark estimates of establishment quality and productivity.

## The Method of Analysis

The data reported here are part of a larger study of human resource management in greenfield sites – new, often purpose-built factories and offices. The main study has three central aims; it examines what happens when greenfield sites turn brown; that is, as they age. The second part is concerned with the impact of ownership and in particular foreign ownership on the nature of human resource management. The third question is concerned with the impact of human resource management.

An overriding question is the extent to which human resource management has become established as a preferred management option, on the assumption that this will be most dearly manifested in new establishments where managers have greater freedom to express their preferred choice. There are three parts to the study; the first is a reanalysis of part of WIRS3; the second is a survey of greenfield sites in the UK; and the third is a number of case studies in some of the surveyed establishments.

For our present purposes we will use data collected from the survey of greenfield sites. The survey was conducted in mid-1993, when a postal questionnaire was sent to just over 1,000 establishments in the UK employing more than fifty staff, including about 800 set up since 1980. We received responses from 393 establishments, subsequently reduced to 344 since some had less than fifty employees. Of the 344, 96 are purpose-built greenfield sites, new plants or offices being used for the first time; 152 are 'refurbished' sites, where there had been a major change of ownership and usually of activity, often following a shut-down period for the refurbishment; and 96 were set up before 1980.

For this analysis, we have restricted the sample to the greenfield and refurbished sites set up after 1980. This cut-off date was chosen as it marks the point at which Thatcherism began to have an impact at work, launching the debate about the new industrial relations. Establishments started since then provide what is arguably the best setting in which to explore the choices managers make about how to operate in the new industrial relations environments. At new establishments, unconstrained by history and tradition in the workplace, managers are most free to introduce the policies and practices of their choice.

Equally, they provide the most exacting test of how far trade unions are able to respond to the challenges they face in the new industrial relations. If they can flourish in such settings, then we can be more confident about their ability to retain a viable long-term role. In operating with new establishments we recognize that there is a different argument that could be made about looking at processes of change in older establishments. However, we believe that the cutting edge of innovations and emerging patterns in human resource management and the new industrial relations is likely to be found in new establishments.

The sample therefore contains 248 post- 1980 establishments of which 166 (66.9 per cent) are non-union and 82 (33.1 per cent) are unionized. These figures are in line with what we might expect from the analysis of WIRS3. Analysis by ownership reveals 104 UK owned establishments, 45 American-owned, 52 Japanese-owned, 19 German owned, and the remaining 24 owned by companies from the rest of the world which in practice means predominantly European Union and EFTA countries. Comparison with WIRS3 shows that the sample is broadly representative in size, based on number of employees and allowing for exclusion of those employing less than fifty staff. It is weighted towards manufacturing industry; indeed 84 per cent are manufacturing establishments, 10 per cent are in financial services, and 6 per cent are other services.

The questionnaire contained four sections. The first asked for background information on issues such as size, ownership, sector, age, and location. The second contained items about the presence of mission statements, human resource management strategy, and the degree of 'parental' influence. The third contained twenty-six items describing a range of contemporary human resource management practices and asked whether they are currently in existence at the establishment and whether they were used one year after start-up. The final asked about a range of outcomes.

These fall into three groups concerned with human resource management, employee relations, and establishment performance. The vast majority of questionnaires were completed either by the head of personnel at the establishment or by the most senior line manager with special responsibility for personnel issues, which in practice often meant the Managing Director, General Manager, or Plant Manager.

**Management and Unions**

In this subsection we examine the impact of trade unions on human resource management strategy and human resource management practices. We do this by comparing the establishments falling into the four trade union categories. These are those with no union (n = 166), those with a single union deal (n = 31), those with a single union but no single union deal (n = 18), and those with multiple-unionism (n = 33). In the questionnaire we were unable to explore the content of the single union deals, so there are risks in assuming that they are similar in nature. However, the question was quite explicit in asking whether there was a single union agreement.

How helpful is a union presence? One indirect way of exploring the impact of the unions was to gauge whether managers considered their presence to be helpful to the achievement of company goals. Sixty-six per cent of managers in establishments where unions were recognized considered the unions to be helpful. This ranged from 70 per cent in the case of single union deals to 55.6 per cent where there are single unions but no special deal. Multi-union establishments fell between the others with 62.5 per cent considering them helpful. The differences are not significant so we must be cautious, despite the apparent trend, in concluding that unions in the context of single union deals are seen as more helpful.

This is a somewhat surprising result if we accept the popular assumption that single union deals are explicitly designed to foster cooperation. It suggests that single union deals, assuming they have been correctly identified, do not have the clear-cut advantages sometimes claimed for them by their enthusiastic advocates. On the other hand, with two-thirds of managers taking the view that the unions are helpful, it is possible that new establishments provide an opportunity for managers to develop the kind of cooperation they want irrespective of whether or not they have a single union deal.

Unions and human resource strategy The questionnaire contained a section of items on aspects of policy and strategy. The responses in this section are important in setting a key part of the context for human resource management. It is hypothesized that those who take strategy more seriously will have better outcomes. However, as noted elsewhere the content of the strategy will be as important as having a strategy. The comparison of the 166 non-union establishments with those where various union arrangements were recognized. In this table we present the descriptive statistics, together with a Chi2 test of differences between the categories.

**Table: Human Resource Strategy**

| | *Numbers saying yes* | | | | |
|---|---|---|---|---|---|
| | *Non-union* | *Single union deal* | *Single union* | *Multi-union* | *Chi2* |
| Mission statement | 80(50.96) | 22(84.62) | 14(77.78) | 22(75.86) | 0.000 |
| If yes: | | | | | |
| Explicitly refers tohuman resource issues | 47(58.75) | 19(86.36) | 11(78.57) | 16(72.73) | 0.060 |
| Altered since firstwritten | 24(39.34) | 9(45) | 1(9.09) | 7(36.84) | 0.224 |
| Human resource-strategy suppor-tedby top site-management | 82(50.31) | 23(76.67) | 11(76.11) | 16(53.33) | 0.059 |
| Strategy altered sincefirst written | 68(42.5) | 11(36.67) | 9(50) | 16(53.33) | 0.548 |

*The first no. in each of the columns is the frequency, the second (in brackets) is the percentage.*

This controls for background variables and is a more rigorous test of differences between the categories. All types of unionized establishment are more likely to have a mission statement than non-union establishments. However, when we control for factors such as size and ownership, the difference is only significant for establishments with single union deals. Where there is a mission statement, it is more likely to include explicit reference to human resource issues in non-union establishments. Although the Chi2 result falls just short of significance, the multivariate test is significant and reveals that once again the differences can be accounted for mainly by the establishments with a single union deal.

The third key issue is the presence of a human resource strategy, formally endorsed and actively supported by the top management team at the establishment. Once again the unionized establishments are more likely to report the existence of such a strategy, although in both tables the results fall just short of significance.

The differences can be accounted for mainly by the establishments with single union deals. One indication of an effective strategy is that it is reasonably consistent over time. Although the differences are not significant, the results indicate that where a mission statement or a human resource management strategy exists, the nonunion establishments tend to be more likely to have altered both.

The results from this first set of data are reasonably clear-cut. Those new establishments where a union is recognized are more likely than non-union establishments to have a mission statement and to include in it specific reference to human resource issues, and more likely to have an explicit human resource strategy. These differences remain when we control for a range of background factors so they cannot be accounted for by variations in size, sector, or ownership. However, the presence of all these reflections of a strategy varies within the unionized establishments and is much the most likely to be found where there is a single union deal.

We cannot establish cause and effect. It is possible that those who think strategically opt for a single union deal. Alternatively, agreement to consider a single union deal forces establishments to confront related strategic human resource issues. It is probably most plausible to suggest that since we are dealing with new establishments, the development of human resource strategy and the planning of a single union deal go hand in hand. In this context, the role of the parent, as Marginson et al, have indicated, appears to be important in shaping attitudes towards trade union recognition and the form it takes. Whatever the reasons, the key finding is that it is the unionized rather than the non-union establishments that take the lead in developing human resource strategy.

### *Unions and Human Resource Practices*

The data indicate that a union presence is associated with a greater likelihood of a human resource strategy and a mission statement. However, it is wise to be somewhat sceptical about both unless they are clearly reinforced by a set of relevant practices. This subsection therefore takes us a step further by examining the presence at the new sites of the sort of practices commonly associated with human resource management. The list is not exhaustive and it concentrates on human resource practices rather than some of those that might be associated with the more narrowly defined industrial relations aspects of the new industrial relations. This reflected the key focus of the study and also our knowledge that most of the establishments in the sample would be non-union and therefore issues like pendulum arbitration would be irrelevant.

Perhaps the most interesting result is the lack of consistent differences between union and non-union establishments. In both sets of new establishments, the use of a majority of the innovative human resource management practices is now the norm. Nevertheless significant differences emerge on seven of the items. Two of these concern status and harmonization. Here the differences are not so much between union and non-union as between non-union and single union deals on the one hand and other forms of union recognition on the other.

However, in both cases it is the non-union establishments that are most likely to report these practices; and, the differences between the non-union and single union deal establishments are significant. Therefore, although establishments with single union deals are more like the non-union establishments, they still fall some way short on single status. The pattern is somewhat similar for two other items, merit pay and appraisal. Non-union establishments are well ahead of all forms of unionized establishment in the use of merit pay. The differences are much less marked on appraisal where it seems that the multi-union establishments are less likely to operate it.

**Table: Human Resource Practices**

| | *Non-union* (%) | *Single union deal* (%) | *Single union* (%) | *Multi-union* (%) | *Chi2* | *Observations* |
|---|---|---|---|---|---|---|
| Harmonized terms and conditions | 69.88 | 63.33 | 50 | 36.67 | 0.003 | 244 |
| Single status | 55.35 | 40 | 29.41 | 23.33 | 0.003 | 236 |
| Internal promotion the norm | 83.73 | 83.33 | 73.22 | 83.33 | 0.676 | 244 |
| No compulsory redundancy | 37.58 | 33.33 | 16.67 | 20 | 0.112 | 243 |
| Trainability as a major selection criteria | 67.48 | 90 | 52.94 | 53.33 | 0.01 | 240 |
| Use of psychological tests for all selection | 17.47 | 16.67 | 16.67 | 26.67 | 0.67 | 244 |
| Realistic job previews during recruitment | 57.23 | 62.07 | 62.5 | 43.33 | 0.432 | 234 |
| System to communicate values to new staff | 68.07 | 80 | 83.33 | 70 | 0.361 | 244 |
| Deliberate development of a learning organization | 57.32 | 75.86 | 66.67 | 53.33 | 0.221 | 241 |
| Minimum annual training requirements for all | 10.84 | 13.33 | 5.56 | 23.33 | 0.212 | 244 |
| Flexible job descs. not fixed to one task | 72.39 | 86.21 | 72.22 | 80 | 0.39 | 240 |
| Jobs designed to make full use of skills | 51.55 | 43.33 | 41.18 | 46.67 | 0.733 | 238 |
| Team working for majority of staff | 73.78 | 79.31 | 72.22 | 63.33 | 0.559 | 241 |
| Staff involved in setting performance targets | 57.93 | 50 | 50 | 40 | 0.296 | 242 |
| Staff responsible for | | | | | | |

| | | | | | | |
|---|---|---|---|---|---|---|
| their own quality | 83.85 | 90 | 94.44 | 76.67 | 0.319 | 239 |
| Majority involved in quality circles or quality improvement teams | 43.03 | 40 | 61.11 | 53.33 | 0.35 | 243 |
| Regular use of attitude surveys | 23.03 | 30 | 16.67 | 20 | 0.708 | 243 |
| Team briefing/ Information cascades | 62.05 | 76.67 | 55.56 | 66.67 | 0.39 | 244 |
| Information on market position/ company performance | 78.18 | 90 | 66.67 | 73.33 | 0.234 | 243 |
| Merit pay for all staff | 64.85 | 37.93 | 38.89 | 30 | 0.000 | 242 |
| Formal appraisal for all at least annually | 72.89 | 68.97 | 61.11 | 43.33 | 0.014 | 243 |
| Human resource policy integrated with business strategy | 56.33 | 89.66 | 58.82 | 53.33 | 0.007 | 234 |
| Human resource policies integrated with each other | 55.06 | 82.14 | 47.06 | 50 | 0.033 | 231 |

The three remaining items are those where establishments with a single union deal stand out as most likely to have adopted a practice. One is the use of trainability as a major selection criterion; the others are concerned with integration of strategy. Establishments with single union deals are much more likely to claim that human resource policies are integrated with business strategy and that the various human resource policies are integrated with each other. This would fit with the earlier claims to be more likely to have a human resource strategy.

Taking the set of practices as a whole, it appears that they are most likely to be reported in establishments with a single union deal, closely followed by non-union establishments. However, the other unionized establishments are often little different, indicating that a union presence is no bar to most human resource practices. Despite this, the exceptions may be important. Unionized establishments are less likely to have progressed towards single status and less likely to be using appraisal-linked merit pay. These touch on traditional trade union territory and it would seem that in this territory they are still able to exert some influence on workplace practices.

### *Unions and Types Strategy*

There is some evidence from the preceding analysis that unionized workplaces, and more particularly those with a single union deal, are more likely to have developed a coherent human resource strategy. However, not all establishments have a strategy and not all have introduced human resource management practices. To explore whether a union presence is compatible with the kind of high utilization human resource strategy sometimes associated with best human resource practice but also often seen as inimical to a trade union presence, we can reclassify establishments.

The basis for this classification was introduced earlier. Those establishments labelled Good have a human resource strategy, defined in the questionnaire as being formally endorsed and actively supported by the top management at the site; and also a high use of human resource practices, defined arbitrarily as more than half of those listed in Table given below. The Bad are the opposite in that they have no strategy and use less than half the practices listed. The Ugly have a strategy but use less than half the practices while the Lucky have no strategy but use more than half the practices.

If strategic integration is at all important, we would expect the Good to report better outcomes than the Bad. If strategic integration around a distinctive set of human resource practices confers an advantage then we would also expect to see the Good report better outcomes than the Ugly and Lucky. By comparing across the groups we can also identify whether adoption of practices without a strategy — the approach of the Lucky — also has an impact on outcomes. In our total sample of 245 establishments, 107 (43.7 per cent) were classified as Good, 70 (28.6 per cent) as Bad, 28 (11.4 per cent) as Ugly, and 40 (16.3 per cent) as Lucky.

The key question for the debate about human resource management and the new industrial relations is whether the Good are compatible with unionism.

**Table: Unions and type of human resource strategy**

| | *Good* | *Lucky* | *Bad* | *Ugly* |
|---|---|---|---|---|
| Union (%) | 50 | 6.1 | 29.27 | 14.63 |
| Non-Union (%) N | 40.49 | 21.47 | 28.22 | 9.82 |
| Chi2 sig. | 0.157 | 0.002 | 0.864 | 0.263 |
| Observations | 107 | 40 | 70 | 28 |
| Single union deal | 63.33 | 0 | 23.33 | 13.33 |
| Single union no deal (%) | 50 | 5.56 | 33.33 | 11.11 |
| Multi-Union (%) | 16.67 | 13.33 | 33.33 | 36.67 |
| Chi2 sig. | 0.099 | 0.014 | 0.815 | 0.717 |
| Observations | 107 | 40 | 70 | 28 |

***Notes:*** *The percentages given are based on a total sample of 245.*

Single-Multi-Union Chi2 scores calculated in comparison with non-union category.

The results confirm that a union presence is compatible with a high utilization model of human resource management. Indeed, if we examine the distribution, a higher proportion of union than non-union establishments fall in the good category. This is due to the greater likelihood that they will have a human resource strategy. In contrast, more of the non-union establishments fall into the lucky category. They have adopted the practices but have not developed a strategy.

The multivariate analysis confirms this pattern but reveals where the differences lie. It is the establishments with a single union deal that are significantly more likely to fall within the Good category while the non-union are significantly more likely to be Lucky. No group stands out as more likely to be Bad or Ugly, although, contrary to expectation, there is a slight tendency for them to be unionized rather than not.

Summarizing the results to date, we have shown that at new establishments, those set up in the 1980s or more recently, industrial relations, manifested in a trade union presence and human resource management are able to exist side by side. However, we can go further than this. It appears that, more particularly in the case of single union deals, it is less a matter of the systems coexisting as of being integrated through a coherent strategy.

Indeed, unionized workplaces are more likely than their non-union counterparts to have a human resource strategy. There do appear to be some differences between the types of union presence. Without a single union deal, there is a slightly lower use of human resource practices and slightly less evidence of the sort of strategic pursuit of a high utilization policy categorized as the Good.

We have shown that with perhaps two exceptions, represented by single status and appraisal-related merit pay, the unions do not inhibit human resource management practice. The next key question is whether they have any impact on performance.

### *The Impact of Unions*

If we wish to conduct a rigorous test of the impact of unions on performance and other outcomes, it is firstly necessary to see if there are links between human resource policy and practice and outcomes. If there are, then it will be necessary to hold this factor constant in order to ascertain the effect which unions have on performance per se, irrespective of the policies which are being used. The wider and controversial literature concerning the impact of unions on performance suggests that on balance they act as a drag. However, it is plausible to hypothesize that where a union presence is part of a planned human resource strategy in a new workplace, this is less likely to be the case.

The first step is to examine the impact of human resource policy and practice on outcomes. This is an important and interesting topic in its own light. For this purpose, we retain the integrative distinction between the Good, the Bad, the Ugly, and the Lucky. These results show that there are consistent differences between the policy types and it will therefore be necessary to hold policy effects constant when testing for union effects. While Table given below has been included in order to demonstrate this necessity, it is also of great interest in itself.

It shows the strength of the links between the use of strategically integrated human resource policies and performance. Specifically, the good establishments, those with a human resource strategy and a high uptake of human resource practices, consistently report better outcomes. At the other extreme, those with the poorer outcomes, revealed most clearly are the Bad, those without a strategy or much use of human resource practices. The Ugly and the Lucky both report consistently poorer performance than the Good on all three types of outcome. This result will be of great encouragement to those who are attempting to implement a high utilization human resource strategy. This is the first UK. study to date which demonstrates the benefits of such a strategy so clearly.

We can now hold the human resource policy variable constant while examining the impact of unions on outcomes. The resulting multivariate analysis is shown. First, however, we can examine the descriptive results.

The results reveal few significant differences between the various categories. There are some exceptions. Establishments with a single union deal claim to have weathered the recession more successfully than multi-union establishments. Industrial disputes are predictably less likely in non-union establishments. Finally there is a trend towards higher quality of staff in single union deal establishments compared with the multi-union.

Only when the controls are imposed do the differences become clearer. The unionized establishments, taken as a whole, report poorer outcomes on almost all variables.

**Table: Human Resource Strategy and Outcomes**

| | *Good* | *Lucky* | *Bad* | *Ugly* | *Chi2* | *Observa-tions* |
|---|---|---|---|---|---|---|
| Human resource outcomes | | | | | | |
| Commitment of lower grade staff | 3.776 (0.731) | 3.675 (0.764) | 3.143 (0.785) | 3.429 (0.742) | 0.001 | 245 |
| The quality of staff employed | 4.056 (0.596) | 3.9 (0.709) | 3.559 (0.632) | 3.929 (0.716) | 0.000 | 243 |
| Quality of work of lower grade staff | 3.972 (0.621) | 4.05 (0.714) | 3.671 (0.607) | 3.75 (0.752) | 0.031 | 245 |
| Quality of human resource policies andpractices | 3.701 (0.633) | 3.154 (0.63) | 2.706 (0.875) | 3.333 (0.733) | 0.000 | 241 |
| The flexibility of staff | 4.234 (0.681) | 4.05 (0.677) | 3.681 (0.795) | 4.107 (0.875) | 0.001 | 244 |
| Ability to move between jobs as needed | 4.085 (0.692) | 3.8 (0.758) | 3.557 (0.792) | 4.036 (0.838) | 0.002 | 244 |
| Flexibility to adjust workforce size | 3.424 (1.121) | 3.25 (1.193) | 3.206 (1.087) | 3.185 (1.075) | 0.651 | 241 |
| Line manager enthusiasm for humanresource policies | 3.813 (0.646) | 3.436 (0.718) | 2.806 (0.875) | 3.071 (0.766) | 0.000 | 241 |
| *Employee relations outcomes* | | | | | | |
| Industrial dispute 'yes' (%) | 16.82 | 10 | 18.57 | 25 | 0.43 | 245 |
| Labour turnover in 1992 | 7.18 (7.826) | 9.375 (10.166) | 12 (13.263) | 11.423 (13.03) | 0.224 | 219 |
| Absenteeism in 1992 (%) | 4.229 (3.026) | 5.879 (6.684) | 4.681 (3.044) | 6 (5.721) | 0.259 | 186 |
| *Performance outcomes* | | | | | | |
| Quality targets attained (%) | 91.554 (13.177) | 88.565 (25.443) | 88.618 (10.592) | 88.429 (20.887) | 0.068 | 145 |

| | | | | | | |
|---|---|---|---|---|---|---|
| How well was the recession weathered | 4.047 (0.773) | 3.925 (0.656) | 3.716 (0.735) | 3.929 (0.858) | 0.033 | 241 |
| Productivity benchmarked against UK | 4.174 (0.829) | 3.917 (0.776) | 3.441 (0.705) | 3.783 (0.795) | 0.002 | 167 |
| Quality benchmarked against the UK | 4.437 (0.773) | 4.192 (0.694) | 3.714 (0.926) | 4.043 (0.706) | 0.000 | 171 |
| Prod'y benchmarked against World | 3.64 (1.029) | 3.348 (0.982) | 3.172 (0.848) | 3.526 (0.964) | 0.485 | 154 |
| Quality benchmarked against World | 3.988 (0.97) | 3.8 (0.912) | 3.429 (1.034) | 3.7 (0.979) | 0.133 | 158 |

***Notes:*** *Means given (minimum 1, maximum 5) with standard deviation in brackets.*

**Table: Unions and Outcomes**

| | *Non-Union* | *Single Union Deal* | *Single Union* | *Multi Union* | *Chi2* | *Observations* |
|---|---|---|---|---|---|---|
| Human resource outcomes | | | | | | |
| Commitment of lower grade staff | 3.56 (0.79) | 3.6 (0.814) | 3.667 (0.686) | 3.233 (0.817) | 0.7 | 244 |
| The quality of staff employed | 3.884 (0.659) | 3.967 (0.615) | 3.834 (0.857) | 3.733 (0.64) | 0.071 | 242 |
| Quality of work of lower grade staff | 3.928 (0.693) | 3.9 (0.662) | 3.778 (0.428) | 3.633 (0.556) | 0.106 | 244 |
| Quality of human resource policies and practices | 3.259 (0.831) | 3.552 (0.736) | 3.111 (0.963) | 3.241 (0.872) | 0.449 | 238 |
| The flexibility of staff | 4.018 (0.777) | 4.267 (0.691) | 4.056 (0.802) | 3.9 (0.803) | 0.802 | 243 |
| Ability to move between jobs as needed | 3.898 (0.776) | 4.033 (0.765) | 3.833 (0.707) | 3.724 (0.922) | 0.676 | 243 |

| | | | | | | |
|---|---|---|---|---|---|---|
| Flexibility to adjust workforce size | 3.252 (1.146) | 3.667 (0.884) | 3.556 (1.097) | 3.103 (1.175) | 0.612 | 240 |
| Line manager enthusiasm for humanresource policies | 3.435 (0.82) | 3.5 (0.777) | 3.222 (1.003) | 3.003 (0.928) | 0.255 | 239 |
| *Employee relations outcomes* | | | | | | |
| Industrial dispute 'yes' (%) | 5.42 | 33.33 | 22.22 | 60 | 0.000 | 244 |
| Labour turnover in 1992 (%) | 9.619 (10.178) | 12 (14.397) | 6.706 (6.864) | 6.261 (12.02) | 0.754 | 216 |
| Absenteeism in 1992 | 4.815 (4.986) | 4.552 (3.101) | 5.231 (3.468) | 4.826 (1.969) | 0.592 | 184 |
| *Performance outcomes* | | | | | | |
| Quality targets attained | 89.13 (18.151) | 93.571 (6.896) | 90 (6.305) | 89.133 (13.856) | 0.84 | 145 |
| How well was the recession weathered | 3.963 (0.767) | 4.214 (0.686) | 3.889 (0.676) | 3.433 (0.679) | 0.021 | 240 |
| Productivity benchmarked against UK | 3.964 (0.838) | 4.211 (0.787) | 3.818 (0.874) | 3.591 (0.796) | 0.547 | 238 |
| Quality bench-marked against the UK | 4.202 (0.854) | 4.318 (0.716) | 4.273 (0.786) | 4 (0.894) | 0.23 | 237 |
| Prod'y bench-marked against World | 3.569 (1.02) | 3.579 (0.838) | 2.9 (0.994) | 3.333 (0.966) | 0.146 | 234 |
| Quality bench-marked against World | 3.838 (1.02) | 3.762 (0.7) | 3.7 (1.337) | 3.85 (0.988) | 0.314 | 233 |

***Notes:*** *Means given (minimum 1, maximum 5) with standard deviations in brackets.*

On a number they are significant. However, as expected, there are variations according to the type of union arrangement. The rest indicates that the poorer outcomes are most likely to be found at the multi-union establishments. In particular, they appear to have poorer human resource outcomes.

In contrast, the only significant factor among the single union establishments is the greater likelihood of industrial conflict compared with the non-union establishments. Indeed, on issues associated with flexibility they appear to be at an advantage.

What these results indicate is that the presence of a union still acts as a modest but sometimes significant drag on performance. The effects are greater for multi-unionism and least for single union deals. Despite the earlier evidence of a willingness on the part of union establishments to embrace human resource practices, it seems that the unions still exert some influence on workplace outcomes. Finally, it is worth noting that the human resource strategy types appear to exert more influence than the unions. Performance is poorer in the Bad establishments than in the multi-union establishments.

The first key question we set out to explore through the study of greenfield sites is whether human resource management and trade-unionism can coexist. The answer from this study is an unequivocal yes. Most human resource management practices are just as likely to exist at unionized establishments as at those without unions. There are some variations on this general pattern.

The first important variation is the finding that the presence of a trade union is associated with a greater use of a human resource management strategy and a mission statement, which, in addition, is more likely to refer explicitly to human resource issues. This needs to be qualified by the analysis of types of trade union presence. A strategy and mission statement is particularly likely to exist where there is a single union deal. We cannot tell from this cross-sectional data whether the union presence encourages managers to think strategically or whether those who think strategically opt for a single union deal.

Although we suspect that the causal direction varies from context to context, since the choice of whether to recognize a union is an increasingly open one, we suspect that management thinks strategically about both human resource management and the new industrial relations and decides to opt for a single union deal. Multiple unionism, by contrast, may come into operation in those establishments where a parent company already has a central collective agreement with a number of unions. It follows that the majority of such cases are likely to be British-owned. Examination of the national ownership patterns confirms that this is indeed the case. The UK- and USA-owned establishments where any union is recognized are the least likely to report a single union deal.

The pattern across the range of human resource management practices also reveals some specific differences and helps to sharpen the distinction between the new industrial relations, reflected in single union deals, and the traditional industrial relations reflected in multi-unionism. Any type of trade union presence is associated with less use of single status and use of performance appraisal and merit pay for all staff. Single union deals on the other hand are associated with a set of practices broadly similar to non-union establishments but with the added advantage of having a more coherent human resource strategy. These results are strongly supported by Millward's analysis of the new industrial relations based on WIRS3. He finds that establishments with single union deals are consistently more likely to have a range of innovative practices, implying once again that they think strategically about single union deals and human resource management issues together.

The second major question we have explored is whether a union presence facilitates or constrains aspects of performance. The general conclusion is that unions inhibit performance and multi-unionism inhibits it more. However, this conclusion requires some qualification since single union deals have far less impact on performance, compared with non-union establishments.

The similarity between non-union establishments and those with a single union deal brings us back to the question of whether this type of unionism is an empty shell. It does not appear to constrain management. Indeed, it is associated with what managers believe to be greater commitment to the organization among lower level staff and with greater flexibility than even non-union establishments. In contrast, multi-unionism is associated with poorer outcomes on all variables except labour turnover and absenteeism; and on five of the outcomes, the differences with non-union establishments are significant. Thus multi-unionism is associated with poorer performance. This confirms the economic research on the impact of unions.

Before reaching the general conclusion that multi-unionism is bad for performance, we should recall the data on human resource management types. The Bad establishments are more clearly associated with poor outcomes than the multi-union establishments, implying that decisions about human resource strategy are more important for outcomes than decisions about multi-unionism — assuming that managers take decisions about these issues and that in practice the two can be disentangled. In one sense, this marginalizes the union issue. On the other hand, unions may always have been marginal to performance in the great majority of organizations although industrial relations specialists, with their distinctive focus on unions, have been understandably reluctant to acknowledge this.

To summarize, the new trade-unionism, reflected most strongly in single union deals, is compatible with human resource management. There is more of a question mark against multi-unionism. This raises the question of why any company will recognize a trade union at a new establishment. A single union deal has very little impact compared with non-union establishments suggesting that they turn unions into empty shells. Multi-unionism has a somewhat negative impact. In our sample of post- 1980 establishments, approximately a third recognized one or more trade unions. However, this fell to 20 per cent in the 'pure' greenfield sites compared with 42 per cent in the refurbished sites. The great majority of managers have already decided that there is no value in recognizing a trade union. So why do others do so?

The evidence from our case studies supports the more extensive data from the CLIRS2. This indicates that unions will be recognized in those companies which have a centralized system of collective bargaining which they wish to retain. Secondly, as our comparison of greenfield and refurbished sites suggests, unions may be recognized at those workplaces which are taken over, even if shut down for a while and refurbished, and where a union was already recognized. It is possible that in some cases there may be scope for the operation of individual values. Some managers, including perhaps personnel managers in particular, may value the presence of a trade union as a counterweight to arbitrary management treatment.

Since we have found little evidence of any trade union official presence in our case studies, it appears that the personnel manager may act as promoter and recruiter for the union. However, this is likely to become less common. The evidence from this study suggests that as we learn more about the impact of the new industrial relations, in the absence of any change towards a government that more actively encourages them, the outlook for trade unions is bleak.

The practices and process of 'new industrial relations' and human resource management have become the primary agenda of industrial relations research and teaching whether prescriptive or critical; notwithstanding this primacy new industrial relations and human resource management are of no use in themselves; they are propagated as mechanisms to rejuvenate the British economy, its manufacturing sector in particular, and connect with current dynamics in capitalist production. Without an evaluation of the problematic nature of the wider dynamics of capitalist production new industrial relations and human resource management are both abstract and decontextual.

In the period since 1945 the dynamics of capitalist production have been generalized under two broad headings. The post-war period is generalized as 'Fordism', centred on the mass production of standardized commodities, institutionalized collective bargaining, and Welfare State capitalism. The contemporary period is generalized as 'Post-Fordism' premissed on the demise of mass consumer markets, the rise of niche markets, and the erosion of social democracy in the institutional base of the State. In particular, it has rejected collective bargaining and trade union recognition as 'good' industrial relations.

If we accept that Fordism and Post-Fordism generalize periods in capitalist production it is equally necessary to question the degree to which national pathways in capitalist production measure up to the generalization. We contend that national pathways predominate over generalized descriptions in the development of capitalist production. In consequence we must evaluate the relationship between capital, labour, and the State within national pathways in order to illustrate how historical formation within particular nation states weakens the viability of generalized description.

We suggest that the British State has been subject to a formative influence of libertarian laissez faire which emphasizes freedom and liberty from centralized and institutionalized measures enacted by the State. In the post-war period plural industrial relations and voluntary regulation epitomize this influence. Equally during the post-war period the British State was subject to the contextual influence of social democracy and plural public policy manifest in 'good' industrial relations as collective bargaining and trade union recognition. The contemporary erosion of social democracy and 'good' industrial relations has separated the State from an active interest in capitalist accumulation; in fact the disengagement of pluralism in industrial relations has wound up the contextual influence of social democracy and returned the formative influence of libertarian laissez faire as contemporary contextual influence in the State, its accumulation strategy, and public policy on industrial relations.

However, the disengagement of pluralism, an accumulation strategy based on flexibility, and redefined 'good' industrial relations are all caught in the permanent yet unfolding contradiction of libertarian laissez faire; that is, a continuity in historical formation within a particular nation state and the predominance of this over generalized pathways in capitalist production. We contend that new industrial relations is in the British case isolated and disengaged from contemporary material dynamics other than promoting what can be termed 'extra flexibility'. This isolation illustrates the weakness of prescriptive generalization in capitalist production because Post-Fordism and Fordism are based on a presumed role for the State, which we suggest never developed in the British State.

This seeks to illustrate the isolation of new industrial relations as informed by human resource management from market and production strategies which are portrayed as the (future) basis of capitalist production in the UK. This develops a wide-ranging polemic and is eclectic in its discussion with references to the State and its current strategy of disengagement from active involvement in capitalist accumulation.

Since 1945 'good' industrial relations have been a central feature of public policy. For much of the post-war period 'good' industrial relations was constituted in terms of plural State institutions presiding over an economy where collective bargaining and trade union recognition were functional elements within an accumulation strategy centred on Fordism. By 1979 'good' industrial relations had become 'bad' industrial relations; almost overnight the Thatcher Government rejected the pluralism in the post-war settlement between capital and labour. More significantly the Thatcher Government came to power when the period of capitalist development generalized as Fordism was exhausted.

The contemporary State has initiated a libertarian, that is individual accumulation, strategy, disengaged pluralism in industrial relations, and sought to roll back much of its previous social democratic orthodoxy in areas such as employment policy, the Welfare State, nationalized industry, and industrial relations. Good industrial relations have been reconstituted and now emphasize the managerial prerogative and less industrial action as the basis of good.

This contends that the contemporary State's method of operation, disengagement from social democracy, actively frustrates its efforts to generate a positive flexible Post-Fordism in the UK. This asserts that flexibility is a means to an end in the movement between stages of capitalist development whereas in the UK it has become an end in itself. In consequence, in the UK, flexibility is not a bridge between Fordism and Post-Fordism but a method of making the entrails of Fordism more flexible, thereby contributing to the development of a neo-Fordist low wage, low productivity, yet flexible, economy. Hence our contention that sovereign national pathways to capitalist development predominate over generalized periodizations. In order to develop this overall argument the discussion which follows is divided into four sections.

In Section 2 formative and contextual influences on the British State are briefly introduced in order to specify the limited nature of the British State. Section 3 evaluates the process of contemporary State disengagement from the post-war social democratic orthodoxy; the strategy of Conservative governments and their attempts to reconstitute good industrial relations is located in the process of disengagement. Section 4 evaluates new industrial relations, new market and production strategies, and suggests that institutional disengagement by the State isolates new (improved) industrial relations from new market and production strategies. In consequence typology-normative description of market and production strategies are removed from their actual constitution in the UK's national pathway. Section 5 builds on the arguments of the previous sections to illustrate the limited nature of new industrial relations in the generation of flexibility and sustainable improvement in productivity.

### *Formative and Contextual Influences*

As a precursor to a more detailed evaluation of new industrial relations we briefly discuss formative and contextual influences on the British State. The aim of this section is to illustrate how a renaissance of formative influences on the State in terms of its public policy actually frustrates overall economic performance. The formative influence on the development of the British State is libertarian laissez faire. As an economic and political doctrine it eschews a centralized state and highlights voluntary regulation in all spheres through contract and status. Notwithstanding its formative influence, laissez faire was discredited as the industrial revolution progressed during the nineteenth century. From the 1870s a contextual influence emerged on the State; social democracy and collectivism developed in response to industrialization and collective experience in the employment relationship.

For example, between 1871 and 1906 trade unions were legalized so that their activities were given immunity from prosecution in specific instances. Additionally between 1832 and 1928 the franchise was extended to all adults over the age of 21. Lastly, between 1908 and 1911 the Liberal Government introduced the beginning of what later becomes a fully fledged Welfare State. In addition to these examples of collectivism and social democracy both concepts reached their height in the formulation of plural industrial relations as public policy in the post-war period. For a general survey on the emergence of collectivism in the UK, see Greenleaf.

For much of the period since 1945 industrial relations were worked out plurally between employers and employees free from substantive legislative interference by the State. In substance pluralism in industrial relations was extra-contractual and socio-political in its constitution. By extra contractual we mean it operated beyond the influence of individual contract, in consequence its method centres on the negotiation of collective agreements on the individual enforcement of contract. Pluralism was socio-political in its constitution because in public policy it was geared towards collective bargaining, trade union recognition, and State absenteeism with minimal negative use of the law; Kahn-Freund referred to this as 'collective laissez faire'.

The formative influence of libertarian laissez faire on the British State facilitated the development of voluntary industrial relations, projecting freedom from the State in the institutional base of industrial relations. Voluntary method in industrial relations illustrates the political foundation of laissez faire which prescribes a preference for voluntary regulation over State regulation. In the post-war period this equated to autonomous collective bargaining between employers and employees.

The central point in the making is the contradictory effect the formative influence of libertarian laissez faire has had. In many respects voluntary industrial relations replicated the formative influence of libertarian laissez faire by limiting active and positive State regulation of industrial relations, in particular the negative use of the law. By this we mean that voluntarism, that is collective laissez faire, encouraged a form of decentralized production politics where capital, labour (and the State) sought to keep the State out of their internal affairs and relations. Perkin argues that a pattern of preindustrial class-formation, emphasizing maximum material freedom from the State was reproduced in industrial society. Barrington-Moore refers to this as a peaceful bourgeois revolution expressing a continuity of interests in and between capital and free labour vis-a-vis the centralized State apparatus in the form of Monarchy or Parliament. I. Clark (forthcoming) illustrates this argument in relation to the development of State policy on productivity in the post-war period.

Notwithstanding the above, institutional freedom only extends to the method of industrial relations. Within a capitalist economy the State is always present in the institution of industrial relations; the State apparatus defends and maintains private property, capitalist reproduction, and the contractually determined employment relationship, that is the naturalized framework of capitalist production. A contradiction in industrial relations is its complete separation from the dynamics of capitalist production. Rule-making in capitalist production is beyond economics but central to industrial relations, this defines the fictitious nature of voluntary industrial relations; their method may be voluntary but their institution results from the framework of capitalist production.

Since 1979 the State has not been rolled back per se, it is the contextual influence of social democracy and collectivism which has been curtailed. As a result the formative influence of libertarian laissez faire has been repopularized in order to halt socio-political advances made by labour during the post-war period.

In essence the Thatcher-Major Governments have sought to restructure capital by eroding social democracy and reconstituting public policy as individual and liberal. A major element in this policy has been the removal of 'market rigidities' such as trade unions, elements of the public sector, and within employment inflexible collective agreements constituted beyond contract. A by-product of reconstituting public policy has been an effort to generate new industrial relations informed, initially by macho management and latterly by new management techniques amalgamated in 'human resource management'. In both cases individual contractual reward and regulation are highlighted. We now proceed to a more detailed discussion of new industrial relations.

### *The New Generation*

The previous argued that since 1979 the formative influence of libertarian laissez faire has been paramount in the State's efforts to restructure the UK's industrial capitalism. In addition it was argued that voluntary industrial relations, constituted collectively or individually, replicate the libertarian bias in the British State which emphasizes freedom from centralized State action and regulation. The absence of centralized State action and regulation has been projected as vital to the generation of new industrial relations; this in turn has led to a rejection of pluralism and social democracy in the institutional base of the State. Both of these were primary contextual influences on the post-war State and public policy on industrial relations. This section examines the State as a functional entity which seeks to structure class conflict and provide co-ordination for the market by facilitating capitalist accumulation.

The period of capitalist development which followed the Second World War is generalized as Fordism; within this, economic co-ordination and class struggle necessitated the promotion of plural industrial relations and a Welfare State. Such innovations accommodated the balance of class forces which were determined by full employment and a diffusion of social democracy in the State. Since 1979 the contemporary State has disengaged this orthodoxy. It has been able to do this with such ease precisely because pluralism and social democracy were constituted beyond the formative influences on the State. One area where the pressure of disengagement has been most prominent is the generalization of new industrial relations.

In terms of our argument we suggest that new industrial relations represents three ideological images propagated by the contemporary State: first, the promotion of the managerial prerogative, employee compliance, and a low strike level; secondly, a rejection of collective bargaining and trade union recognition as public policy and their replacement with managerially determined regulation and individualism in the employment relationship; thirdly, a prescription for management labour use strategies centred on flexibility and extra-contractual commitment through human resource management. Each image evokes the formative influences of libertarian laissez faire informed by contract and status and rejects contextual influences centred on pluralism, collective bargaining, and trade unions.

Thatcherism emphasized the conservative nature of the British State and repopularized individualism and freedom from the State. Thatcherism sought to reduce financial and institutional dependence on the State and encourage self-reliance, both economically and socially. In so doing it attacked the contextual basis of the post-war State.

By promoting contractual individualism Thatcherism launched a supply side attack on 'obstacles' to productive efficiency such as public debt, State-spending on the products of social democracy, and the social democratic acceptance of privileged trade unions. As Gamble makes clear, Thatcherism unwound the coil of social democracy in the UK's State apparatus (a sociopolitical retreat designed to promote economic advance). A rapid change in public policy on industrial relations in the use of the law and the promotion of individualism became the leading edge of State disengagement from the postwar plural orthodoxy.

The rhetoric of new industrial relations attacks the acceptance of conflict in industrial relations; the failure of pluralist industrial relations as public policy. The substance of new industrial relations represents an effort to contextualize formative influences on the State. In consequence the State has sought to circumscribe or terminate key rights and immunities acquired by trade unions since the late nineteenth century. Pioneers of social democracy such as the Webbs saw the expansion of State activity and institutional recognition on behalf of labour as an imperative; that is, a functional response to the needs of industrial capitalism.

The political erosion of social democracy since 1979 is also propagated on the basis of current imperatives in capitalist development; in crude terms, the orthodox pluralism of 'old' industrial relations was based on the contextual influences of collectivism, union recognition and the absence of law: 'new' industrial relations is based in the formative influence of libertarian laissez faire, State individualism, and freedom from extra contractual institutional regulation. Collectivism sat easily with the functional requirements of Fordism, whereas market individualism is propagated as essential for a successful movement to a Post-Fordist stage in capitalist development.

In order to avoid the charge of functional determinism there are two caveats which illustrate the problematic of function. First, old and new industrial relations are constituted through public policy; in both cases the extent to which the reality measures up to constitution is questionable (for a brief discussion of the limits in the post-war settlement see Eldridgeet al.; for the limits of the contemporary settlement see Hutton. The second caveat concerns the generation of new industrial relations and its role in the movement from Fordism to Post-Fordism. As Zeitlin points out, States are not rational actors operating as historical subjects in defined periods but complex and contradictory associations. Hence there can be no guarantee that action by the State can be coherent or strategic. If this were the case order in industrial relations would be the norm.

The interesting question is how public policy becomes dysfunctional; the role and motivation of the State is a key factor as are its formative limitations. In the post-war period contextual influences on the State, pluralism, and social democracy became almost exclusive. For example, the Donovan prescription for industrial relations reform had no linkage to economic performance other than the social democratic assertion that formalized procedures at company level would arrest the use of restrictive practices, unofficial industrial action, and informal sectionalism. Since 1979 public policy has sought to sweep away social democracy and pluralism in industrial relations precisely because it inhibited economic performance via its method of extra-contractual (collective) rigidity.

In both periods public policy became dysfunctional; first, it failed to address the issue of management. In the 1960s management practice was largely ignored by the Donovan proposals. Flanders argued that procedural reform would improve management; however, as Hyman point out management did not necessarily improve its own practice in terms of cost and production control or work study. In the contemporary period management is assumed to be improved by measures which promote the managerial prerogative. However, British management practice was not necessarily connected to the broader material dynamics of Fordism or Post-Fordism.

A second reason for State policy becoming dysfunctional centres on the form of the State; in the post-war period contextual influences were determined extra-contractually whereas in the contemporary period extra-contractual influences have been curtailed. The contradiction for the State is its limited form. In the era of pluralism the State could not structure an integration of formative and contextual influences, whereas today the State has rejected the latter and seeks to operate through the former.

Hence human agency within the institutional base of the State has gone from social democracy without a consideration of economic performance to a singular consideration of capitalist accumulation without a consideration of social democracy or comparative economic performance. Use of law and the rejection of anything approaching good industrial relations in public policy are the dysfunctional consequences of State policy: the absence of the latter and pivotal role of the former have enabled the State to go back to its formative influences of contract, status, and the market.

All three now drive human agency within the State's institutional apparatus. For example, in the pluralist era 'status rights' were determined extra-contractually through the acceptance of collective bargaining, trade unions, and the minimal use of the law. In the contemporary era 'status' is not attached to anything collective, but instead, the individual contract of employment, which the prescription behind human resource management encourages individual employees to go beyond in order to progress up a single status hierarchy.

By disengaging from an institutional interest in good industrial relations the State has no industrial relations or overall industrial strategy which can lever the UK economy into Post-Fordism other than the purported benefits of market-oriented flexibility and statistically engineered improvement in productivity. As Zeitlin points out, functional explanations become tautological if any development can (retrospectively) be advantageous or compatible with functional requirements in capitalism. The critical issue is the disconnection of cause and positive effect. Changes in the use of law and the generation of new industrial relations as enterprisebased public policy are largely negative in their effect because in the UK they fail to connect with production and market strategies essential in a movement to positive Post-Fordism.

In the main, new industrial relations operates in Fordist product and market strategies which in the majority of areas encourage low productivity and low wages. Business operates in a climate of perennial uncertainty and instability which in the absence of an overall industrial strategy encourages short-term responses to marketing, production, and management in general. As enterprise responses such moves are expressions of rational self-interest; however, the absence of an overall industrial strategy, other than the pursuit of flexibility, provides no positive dynamic for employers to follow.

### *The Basis of Relations Change*

The first Thatcher administration visualized trade unions as operationally uncontrollable and restrictive. Trade unions were held to be uncontrollable in the sense that industrial action was often unofficial, secondary, and involved the use of mass picketing. In addition highly particular restrictive practices were generalized to be operative throughout the economy. Such practices created inflexibility and rigidity in the supply side of the economy blunting its efficiency. Inefficiency manifested itself in a failure to use new technology in a competitive manner.

Supply side measures attacked obstacles to productive efficiency such as trade unions. Early legislation was designed with two purposes in mind: first, to challenge established patterns of behaviour and conduct in industrial disputes, and secondly, to improve the managerial prerogative. The latter effect is a function of the former; measures such as secondary picketing and unofficial industrial action were often traditional responses to managerial unreasonableness and unilateralism. In the new legal environment of the trade union as legal personality, fines and possible sequestration make such action less likely. Hence in operational terms the likelihood of trade union financial loss facilitated a potential improvement in the managerial prerogative.

The Employment Acts of 1980 and 1982 were not primarily directed at the internal activity of unions or their (restrictive) practices but at their conduct within industrial disputes. The 1980 Act outlawed secondary industrial action and secondary picketing whereas the 1982 Act made the continuation of these now illegal activities more pressing by narrowing the definition of a trade dispute and restoring the legal personality of trade unions. As Brown and Wadhwani comment, these changes substantially weakened the position of unions which traditionally relied on secondary action.

Thus, the first attack on the working of established industrial relations was to weaken its mode of operation in times of dispute. The second attack can most effectively be seen within the wider attack on, and rejection of, elements within the supply side of the post-war settlement.

The attack on the post-war settlement and the supply side in particular was the Thatcher Government's response to the failure of economic and social regulation in the orthodoxy of the social democratic State; that is, the capacity of the State to manage this orthodoxy. The presence of near full employment was visualized as reducing pressures on employers to be efficient thereby resulting in uncompetitive productivity levels especially in manufacturing.

In addition the restrictive nature of trade unions stifled enterprise and the effective operation of market forces. Initially the strategy of attack was to shake out the manufacturing sector by severe deflation, an indirect effect of which was to promote the managerial prerogative on the basis of 'macho management' which later appeared more reasoned in 'new industrial relations' centred on the idea of human resource management. By implication the Government argued that the manufacturing sector would re-emerge leaner, fitter, more flexible, and free of the rigidity imposed by previously acceptable restrictive practices. Crouch sees this as a 'rejection of compromise': what we have termed the social democratic orthodoxy in the post-war settlement. Crouch argues that the State has rejected the need for good industrial relations and failed to institute anything in its place.

Whilst Crouch is generally correct it must be pointed out that human agency which is driving the contemporary State does not want to institute anything in the place of good industrial relations; precisely because the basis of the comtemporary State's effort to generate new industrial relations is institutional disengagement from the employment relationship; an effect of which is a loss of political citizenship for trade unions.

Efforts to politically reconstitute good industrial relations are a response to the incapacity of the social democratic orthodoxy in the post-war State. It is best visualized as an effort to modify the working of market forces to counter the tendency for the rate of profit to fall. For sustainable success such a policy must be grounded in a solid industrial policy.

Lane has argued that since 1979 the State has disengaged itself from industry and the circuit of capital precisely because of its overt free market ideology which denies the need for an active industrial policy. This is exactly the case because current accumulation strategies and industrial policy express the contradiction of the formative influence on the State; that is, the libertarian bias of freedom from State regulation. Jessop et al. has highlighted this as a central flaw in the libertarian accumulation strategy of the contemporary State.

Dynamic efficiency within any accumulation strategy requires the active that is collective, cooperation of both parties in the employment relationship. The political reconstitution of good industrial relations expressly avoids this via its rejection of pluralism. This point can be amplified through a brief discussion of these changes at the level of the firm.

### *Relations at the Level of the Firm*

The rejection of the post-war settlement and higher levels of unemployment, together with the empty libertarian accumulation strategy, has placed economic uncertainty at the centre of corporate strategy. As Hyman argues the primary effect of this uncertainty is budgetary pressure supplemented by management empowerment-prerogative to introduce new initiatives in industrial relations centred on labour control under the label human resource management.

Hyman's point is reinforced by Streeck who highlights the attack on 'status rights' within the contract of employment which new industrial relations promotes via its location in the wider reassertion of market principles. The message of human resource management replaces the notion of social stability and extra-contractual status (in collective bargaining) with the promotion of cooperative 'extra' flexibility based on individual status and extra-contractual obligation, what Storey terms going beyond contract.

The template of so-called 'soft' human resource management focuses on the individual to legitimize more authoritarian employment practices which undermine the institutional framework of 'old' industrial relations. However, the devices of contractual regulation, extra-contractual obligation, and individual status are insufficient to raise productivity and counter the tendency for the rate of profit to fall. An active industrial strategy is essential to focus the material objectives behind greater flexibility and improved productivity; in the absence of this the pursuit of flexibility has become an end in itself not a means of capitalist regeneration.

The contemporary libertarian accumulation strategy centres on the deregulation of markets, especially the labour-market, privatization, the stimulation of small businesses, and the enterprise culture. It is based on a highly particular stereotypical image of private sector capitalism which the individualist and contractually bound State generalized as the norm.

In summary it can be concluded that elements of new industrial relations have been introduced but there are two caveats; first, if we evaluate new industrial relations in terms of the historical development of the British State and its formative influences, the disengagement of pluralism in industrial relations further separates the State from active involvement in capitalist production; that is, new industrial relations cannot by itself connect with contemporary material dynamics.

Secondly and relatedly, in the absence of an active industrial strategy new industrial relations largely operate in a vacuum; that is, the atomized firm and individual accumulation strategies. In the following section we can address the question of why we need new industrial relations by examining product, employment, and labour-market changes in more detail.

### *The Need for New Industrial Relations*

The previous made clear that the generation of new industrial relations is of no use in itself. The management and regulation of employment; that is, its industrial relations is a requirement of industrial capitalism and its wider production dynamics. In consequence it is necessary to examine wider economic and social restructuring which are alleged to be the crucial impetus for the dissemination of new industrial relations.

The central components of economic and social restructuring are twofold: first, new forms of production and associated market strategies, and second, social restructuring. The former is generalized in terms of flexible specialization and a movement to 'Post-Fordism' whereas the latter is generalized as 'flexibility' in civil society and its prevailing attitude to work.

This section briefly details both flexible specialization and flexibility and then evaluates each in terms of the UK's contemporary accumulation strategy and the historical development of the State. It propagates an argument which suggests that, in the UK at least, flexibility does not measure up to either dominant model; as a result, we contend that in the UK flexibility is constituted in the entrails of Fordism.

In consequence the substance of new industrial relations cannot connect with market and production strategies on which it is premissed. Hence in large measure it is rhetorically based to justify deterioration in the quality of the employment relationship. However, because of its individual constitution new industrial relations do benefit some workers who are empowered to go beyond contract; that is, become more flexible.

### *Conventional Flexibility*

As a theory of production flexible specialization concentrates on changes in the production process which result from the application of new technology and computerized production equipment. The demand side dynamic of flexible specialization is the saturation and collapse of mass Fordist markets together with the promulgation of more determined consumer sovereignty. The supply side dynamic of flexible specialization represents a market strategy based on the pursuit of niche markets.

The economics of flexible specialization are simple: improvements in the technological base of production enable niche markets to be pursued because the fixed costs of set-up times can be drastically reduced, thereby enabling small batch customized products to be profitably produced at standardized prices. The primary advocates of this strategy, Piore and Sabel, see flexible specialization facilitating the re-emergence of craft products and in consequence multi-skilled craft workers; for a critical review of evidence for the UK see Nolan and Walsh.

In the absence of stable accumulation and production strategies based in Fordism, alternatives such as flexible specialization are propagated as the harbingers of economic and social stability in a movement to Post-Fordism. We can now turn to flexibility as a labour utilization strategy at the level of the firm.

Flexibility as a management-use strategy for labour was first repopularized in a typology presented by Atkinson. This typology centred on management segmenting its labour force into a core, with structured internal labourmarkets and a periphery of plug-in-unplug jobs. Hutton refers to these groups as privileged: the 40 per cent of the labour-market whose market power has increased since 1979 and the marginalized and insecure whose market position has deteriorated since 1979, as a result of flexibility and new industrial relations. Segmentation leads to the possibility of functional flexibility in the core and numerical flexibility in the peripheral groups.

Hyman argues that flexibility has become the theme of the 1980s wherein industrial relations is integrated into business strategy in order for management to cope with economic uncertainty. If we accept that flexibility is the main theme in contemporary business strategies we must add that it represents one result of the State's disengaged accumulation strategy. This positions the management of macroeconomic uncertainty at the level of the individual firm.

It is important to make clear that in the UK flexibility is a management strategy (flexible firm) and more. Flexibility also refers to labour-market outcomes which result from deregulation, the enhanced managerial prerogative, human resource management, and the disengagement of the social democratic State. We term this 'extra flexibility' in order to distinguish it from flexibility inherent to the flexible firm and flexible specialization.

Jessopet al. generalize flexible specialization and flexibility into a post-recession settlement which forms the basis of a movement to Post Fordism in the UK; that is, it is a functional response to the needs of British capitalism. The effect of this movement, the success of which is highly uncertain, impacts on industrial relations in three ways. First, industrial relations have become less collective and more differentiable. Core workers who presumably are the focus of new industrial relations are themselves integrated into the organization for which they work by their location in secure internal labour-markets. The mechanics of human resource management are prescribed to be the basis of this integration for a hopeful account of these developments).

Secondly, collective industrial relations are of declining significance; as a response to heightened uncertainty in market conditions, the wage relation itself is made more flexible for both the core and the periphery. WIRS3 data concludes that the majority of workers do not have their pay determined as a result of collective bargaining. For manual and non-manual workers in 1990 the figures were 45 per cent and 24 per cent respectively whereas in private services the figures for manual and non-manual workers were 32 per cent and 27 per cent.

Only in the public sector did the majority of manual and nonmanual workers have their last pay increase determined by collective bargaining (78 per cent and 84 per cent respectively). Where pay was not determined through collective bargaining the most significant determinant was management at establishment level. A third effect of the post-recession settlement on industrial relations is the disappearance of many full-time jobs, some of which are reconstituted via subcontracting, or the use of non-standard labour in the form of agency workers and part-timers.

For Boyer these types of labour-market and industrial relations flexibility are essential because capitalism has moved beyond Fordism. In consequence methods of industrial relations regulation and the quasi-right to full-time employment are unsuitable in Post-Fordism or neo-Fordism stages of capitalist development. We can now evaluate flexible specialization and the generalized flexibility thesis within the UK's current accumulation strategy and the stance of the State.

### *Economic and Social Restructuring*

The libertarian accumulation strategy espoused by the State during the 1980s and 1990s is centred on extra-flexibility popular (individualist) capitalism and the enterprise culture. It assumes social and economic stability will result from the stance of the State; that is, its disengagement from the economy and further separation from civil society.

Within the libertarian accumulation strategy flexible specialization and flexibility are more or less left as free-standing strategies with which the mechanics of new industrial relations can connect. In short the chimeric content of the contemporary accumulation strategy has generated an enterprise strategy based around numerical flexibility between core and peripheral workers. The potential benefits of flexible specialization have been relegated to a concentration on changes in current production and labour processes which in themselves create functional flexibility.

Hence both flexibility as a labour-use strategy and attempts at flexible specialization place the emphasis on labour input in isolation from the wider context of such movements. Lane argues that flexibility in the UK has been brought about by an overall reduction in terms and conditions of employment, with functional flexibility pushing more labour into the periphery. In consequence the potential benefits of new industrial relations and human resource management are irrelevant to large sections of the employed labour force because they are not in its locus.

Elger argues that flexibility in British manufacturing is based in job intensification and job enlargement not multi-skilling. Knell concludes that foreign-owned multinational firms who invest in British regions do not necessarily bring flexible specialization to such regions but adapt production to local flexibility as generalized by the accumulation strategy of the host State; that is, in the UK low productivity, low value production by marginalized and insecure labour. As a result flexibility becomes functional and rhetorical.

Flexibility is functional in the sense that its actual dissemination as distinct from prescribed type is seen by the State as a response to the imperative and pressures of capitalist accumulation in the movement to Post-Fordism. Such passive facilitation is rhetorical in that as a response it solves problems in a deterministic manner. In short the passive response of the State, evident in the absence of industrial strategy, coordinates production dynamics and resolves industrial relations conflict in civil society precisely because it meets the changing requirements of British capitalism as defined by the laissez faire State.

That is, an accumulation strategy based on flexibility and low wages is likely to reproduce a Hong Kong style economy with the worst traits of the deregulated US labour-market, wherein regions seek to attract foreign-owned non-European multinationals.

Besides providing employment this is likely to reduce indigenous profitability in similar sectors by exposure to greater international competition (premissed on flexibility and low wages) creating pressure for further financial engineering to remain competitive via flexibility and reductions in labour numbers and standards. This is likely to reduce the level of capital stock per employee, reducing the need for investment in human capital.

Sadly, this course of action has led to an evaluation of economic performance solely in terms of the productivity of human labour in the absence of attention to longer term capital renewal, precisely because generalizing low wages (by European Union standards) but high (in comparison to the recent past) productivity is the basis of the contemporary accumulation strategy. The absence of the potential for class conflict or even a collective employee voice mechanism has resulted in extra flexibility being conflated and generalized as a direct result of flexibility as presented by Atkinson.

Storey describes the presence of human resource management under four headings: beliefs and assumptions, the pre-eminence of line managers, strategic aspects, and key levers. All four are premissed on a 'can do' outlook which eschews and goes beyond contract, a movement which empowers employees and management to become more committed to their organization. We term this an individual status-obligation fulcrum.

The fulcrum and its mechanisms listed under the four headings may well define an organization as one where human resource management philosophy prevails; however, the whole approach is premissed on the absence of employee interests, a benefit of which is greater flexibility. Clark argues that flexibility is only useful as a means, therefore it must be allied to existing procedures, not seen as an end which was absent in 'old' industrial relations.

The disengagement of the State at the level of the economy combines with the institutional prescription of individualism and individual values which permeate civil society; this combination is dysfunctional. It promotes the managerial prerogative together with entrepreneurialism without stimulating an active context for individualism to operate in. Storey and Sisson argue that much of the individualist prescription in the human resource management literature is decontextualized from the real world; in the case of the UK we can add to this that much of it is decontextualized from the way the State operates.

For example, the voluntarist principle on apprenticeship training was virtually destroyed in the early 1980s as a result of the shake-out in manufacturing industry. Voluntary destruction illustrates a contradiction in new industrial relations as informed by human resource management; its prescription empowers commitment and multi- or re-skilling, but the absence of formally administered and regulated training systems promotes a logic of improving flexibility in current production systems and methods of work organization.

The resultant trend of such inertia is the development of a low productivity, low value-added, low pay manufacturing sector. Hence in respect of decontextualized position there is a double contradiction; new industrial relations and human resource management are decontextualized from the voluntary basis of much of the UK's industrial relations framework; equally and relatedly, management in the UK is unlikely to consider the benefits of human resource management and might prefer not to use it because of its resource demands.

The fact that this point is rarely made clearly indicates the organization specific pathway to new industrial relations and human resource management. The pathway rejects a collective employee voice mechanism as irrelevant because it is based only in input analysis. This is likely to be the case because of an absence of focused industrial strategy on economic and social restructuring, the basis of the State's industrial strategy: placing extra flexibility centre stage in the status-obligation fulcrum of new industrial relations and human resource management at the level of the firm; that is, flexibility based largely in the productivity of human labour.

Core workers are assumed to collaborate with management in the socioeconomic restructuring of the labour process through the mechanics of new industrial relations and human resource management. Individualism, trust, empowerment, quality circles, briefings, and improved communication encourage and empower workers to enter the restructuring process themselves.

Here we can see how flexible specialization, the flexible firm plus extra flexibility have been fused together to create an enterprise strategy derived from direct and indirect pressure on labour independent of market production pressures. This point illustrates the argument presented above that flexibility in the UK is itself an atomized concept and an end rather than a means. Recent empirical evidence seems to confirm that the main thrust of flexibility as a labour-use strategy is not functional and numerical flexibility as prescribed in the Atkinson typology but an exercise driven by cost and financial pressures.

In many cases this resulted in the continued use of nonstandard labour in the form of part-timers, agency or other temporary workers, and subcontracting. Another significant conclusion of the study suggested that many employers were now moving away from the use of non-standard labour and returning to a reliance on standard full-time labour because of the competitive and organizational benefits it brings.

In the UK the focus of economic and social restructuring through flexible specialization and flexibility has been politically mediated through the active disengagement of the State. As Jessop argues, it has resulted in a form of flexibility too flexible for the generation of Post-Fordism by the flexible specialization route. Nolan and O'Donnell assert that this results from a neglect of positive interventionary industrial policy which is essential to conduct and focus individual enterprise strategies. This is the case because individualism permeates the current institutional framework of the State and informs human agency within the apparatus of the State.

Both are crucial to the generation of extra flexibility and the avoidance of a centrally determined industrial policy. Libertarian laissez faire, that is freedom from the State, the basis of the current accumulation strategy, is a political leitmotiv, nothing more. It is a theme without substance which is replicated in much of new industrial relations and human resource management.

Both are rhetorically based in the managerial prerogative and flexibility as an end in management labour-use strategies. Human agency which drives the State has determined to separate the State, civil society, the locus of new industrial relations, and human resource management; in consequence the collective State apparatus cannot focus the accumulation strategy it has determined. The State has, however, succeeded in attaining increased extra flexibility within the employment relationship. As Sisson shows, at the level of the firm, much of this rooting is at the 'soft' end of human resource management.

The short-term benefits of new industrial relations and soft human resource management are likely to be constituted in improved productivity figures and tighter wages costs; however, it is as yet unclear what the economic benefits of this extra flexibility are (other than it being visualized as an end in itself).

We can follow Boyer in suggesting that flexibility within economic and social restructuring can be either positive or negative. In the UK's case it appears to be negative in the sense that flexibility represents movement within current structures and does not represent a transition to something new. The form of the State and the absence of positive interventionary industrial and employment strategies are central to this process.

In the light of this argument we can now proceed to discuss the limited potential of new industrial relations in the generation of increased flexibility and improved productivity in the wider context of the UK's neo-Fordism.

Chapter 3

# Management of Pay and Performance

## PAY AND REWARD SYSTEMS

Budget tourism is in and the Indian Government is planning to use the opportunity. A change in its policy of auctioning hotel sites, with sops for attracting big players of the Indian hotel industry, is on the anvil. A significant change will be a more liberalised payment-of-land-cost plan, with a focus on budget hotels. This will require resizing of hotel plots, as, so far, hotel sites are auctioned within set parametres of shop-cum-office sites.

At present, bidders at hotel-site auctions have to pay the land cost within three years from the date of auction. The change will mean this schedule extended to between 15 and 20 years. Several leading hotel groups have shown interest in setting up hotels, but back off everytime they are asked to pay the cost of land within three years of auction. Industry pundits have told the Administration that it took upto six years for a new hotel venture to break even, so, the payment should be staggered. The first two years are spent just in construction, which means no recovery.

The Administration, by extending the payment schedule, will end up getting more from increased number of bids and interest spread over more time. The idea of revenue sharing between the Administration and a chosen hotel chain has been dropped, as a similar system has not worked well in New Delhi, with major hotel groups defaulting on payment. The hotel industry wants to go in for budget tourism, for which, the want fresh sites and not disputed property.

This develops some of the issues introduced in surrounding one of the most important sets of employment rules - pay and pay determination - but in the reverse order because pay is the outcome of the process of pay determination. As Rubery observes, 'Payment systems are a mechanism or a medium through which the employment relationship is constituted and codified development of a new payment system may be seen as part of a reconstitution of power relations'. In particular we show how pay and reward systems constitute one of the central facets of a managerial cost-control approach, with a strong gender effect.

Pay defines a worker's status and standard of living, and can affect motivation and commitment to work, so low pay may be detrimental on a number of grounds. Pay may be used by employers to signal they are good employers, to attract the best workers, to maximize control, to motivate workers, to improve performance, and as part of a change management programme. While some of these objectives are allied to higher pay, we must not assume that employers will apply all, or any, of these principles to every occupational group within the same organization. We have already noted that more beneficial conditions may be applied to a privileged core, while the rest of the workforce is subjected to less favourable and more controlling conditions, including low pay.

The term 'total reward system' has traditionally been used to describe remuneration in the HI. Employees in hotels and restaurants, but not necessarily in other sub-sectors, are assumed to receive all or most of the following variable reward system:

basic pay + subsidized lodging + subsidized food + tips or service charge + 'fiddles' and 'knock-offs'.

The wider application of this package may well have been overstated in an attempt by employers to justify that employees are not really low-paid. The stark reality is that the HCTS is low-paid, regardless of how pay is measured. Most of the elements of the total reward system can be applied to workers in other sectors, who may benefit from other more favourable monetary and non-monetary benefits. Hence shop workers can 'fiddle' by short-changing customers, while there are a host of occupations where workers can readily pilfer small items from their employer such as pens, sellotape and stationery. Tipping is common practice in hairdressing.

The unpredictable and variable nature of the total reward system says a great deal about the nature of the employment relationship in the HI. In spite of the legal and institutional framework, managers are able to exert strong control through individual contract making, and unilateral management determination of pay. Informal practices are not the preserve of any particular type of workplace or activity. In fast food stores practices involve the distribution of rewards and favours according to informal systems of individual bargaining, including access to days off and favourable rosters. An informal deal may bind a worker to a tacit understanding that may later be used as a sanction against her/him. The lack of transparency about reward systems reduces workers' bargaining power by isolating individuals. It is not surprising that the HI sustains high quit rates in these circumstances. Reward is not seen as a component part of culture change.

Apart from keeping pay low, there are other circumstances and conditions under which managerial control may be intensified. For example, control on wage costs and employee performance is achieved through high reliance on tips, particularly in pubs and bars. Work intensity is maximized by the provision of live-in facilities, enabling staff to be summoned to work at short notice. Tightening up on a 'blind eye' approach to 'fiddles' and pilfering when business slackens and dismissing the miscreants can be used to control employee numbers, e.g. strawberries at the Wimbledon lawn tennis championships. On the other hand managerial control has been weakened by the poor economic situation in Russia. The lack of funds to pay employees has led to demands for copious time off.

## Regulation and Determination

Global commitment to a minimum wage and the equalization of pay between men and women provide the central foundation to the regulation of the pay of many HCTS workers. Both principles have been given legal effect in many countries throughout the world. While law-abiding employers will pay at least the minimum rate, and uprate it as required, the issue of narrowing the gender pay gap is far more problematic. We also consider how far collective bargaining has served the interests of employers and workers, although that its application and effects can be patchy and largely ineffectual. Hence the primary actor in pay determination is management.

### *Minimum Wages*

By 1980 the ILO's minimum wage Convention had been ratified by 194 countries to the benefit of many hospitality and tourism workers. Large swathes of the British HI were within scope of wages councils system between the mid-1940s and mid-1990s. Abolition of the system in 1993 led to the deterioration in pay in the HI.

Although the objectives of a minimum wage can vary, one purpose is to provide a pay floor. However, the level at which the wage is set affects its 'bite'; a wage set very low and sporadically up rated will be largely symbolic. Three-quarters of minimum wage workers in the US work in the HI, and industry leaders are renowned in their fight to hold down the wage. Lower-level jobs in the HI in the US are paid at the same level as other industries, ostensibly because of minimum wage laws. In Australia and Singapore one-third and two-thirds of hotel workers respectively are paid above the minimum.

Favourable differential rates may apply to casuals and young workers, reinforcing their importance as integral to cost-minimization. Under the award system in Australia casuals receive a loading (about 20 per cent) above standard rates and a minimum pay guarantee (2-3 hours) in lieu of annual and sick leave, but are not entitled to premium payments for weekends. It is alleged that McDonald's dismiss workers when they reach the age of 20 to avoid paying full adult rates. Most other studies have found no evidence to support the employment of young workers as a means to evade the minimum wage.

### *The Minimum Wage*

The introduction of a NMW in the UK has caused a pay spike at the minimum rate, showing that workers actually benefited from its introduction. The arrival of the NMW has not been a discrete event in a stable world. Individual firms do have scope for discretion, and to take random, opportunistic decisions. However, there has been a tendency for hospitality firms to take a 'low road' approach. Hotels have tended to adopt a cost-minimization strategy rather than pursue a quality enhancement route.

### *Case Study: Introducing the UK National Minimum Wage in Hospitality*

The NMW was introduced in April 1999. Two rates were set - a full adult rate of £3.60, and a lower development rate for young workers aged 18-21 and adult trainees in the first six months of a new job. By October 2003 the full rate was £4.50 and the development rate £3.80. Rates of £4.85 and £4.10 have been provisionally accepted to apply from October 2004, subject to the LPC's advice in light of economic circumstances.

The NMW has been introduced successfully, with employers given plenty of warning about forthcoming increases. The HI has been disproportionately affected because it has the highest proportion of low-paid jobs, particularly among females, and employs large proportions of young people, the group most likely to suffer unemployment effects. Twenty-three per cent of hospitality jobs, 300,000 in total, benefited from a major hike in the NMW of 40p in 2001.

Waiting and bar staff are among the occupational groups most affected. The impact on the wage bill of 0.7 per cent is less than at the time the NMW was introduced.

Employment has increased by 200,000 since 1999. Many firms have deployed a wide variety of coping strategies, including increased cost control, adjusting hours, employment restructuring, increasing prices and reducing profits. A pay spike at the level of the full adult rate has developed, with a mezzanine floor some 30-40p higher, reflecting tight labour market conditions in some parts of the country. Small firms have been more affected, because large companies' pay was already at or above the NMW rates.

The youth development rate is below the market rate and most employers pay the full rate at age 18. Most employers are likely to welcome the introduction of a lower rate for 16- and 17-year-olds in 2004, subject to the LPC's recommendations. There has been little take-up of the adult development rate, mainly because firms find it hard to recruit at this rate, recruits already have the skills and it is unfair/divisive.

In the UK three aspects of the NMW have particular resonance within the HI: tips and gratuities, an accommodation offset and the differential treatment of young workers. Employers may use tips or a service charge collected through the payroll to 'top up' hourly pay to the NMW, whereas cash tips paid to and kept by workers do not count. As there was a limited call to the LPC's suggestion that the rules for treatment of tips and gratuities be reconsidered, this remains unchanged.

An accommodation offset of £24.40 per week can be deducted from the NMW to pay for accommodation. Where accommodation is for less than a full week, the offset must be a corresponding reduction, which replaces specified hourly and daily rates. Employers can charge more provided the deduction does not bring the hourly rate to below the NMW. The BHA estimates that the average cost of accommodation is

£42 per week, and that employers typically charge between £40 and £50. Other sources suggest wider weekly variations of between £20 and £95 and £35 and £65.

While youth pay is generally lower than adult pay (LPC, 2003), many employers have been uneasy about the exclusion of 16- and 17-year-olds from any form of minimum wage protection. Some believe that the absence of regulation will lead to a vulnerable group being exploited by ruthless employers, while others consider exclusion is discriminatory or not justified on grounds of equity. The government's decision to ask the LPC to consider the case for introducing a minimum wage rate for workers of these ages is likely to be uncontroversial. Some 25 per cent of students in employment aged 16 and 17 work in the HI, and a number of major fast food employers, including Burger King, already apply the full NMW rate from age 16.

The government's continued rejection of the LPC's advice to apply the full NMW rate at age 21, rather than 22, remains an anomaly and irrelevance for most firms. Yet there are still pockets in the economy where employers use the lower youth rate, including rural North Wales. The method of job evaluation, which can be used to determine equal value claims for equal pay, offers one way to establish the reasons for the differences in adult and youth pay and to assess whether differences can be objectively justified. This approach, based on job content and employee attribute analysis, has been used in North Wales, as Case study illustrates.

### *Case Study: Small Hospitality Firms in North Wales*

Employers perceive a positive relationship between age and employee attributes, rating under 18s' attributes consistently lower than the rest of the workforce. Some attributes such as solving problems, making decisions, and interpersonal skills are developed through experience, hence lower pay. In most cases work also involves fewer tasks and responsibilities. The exception is fast food, where workers of all ages receive the same starter rate, as they are subject to the same tasks, responsibilities and working conditions.

Workers aged 18-21 are to an extent disadvantaged on lower pay, because they appear to be performing the same tasks as older workers. Employers appear to place more emphasis on the possession of higher personal attributes by older workers.

The LPC was placed on a permanent footing in 2001, with a view to monitoring the impact of the NMW and making uprating recommendations. The pattern has been to recommend increases on a two-year basis from October, with the proviso that the second stage increases are reviewed nearer the time. Although the initial NMW rate was set 'prudently' because of the unknown effects, subsequent increases have been above average earnings. These have been of most benefit to workers on lowest docile earnings who are less likely to get incentive or overtime pay. Assuming the 2004 increase is implemented; estimates suggest that the NMW will have increased from 88.7 per cent to 94.5 per cent of half median male earnings in its first five years.

The principle of equal pay for equal work regardless of gender is more recent than a minimum wage, emerging from 1951 ILO Convention on Equal Pay. Equal pay was integral to the Treaty of Rome 1957 and has been addressed in subsequent EU Directives. In Britain the Equal Pay Act 1970 enabled equal pay claims to be made between men and women on the basis of like work or work rated as equivalent under a job evaluation scheme. The Act was amended in 1983 to allow women to claim equal pay for work of equal value, even where no job evaluation scheme was in place. Hence a female canteen worker could claim her job was of equal value to a male painter and decorator. Same sex claims between part time and full-time workers were not possible until the Part-time Employees (Prevention of Less Favourable Treatment) Regulations were introduced in 2000. However, minimum wage and equal pay legislation have had a limited effect on pay relativities.

In 2003 implementation of a provision of the Employment Act 2002 introduced an equal pay questionnaire in equal pay cases at employment tribunal, to make it easier for applicants to request key information from the employer when deciding whether to bring a case. Completion is not compulsory but failure to reply may lead to inferences from the tribunal.

### *Institutional Constraints*

Men earn more than women, because every labour market in the EU is gender segregated. Full-timers earn more than part-timers, although the differential is smaller among women than among men. Strong collective bargaining and minimum wage regimes reduce the percentage of low-paid workers, but the benefits of regulation do not extend to women, especially parttimers, as much as to men. There is also a strong sectoral effect whether or not national arrangements are in place.

'It is extremely unlikely that both differences in systems of wage determination between countries and changes to wage structures would not have consequences for the relative pay of women and men'. Hence in the US, Canada and UK where pay determination systems are decentralized and fragmented, between 19 and 25 per cent of the full-time female labour force is low-paid compared to 6 per cent in Scandinavia where solidaristic bargaining prevails. That said, women executives in the US have lower starting salaries than their male counterparts, and pay inequality persists where directors are believed to be able to 'get more for less'. Whitehouse et al. (2001) conclude that the prosecution of pay equity cases has been limited by progressive decentralization in Australia and Britain, although in different ways.

The failure of minimum wage systems to deliver gender equity in the EU arises from strong political pressure not to increase minimum wages as a symbol of wage restraint and to promote a more flexible labour market. Unusually, a stated objective of the UK's NMW was to promote gender equality; over 70 per cent of beneficiaries were women, and around two-thirds of jobs below minimum wage levels were part-time. The gap between male and female hourly pay has narrowed, particularly among part-timers, but still remains at 82 per cent for full-timers and 89 per cent for part-timers.

In Western Europe collective agreements reached at multi-employer (sectoral and economy-wide) have coverage that is greater than union density. This is because even firms with few union members participate in sectoral bargaining and statutory procedures extend the terms of the agreement to all employers in the sector. Selected examples from EU countries are shown in Case study. In the US the wages of highly unionized occupations in the hotel, gaming and restaurant industry in Las Vegas are significantly higher than the wages of identical non-union occupations in Reno.

In the US the Fair Labour Standards Act 1938 created two classes of employees - those paid for the hire of their labour and those undertaking administrative, professional or executive duties that are paid a salary. The latter are exempted from minimum wage laws. Incorrect classification of employees can be costly.

### The Role of Managers in Pay Determination

The nature of skills (readily available and transferable) and unpredictable demand tend to create a low market rate for jobs. We identify how British managers are able to exercise considerable discretion over pay within the legal and institutional frameworks outlined above.

Which managers are involved in determining pay will depend on whether workplaces are multi- or single-site; in the WERS sample over three-quarters of HI workplaces are multi-site. In just under half the HI workplaces higher-level managers beyond the workplace and the Board of Directors are directly involved in determining the pay rise, although workplace management is involved in 37 per cent of cases. Where the decision about pay change was made at the establishment (one in eight HI cases), higher-level managers are not consulted in two-thirds of cases. While hotel managers are most likely to be involved, a majority consulted their higher-level colleagues. While pay is largely management-determined in AIS and the PSS, HI workplaces, unsurprisingly, are significantly less likely to involve union representatives in this process.

Pay setting arrangements for different occupational groups differ within AIS, the PSS and the HI, and by size of workplace and sub-sector. One must be careful about drawing too many inferences from these because the limited presence of some occupational groups means that numbers of cases can be very small. Even so, higher management clearly takes a leading role in setting pay in the HI, suggesting strong emphasis is placed on organizational cost control.

## Case Study: Pay Determination in the European Hospitality Industry

### *Spain*

In 1996 a binding four-year sectoral agreement replaced a labour ordinance which contained a cumbersome pay structure. The new agreement lays down basic conditions regarding grading systems, disciplinary procedures and training, which is monitored by a joint committee of the signatory partners. Pay is determined by an extensive network of collective agreements. Some 555,083 workers (71 per cent of the total HI workforce) were covered by 104 company and 47 provincial agreements.

### *India*

Indian Hotels Company Ltd (IHCL), better known as the Taj group, has set a global benchmark by registering an 80 per cent loyalty with its staff, at a time when turnover in hospitality staff is at a high due to international hotel chains setting up shop in India, says a Gallup survey. The company's employee turnover rates are amongst the lowest in the industry and IHCL senior vice-president (HR) Bernard Martyris attributes it to the high loyalty factor amongst the employees. According to him, the accessibility of senior staff, quick responses to employees' grievances and needs keep the company's employee rolls firm.

Mr Martyris also said despite the group not offering the previously available job security, turnover is still low because it has, in turn, increased pay by 30-35 per cent. Till recently, the Taj was not a good paymaster. And the poor pay structure for the operation staff is the main reason for turnover in our industry. In a year or so, we will be the best paymasters in the country. The company was to conduct a wage revision during the last fiscal, but due to the September 11 terror attacks and its fallout, was unable to do so. Along with pay, IHCL is also targeting not only fast-trackers but also its solid citizens. This, according to Mr Martyris, is the only way to retain employees.

He also attributed the strong affinity of employees to the company, to an internal union. "The very fact that we don't have external influences in our unions is pointer enough. Our unions are powerful and fight for employee rights, but they always take into consideration the interests of the company," he points out.

Along with programmes of tracking employee satisfaction, the Taj group has also put into place systems such as STAR (special thanks and recognition system), wherein employees are encouraged to contribute ideas and are recognised for any special service they render. The patented programme recently won the international Hermes award.

### *Italy*

In 1999 four new collective agreements set minimum pay and conditions for three years, including increases to the number of atypical working arrangements, new options for managing working time and measures to improve training. Some 800,000 employees are covered by the agreements, but in some areas half of employment is in the black economy. The right to bargain locally has been recognized since 1993. In practice company bargaining has continued for organizations employing more than 15 employees.

There is a new option for smaller companies and companies where it has not been customary to bargain regionally. To encourage firms to enter the formal economy special clauses may be negotiated at this level, allowing agreed pay increases to be implemented in an alternative way.

*Sweden*

Sectoral agreements are combined with local agreements. Employers who are not members of the main employers' organization may be bound by the terms of the sectoral agreement through signing an auxiliary agreement. This is common among small companies who are not members of an employers' organization, and for around half of those workplaces with union members who have no company agreement. Although collective agreements set minimum pay, most employees earn above these amounts.

*Germany*

Collective agreements have the force of law, acting as a minimum wage, and cover 80 to 90 per cent of the German workforce, although trade union membership is low. McDonald's and other fast food establishments broke away from the HI collective agreement by establishing a new employers' federation Bundersverband der Systemgastronomie (BdS) and negotiating separately with the Gewerkschaft Nahrung Genuss Gaststatten (NGG).

The fast food collective agreement on pay and conditions includes pay in lieu, overtime, sick pay and the washing of uniforms. The lack of works councils in stores means there is no guarantee that the agreement will be adhered to.

*Netherlands*

Employees are covered by a three-part national collective agreement. Part A contains conditions that are binding on the whole sector. Parts B and C give individual establishments the option to negotiate at local level with a works council or other representative body provided the agreement is superior to the sectoral agreement. There is one pay scale covering eleven grades, and 120 job categories have their own job descriptions.

A two-year agreement reached in 1998 provided for pay increases in 1998 and 1999, new early retirement provisions in 2000, greater scope for local level negotiations and changes to working time arrangements.

### *UK*

There is no state-sponsored collective bargaining, so most employers are guided by the NMW introduced in 1999. Two of the largest hotel companies, Jarvis and Thistle Hotels, have entered into company collective agreements. The Jarvis agreement includes a probationary hourly rate (first three months) set at the same rate as the NMW, and a minimum rate that is 18p above the NMW, both applicable at age 18. Premiums apply for designated night work (63p per hour) and unsocial hours (59p per hour). Higher rates apply in London and within the M25 orbital.

Although two-thirds of HI workplaces in WERS have an annual pay review, workers in the LOG in these workplaces are significantly less likely to benefit from an annual pay review than their counterparts in AIS and the PSS where nine in ten workplaces operate an annual review. However, workers in the LOG in one-fifth of HI workplaces are significantly more likely to benefit from more frequent pay reviews. Pay is reviewed less than once a year in 10 per cent of HI workplaces, especially in restaurants (over one-quarter). One in 12 HI workplaces had not actually changed pay at the last review. Workers were most likely to have received an increase of between 3 and 4 per cent, although settlements in hotels were more typically at 4 per cent and above. The HI had slightly more cases of the lowest and highest increases at the last pay review.

In the interim six-year period between the abolition of wages councils and the introduction of the NMW, the lack of a reference point for reviewing pay created pay inertia among small HI firms, widening the pay gap between them and larger companies. Some two years after abolition pay had stayed the same or decreased in nearly one-third of the companies surveyed. In the absence of the review date specified in the wages order, almost half the firms had no fixed review date. Personnel directors stressed that the single major change since abolition was a new flexibility in their company's approach to pay-setting, largely in relation to skills pay, thus widening pay differentials above the minimum rate.

As there was nothing to prevent the paying of higher rates under the wages councils, this may be a reflection of a relative decline in pay for those on minimum rates. The main determinants of pay reviews were the local labour market and competitors' pay rates, followed by company economic performance and cost of living/inflation. Wages councils clearly had a significant impact upon pay determination procedures, pay levels and pay structures in the HI.

Even in the two-year period leading up to the introduction of the NMW, many HI firms did not adjust pay in advance, waiting until 1 April 1999 when it became a legal necessity. In the early stages of the NMW only 50 per cent of small HI firms increased pay annually. Pay increases were highly variable and unstructured. Nevertheless, the NMW, as noted above, has been an important influence on HI workers' pay in conjunction with tight labour market conditions. Many firms across the HI, particularly pubs and restaurants, have moved their anniversary dates to October and now review pay to coincide with increases in the NMW.

The major hotel companies have more highly variable review dates. Adverse business conditions in the hotel sector following the foot-and-mouth epidemic and the slump in international tourism and business travel post-11 September caused a number of the major companies to cancel or delay their pay review. Others froze recruitment, allowing turnover and natural wastage to reduce staff numbers.

However, skill shortages in a tight labour market created recruitment and retention problems in key jobs, with pay rises for those affected. However, in many of the large chains, including De Vere, Hilton International, Jarvis Hotels, Thistle Hotels and Whitbread starter rates were at or very close to the NMW rate of £4.10. The median pay of waiting and bar staff, room attendants and commis chefs was 30-40p an hour above the NMW.

**Table: Pay-setting Arrangements for Different Occupational Groups in Context and by Size of Workplace (%)**

| | *AIS* | *PSS* | *HI* | *<25* | *25-49* | *50-99* | *100+* |
|---|---|---|---|---|---|---|---|
| Managers/ administrative | HM (43) | HM (50) | HM (60)** | HM (57) | HM (71) | HM (60) | HM (50) |
| Professional | WM (27) | WM (39) | WM (30) | IN/SOW (45) | WM (46) | WM (55) | HM/WM (48) |
| Technical/ scientific | WM (36) | WM (38) | HM (51) | OCB/HM (50) | HM (100) | HM/WM (50) | WM (58) |
| Clerical and secretarial | WM (34) | WM (42) | WM (36) | SOW (41) | HM (68) | WM (61) | WM (49) |
| Craft and skilled manual | WM (37) | WM (37) | HM (38) | IN (59) | HM (72) | WM (65) | WM (56) |
| Personal service | HM (32) | HM/ WM (39) | HM (37) | HM (30) | HM (67) | WM (58) | WM (47) |
| Sales | HM (45) | HM (50) | HM (61) | HM (65) | HM (66) | HM (50) | WM (56) |
| Operative and assembly manuals | WM (41) | WM (42) | HM (83)* | HM (100) | HM (100) | HM (34) | HM/WM (50) |
| Routine unskilled manual | WM (33) | WM (42) | HM (38) | HM (33) | HM (55) | WM (60) | WM (50) |

***Notes:*** *All establishments where any employees in occupational category. The most common method used where any employees in particular occupational groups. HM = higher management, WM = workplace management, CB = collective bargaining with more than one employer, OCB = collective bargaining at organizational level, WCB = workplace collective bargaining, IN = negotiation with individual employees, SOW = some other way. In cases where two arrangements rank first equal, both are shown. *Significantly different at the 5% level from AIS and PSS. **Significantly different at* the 5% level from AIS.

**Table: Pay-setting Arrangements for Different Occupational Groups by Sub-sector (%)**

| | *Hotels* | *Campsites* | *Restaurants* | *Bars* | *Canteens* |
|---|---|---|---|---|---|
| Managers/ administrative | HM (55) | OCB (72) | HM (57) | HM (75) | CB (45) |
| Professional | WM (69) | HM (100) | SOW (93) | IN (70) | IN (75) |
| Technical/ scientific | HM (51) | OCB (95) | WM (100) | HM (100) | – |
| Clerical and secretarial | WM (53) | OCB (72) | SOW (44) | SOW (61) | CB (55) |
| Craft and skilled manual | WM (52) | OCB (78) | HM (56) | HM (54) | WCB (40) |
| Personal service | IN (42) | HM (78) | SOW (39) | HM (85) | CB (78) |
| Sales | WM (63) | HM (100) | WM (51) | HM (80) | CB (71) |
| Operative and assembly manuals | HM (60) | HM (100) | HM (85) | HM (100) | WM (100) |
| Routine unskilled manual | WM (50) | WM (72) | HM (43) | HM (52) | CB (65) |

***Notes:*** *All establishments where any employees in occupational category. The most common method used where any employees in particular occupational groups. HM = higher management, WM = workplace management, CB = collective bargaining with more than one employer, OCB = collective bargaining at organizational level, WCB = workplace collective bargaining, IN = negotiation with individual employees, SOW = some other way. In cases where two arrangements rank first equal, both are shown.*

## Case Study: The Cost of Misclassifying Restaurant Managers under the Fair Labour Standards Act

Employee misclassification cost Waffle House more than $3,000,000. Restaurant managers working an average of 89 hours per week were classified as exempt executives. Factors that counted against the company were:

- Unit managers served as grill cooks on the busiest shift.
- The primary training objective was to become a proficient grill operator, with exposure to management duties and responsibilities coming second.
- Managers often substituted for other employees.
- Other employees regularly stood in for absent managers.

Under the Fair Labour Standards Act the managers were entitled to be paid overtime for all hours worked in excess of 40 per week.

Much of the HI is characterized by the absence of grading schemes, and a lack of well-defined differentials between jobs. This, coupled with the lack of job evaluation, is likely to exacerbate pay discrimination. Loosely defined and variable pay structures can be explained in terms of the interplay between labour and product markets, firms' own choices and shocks such as the NMW.

Managers may structure pay to maximize cost savings by limiting hours and ensuring that employees earn below the threshold for National Insurance Contributions (NICs). An overspend on wages can be compensated by reducing the hours of part-time workers on variable hours contracts and the numbers of casual workers on a daily or weekly basis.

The majority of the major hotel companies have pay progression scales for different departments or employee groups, almost all of which are subject to performance (IDS, 2001). Individual performance reviews are also common in fast food, noted below. Up until 2001 employers were able to increase pay for the lowest paid without any repercussions for those further up the scale. The 40p hike in the NMW in 2001 led to a narrowing of differentials within hotels' pay structures, necessitating increases for junior supervisory staff (IDS, 2002).

The 2001 increase also caused McDonald's to shift from paying adult rates at 16, and to reintroduce age-related pay, with different rates for restaurant crew below 18, aged 18-21 and 22 years and over. While national chains set national rates, a number also have differential location-based pay for the provinces, and London and the South-east, in addition to other tight labour markets such as out-of-town retail parks.

In small independent firms largely informal pay determination provides considerable scope for discretion within a framework of either individual employer- employee bargaining or unilateral management determination, in spite of the NMW. In a low-paying region nearly one-third of small employers were making use of the development rate. As noted earlier, they justified lower pay for young workers who were less experienced, had lower skills and were less productive, but age in itself was not a determinant of pay.

**Case Study: Pay Structures and the Minimum Wage**

The new NMW wage structure did not match the practice of most firms. Firms' initial response was to 'pick and mix' or do the minimum required, which meant increasing some adult workers' pay while leaving others' pay at the same level. Even though young workers were already being paid more than the development rate, their pay was also increased at the same time adult workers' pay was adjusted to comply with the NMW.

Notional adult minima might apply at age 18 or age 21, but managers exercised considerable discretion to give accelerated progression, so there was no strict wage-for-age policy. There was informality and flexibility about how managers determined individuals' pay as they saw fit. Many could not adequately explain the basis of their pay structures and how employees progressed to higher pay.

Most young workers aged 18-21 and many exempt 16- and 17-year-olds were paid more than the development rate.

Differentials were generally maintained because there was still a sizeable gap of £2.00 per hour or more between most workers and the higher paid. In one case the hourly differential between three supervisors had reduced from 50p to 25p. The manager was prepared to restore the differential if asked to do so because it would not be costly.

### *The Components of Remuneration*

Although relatively few countries provide comparable earnings data, as a general rule hotel and restaurant workers across the world earn less than workers in socially comparable positions, and the differential tends to be higher in developing countries and for occupations requiring more skills and responsibilities.

Working conditions in the EU (1996) include potentially problematic areas such as irregular working hours, frequent Sunday work, wages without a fixed element in 25 per cent of cases and widespread absence of overtime premiums; wage levels are generally 20 per cent below the EU average. Similar problems are observed in North America. Even where overtime premiums exist, they may rarely be paid.

We should note major problems with comparative statistics. Tips are not always declared for tax and will not be shown, and differences in the skill and training content of occupations in sub-sectors, such as waiting staff, mean that comparisons may not be made on a like-for-like basis. Weekly earnings show a bigger gap than hourly earnings because men work more overtime.

Women's consistently low pay can be explained by three main sets of factors: occupational segregation by gender, methods of pay determination and the concentration of low pay in certain industries, which makes it especially trenchant in the HI. Broadbridge provides support for arguments, showing that nature of skill and trade union activities have been constructed against women. Rubery warns that trends towards performance-related pay (PRP) pose a potential threat to pay equality as discretion in pay determination increases and there is no clear relationship between earnings and job grade. She also suggests that devolving HRM to line managers who are less aware of gender issues will also impact negatively on pay equality.

The size of the pay difference varies across countries, and there are exceptions. Tourism in North Korea is a low-wage sector but is more advantageous to women in terms of earnings inequality and level of earnings. While women have lower pay expectations at career entry and career peak than men, organizational issues such as a 'glass ceiling' blocking entry into higher paying positions are indicative of discrimination. By placing more emphasis on relationships in the workplace than on status women rule out jobs which might bring higher rewards.

The position in Britain may be even more polarized. A survey of the major hotel companies (2000), which might be expected to be 'market leaders', did find that pay was well ahead of the NMW. Only a minority pay premium rates for night or weekend work, and only two-fifths pay overtime at premium rates. New Earnings Survey (NES) data for the hotel sub-sector consistently show adult full-time earnings at two-thirds of average earnings for the whole economy, with overtime pay, shift pay and bonus payments comprising a very small part of total earnings compared to the rest of the economy. The same is also true for the HI as a whole.

The lowest-paid HI workers (lowest decile) rarely receive overtime or incentives. Low pay is linked to a wide range of factors, many of which are specific to the establishment and its competitive strategy. The incidence of low pay is high in single establishments and low in small establishments that are part of a larger organization. Basic pay is 100 per cent of total earnings in two-thirds of small HI firms.

In 2002 the median pay of waiting and bar staff, luggage porters, room and leisure centre attendants and commis chefs was between £4.41 and £4.50. By contrast head chefs and sous chefs enjoyed relatively good pay, with median rates in South-east England exceeding £11 per hour.

**Table: Patterns of Pay for all Employees on Adult Rates (2002)**

| | *Average gross annual pay (£)* | *Average gross weekly pay (£)* | *Increase April 2001/2 (%)* | *Average hourly pay (excl. O/T) (£)* | *Average total weekly (hours)* | *Average weekly overtime (hours)* |
|---|---|---|---|---|---|---|
| Full-time | | | | | | |
| AIS | 24,603 | 465 | 4.6 | 11.73 | 39.6 | 1.8 |
| HI | 15,762 | 299 | 3.7 | 7.28 | 40.9 | 1.2 |
| Part-time | | | | | | |
| AIS | 7,903 | 148 | 6.0 | 8.09 | 19.6 | 1.0 |
| HI | 5,080 | 93 | 13.3 | 6.11 | 17.9 | 0.6 |

*Source: NES (2002); ONS (2002).*

**Table: Patterns of Pay for Male Employees on Adult Rates (2002)**

| | *Average gross annual pay (£)* | *Average gross weekly pay (£)* | *Increase April 2001/2 (%)* | *Average hourly pay (excl. O/T) (£)* | *Average total weekly (hours)* | *Average weekly overtime (hours)* |
|---|---|---|---|---|---|---|
| Full-time | | | | | | |
| AIS | 27,437 | 514 | 4.8 | 12.59 | 40.9 | 2.4 |
| HI | 18,051 | 331 | 2.2 | 7.87 | 41.9 | 1.3 |
| Part-time | | | | | | |
| AIS | 9,485 | 165 | 7.7 | 10.08 | 19.2 | 1.5 |
| HI | -* | 100 | 17.1 | 7.56 | 17.8 | 0.5 |

*Source: NES (2002); ONS (2002).*

**Table: Patterns of Pay for Female Employees on Adult Rates (2002)**

| | *Average gross annual pay (£)* | *Average gross weekly pay (£)* | *Increase April 2001/2 (%)* | *Average hourly pay (excl. O/T) (£)* | *Average total weekly (hours)* | *Average weekly overtime (hours)* |
|---|---|---|---|---|---|---|
| Full-time | | | | | | |
| AIS | 19,811 | 383 | 4.5 | 10.22 | 37.5 | 0.7 |
| HI | 12,984 | 257 | 4.7 | 6.48 | 39.6 | 1.0 |
| Part-time | | | | | | |
| AIS | 7,593 | 144 | 5.8 | 7.72 | 19.7 | 1.0 |
| HI | 4,822 | 89 | 10.5 | 5.57 | 17.9 | 0.7 |

*Source: NES (2002); ONS (2002).*

**Table: Full-time Annual Male Earnings in Context and by Size of Workplace (%)**

| | *AIS* | *PSS* | *HI* | *<25* | *25-49* | *50-99* | *100+* |
|---|---|---|---|---|---|---|---|
| <£9,000 | 7 | 11 | 47* | 34 | 42 | 56 | 47 |
| £9,000 to <£12,000 | 15 | 18 | 23 | 26 | 31 | 17 | 23 |
| £12,000 to <£16,000 | 24 | 24 | 12* | 9 | 16 | 12 | 13 |
| £16,000 to <£22,000 | 28 | 19 | 9* | 12 | 5 | 8 | 9 |
| £22,000 to <£29,000 | 15 | 12 | 5* | 12 | 4 | 4 | 4 |
| > £29,000 | 12 | 16 | 4* | 7 | 3 | 3 | 5 |

*Source: WERS98.*

**Notes:** *Aggregate percentage of all weighted cases. *Significantly different at the 5% level from AIS and PSS.*

**Table: Full-time Annual Female Earnings in Context and by Size of Workplace (%)**

| | *AIS* | *PSS* | *HI* | *<25* | *25-49* | *50-99* | *100+* |
|---|---|---|---|---|---|---|---|
| <£9,000 | 18 | 24 | 57* | 57 | 58 | 62 | 50 |
| £9,000 to <£12,000 | 25 | 25 | 19 | 14 | 18 | 19 | 24 |
| £12,000 to <£16,000 | 23 | 21 | 13** | 13 | 12 | 12 | 14 |
| £16,000 to <£22,000 | 20 | 16 | 8** | 14 | 6 | 5 | 7 |
| £22,000 to <£29,000 | 10 | 8 | 2* | 3 | 2 | 1 | 2 |
| > £29,000 | 4 | 5 | 1* | 1 | 2 | 0 | 2 |

*Source: WERS98.*

*Notes: Aggregate percentage of all weighted cases. *Significantly different at the 5% level from AIS and PSS. **Significantly different at the 5% level from AIS.*

**Table: Full-time Annual Male Earnings by Sub-sector (%)**

| | *Hotels* | *Campsites* | *Restaurants* | *Bars* | *Canteens* |
|---|---|---|---|---|---|
| <£9,000 | 18 | 69 | 50 | 37 | 34 |
| £9,000 to <£12,000 | 20 | 10 | 28 | 32 | 26 |
| £12,000 to <£16,000 | 14 | 6 | 7 | 17 | 4 |
| £16,000 to <£22,000 | 9 | 7 | 10 | 10 | 3 |
| £22,000 to <£29,000 | 6 | 1 | 1 | 4 | 15 |
| > £29,000 | 4 | 1 | 4 | 1 | 18 |

*Source: WERS98.* **Notes:** *Aggregate percentage of all weighted cases.*

**Table: Full-time Annual Female Earnings by Sub-sector (%)**

| | *Hotels* | *Campsites* | *Restaurants* | *Bars* | *Canteens* |
|---|---|---|---|---|---|
| <£9,000 | 54 | 76 | 54 | 51 | 64 |
| £9,000 to <£12,000 | 21 | 7 | 20 | 27 | 12 |
| £12,000 to <£16,000 | 14 | 6 | 10 | 17 | 10 |
| £16,000 to <£22,000 | 8 | 11 | 12 | 0 | 10 |
| £22,000 to <£29,000 | 1 | 0 | 2 | 2 | 4 |
| > £29,000 | 1 | 0 | 2 | 2 | 2 |

*Source: WERS98.*

***Notes:** Aggregate percentage of all weighted cases.*

**Table: Employees Earning less than £3.50 per hour in Context, by Size of Workplace and Sub-sector (%)**

| | *AIS* | *PSS* | *HI* | *<25* | *25-49* | *50-99* | *100+* |
|---|---|---|---|---|---|---|---|
| None | 67 | 57 | 40* | 47 | 19 | 34 | 40 |
| 50%+ | 8 | 12 | 33* | 34 | 49 | 15 | 8 |
| | ***Hotels*** | ***Campsites*** | ***Restaurants*** | ***Bars*** | ***Canteens*** | | |
| None | 41 | 4 | 35 | 35 | 80 | | |
| 50%+ | 18 | 0 | 31 | 48 | 12 | | |

***Notes:** All weighted cases. *Significantly different at the 5% level from AIS and PSS.*

WERS data indicate a similar disparity across all sub-sectors. Differences in the actual pay levels of full-time employees differ between the AIS, the PSS and the HI, between men and women. The main reason (from a multi-response question) for significant differences in pay levels is hours worked in over two-thirds of HI workplaces. Job grade/classification (59 per cent) and skills/core competences (47 per cent) are of second- and third-order importance.

In AIS and the PSS the two most important factors are job grade/classification and hours worked, with overtime and skills/core competences being the second and third most important factors respectively. Earnings patterns by size of workplace and sub-sector are not clear-cut. The reasons given for these differences are also similarly diverse. In terms of low pay HI workplaces are significantly more likely to have workers earning less than £3.50 per hour and to have half or more workers that are low-paid.

### *Tips*

Tipping is culturally specific and more prevalent in countries characterized by strong needs for achievement and power, where intolerance of uncertainty, anxiety and neuroticism are greater, and where citizens place greater value on status and prestige. In Egypt, the US and Argentina, where people are extroverted and status-seeking, it is customary to tip many service workers. Very few service workers receive tips in Japan, Iceland and Scandinavia, where there is greater emphasis on social than on economic relations.

While one view of tipping is that it is the most efficient way of monitoring and rewarding the efforts of service workers, and may motivate workers to perform well, workers set a price for service that is personalized and difficult for managers to monitor. The relationship between tipping and service quality is weak, even though managers and employees perceive such a relationship.

A range of behavioural variables are thought to affect tips, including good appearance, being on first name terms, particular dress codes and touching and smiling. Uncertainty of pay may be detrimental to job satisfaction and commitment, and even lead to dysfunctional behaviour, e.g. cheating and pilfering. For customers tipping functions in part as a status display, to gain social approval or to compensate poorly paid workers.

The extent to which tips increase gross pay or total reward is highly variable, and appears to be higher where the employee has more control, i.e. takes tips individually. Purcell et al. (1999) found that workers in pubs and bars could enhance their hourly pay by up to £2.00 per hour in larger establishments and by up to £1.00 per hour in smaller establishments. Restaurant workers could only achieve up to

£1.00 per hour, but only for evening work in busy city centre establishments, and also received very few fringe benefits. In hotels where an employee sharing system or employer distribution of tips is the norm, tips amount to less, but other terms and conditions are generally better.

### Case Study: Pay, Income Tax and National Insurance Contributions

Low pay serves the immediate mutual interests of employer and employee as an avoidance strategy for employment taxes, but this may have other longer-term and more damaging consequences. Avoidance maximizes employees' net pay and minimizes employers' labour costs, but employees are not eligible for a range of benefits, including pensions.

In Britain the threshold at which NICs became payable increased to the same level as the income tax threshold in 2000, a year after the NMW was introduced. This combined threshold was £84 per week when the NMW stood at £3.60 per hour. Thus a worker paid the NMW would only become liable for both deductions after working 23 hours, with the employer being subject to NICs only.

Two contrasting effects have been observed.

In 1999 when the NMW and the NIC threshold was still below the income tax threshold, some low-paying employers realigned the hours of their part timers to keep their pay below the NIC threshold. One small firm had to increase the number of employees to cover the same workload over the same hours at mutual cost benefit. This was not 'real' job creation.

In 2000 the changes increased the wage: hour ratio of 'exempt' employees thus providing employers with an incentive to increase their part-time workforce on longer hours.

### Case Study: Tips in Practice across the World

#### *US*

Tipping is almost universal. Waiting staff depend on tips for a living wage, where a set percentage of the bill is automatically expected. Tips can exceed basic pay, and credit card tips often get pooled among staff. Hotel bellmen could double the amount of tips by providing a full service, rather than a limited service.

### *Spain*

Tipping is very common but amounts to no more than a few coins, and credit card tips are almost unheard of.

### *UK*

Staff keep cash tips, either individually or on a pooled basis, and do not pay tax on them, unless they are declared. Staff working in pubs, bars and restaurants are more likely to benefit from tips than hotel staff. Staff are not entitled to receive tips or a service charge that are added to a credit card in addition to the NMW, although employers can use these payments to top up pay to the level of the NMW. This situation was finally confirmed by a ruling of the European Court of Human Rights in 2002. Where tips are paid into a tronc, the tronc master shares them among employees who are taxed on them.

### *Italy*

Restaurants may add 10-15 per cent to meals but customers are normally expected to add 10 per cent. Credit card tips are passed on to waiting staff.

### *New Zealand*

Tipping is not widespread in restaurants. Managers consider that tips are a private transaction between server and customer and are not taken into account when setting pay.

### *Australia*

Tipping usually applies only in high-class restaurants. Credit card tips are usually divided among staff.

## Case Study: The Tronc and Hierarchical Pay in Designer Restaurants

Each employee is awarded a number of points according to their position. Departments are allocated a set percentage of the tronc, which is divided by the total number of points based on total employees per shift. Chefs view the tronc as a bonus to their salary, whereas it is a supplement to low basic wages for waiting staff.

In City Centre Restaurants, which operates chains such as Caffe Uno and Garfunkels, it is claimed that waiting staff in London make so much in tips they could work without being paid a basic wage. Basic rates, set low, are topped up to the NMW with centrally collected tips. Pizza Express introduced a similar system when the NMW was introduced, but soon abandoned it amid adverse publicity. The company now encourages individual staff to keep their own tips, believing it is morally wrong to use tips or a service charge to subsidize wages.

### *Incentive- and Performance-related Pay*

On a global basis variable pay linked to performance is not yet common, but is emerging in countries such as the US, the UK and Australia, particularly among large hotel groups. Incentive pay falls broadly into two categories: PRP and payment by results (PBR). The former normally measures performance against previously determined criteria expressed as targets or objectives and has particular resonance with both a customer service-focused ethos and an HR philosophy designed to generate motivated and committed employees. A payment system that rewards employees for attaining quality goals is more likely to result in improved SQ.

By comparison PBR schemes, which measure fixed outputs, may be more appropriate to the factory production line. However, it is also important not to lose sight of fact that employee control also underpins both PRP and PBR, with PRP reflecting a tightening of the way in which individual performance is regulated. Hence increased performance may be required for the same or less pay where schemes replace non-performance based systems or provide for a derisory performance-related element.

Another set of circumstances driving incentive pay centres upon improving recruitment and retention, and reducing high turnover. Dermody (2002) reports how US restaurants use incentive programmes to retain employees. Schemes are most often tied to business volume and generally offer servers incentives to sell more items. Independent restaurants use creative incentive practices, such as unique gifts and team incentives more frequently than chain restaurants, which apply daily contests with a cash increase tied to individual performance. Few front office or back-of-house staff benefit from such schemes.

Other schemes as part of performance management may be more selective, targeting managers, e.g. Wolverhampton and Dudley, which runs family-friendly pubs, or key workers, e.g. TGI Fridays, Pret a Manger, KFC, Select Service Partner and Welcome Break, which have all succeeded in reducing turnover markedly. Competency-based pay linked to the completion of training modules is also widely used. McDonald's employees can gain an extra 15p increase per hour every four months if they achieve 93.5 per cent performance. In practice only a small minority benefit because performance review sheets are not completed on time or even at all.

Profit-related and sales-related schemes are the most common basis for incentive pay among major hotel companies, 70 per cent of which operate some form of bonus scheme. The criterion of good customer service is less common, with a few instances of chefs being rewarded according to gross profit on food or by minimizing food costs. Profit sharing and share ownership may be segregated by gender as more benefits accrue to full-time workers who are more likely to be male. The criteria for PRP for Flightpath Telephone Sales staff were based on hard skills (e.g. individual sales targets) and soft skills (e.g. handling calls). Supervisors could listen to and tape employees' performance, hence employees' ability to 'deep act' directly shaped their pay.

From WERS variable pay schemes, including dividend-based schemes, are slightly more common in the HI and the

PSS (just over 60 per cent) than in AIS (53 per cent). Above average proportions of large workplaces and bars have such schemes. In all groupings profit-related payments or bonuses are the most common type of variable pay.

While just over half of HI workplaces have profit-related payments or bonuses and deferred profit-sharing schemes, the proportion rises to over three-quarters in large workplaces and bars. Conversely most restaurant workers do not benefit from these schemes. Employee share ownership schemes are also more common in the HI than in AIS and the PSS. Individual or group performance-related schemes are less likely to be found in the HI than in AIS and the PSS.

PRP on its own is not widespread, as it applies in only one in nine HI workplaces, affecting managers and administrative staff in three-quarters of these workplaces. The pattern of usage among other occupational groups is different from in AIS and the PSS. In the HI professional staff and manual workers (craft, skilled and unskilled) are more likely to benefit from such schemes than their equivalents in AIS and the PSS. Conversely clerical and secretarial and sales staffs in AIS and the PSS are more likely to have PRP than their counterparts in the HI. Some of these variations are likely to arise because of the different occupational characteristics of each group. The application of PRP to occupational groups also varies by size of workplace and sub-sector because of their different occupational make-up.

Where PRP applies to non-managerial employees in the HI (N= 15) a greater proportion of them are included in the scheme than in AIS and the PSS. Where PRP has been paid to non-managerial employees in the last 12 months, all have been included in the scheme in just over half of these HI workplaces. Individual performance/output is significantly less likely to be used as the basis for PRP in the HI, where schemes are most likely to be group- or team-based. Individual performance/output is usually measured or assessed by a supervisor, whereas other measures of output are more likely to be used in AIS and the PSS.

## Case Study: Contemporary Incentive, Performance and Competency-based Pay in Britain

The Marriott Hanbury Hall Hotel has profit share for managers and team leaders. Waiting staff can earn extra pay for selling additional coffees and desserts. A variety of non-cash recognition awards are available to reward very good performance. Accor Hotels provides in-house skill-based programmes that link pay increases to the achievement of new skills.

McDonald's moved to a single performance review for merit-based pay in 2002. Staff are assessed between July and September, with the corresponding increase awarded at the end of September. Individual performance pay ranged from 0 per cent (needs improvement) to 6 per cent (excellent). Most received 3 per cent (satisfactory), and others 4.5 per cent (good).

Select Service Partner (UK Rail Division) introduced a new pay structure in 2002 based on completion of relevant training modules. Each stage takes around three months, and the company has applied for recognition under the NVQ scheme.

Pub retailers commonly link pay progression to training. The BII estimates one in four pub workers is studying for an NVQ/SVQ. Pizza Express pays a discretionary bonus to back-of-house staff who are not in a position to earn tips, linked to the profitability of the restaurant.

Pret a Manger pays a weekly bonus worth 75p per hour on top of basic rates for every hour worked. Mystery shoppers visit all shops and award points for efficiency, quality and speed of service. The shop has to score 90 per cent or over to qualify. A card for outstanding service worth £50 in cash can also be awarded.

A contract catering company paid £100 to a supervisor whose idea of filling confectionery machines with home-made or branded cookies increased gross profit from 18 per cent to 40 per cent. Staff could also earn £100 for leads to new business, plus a further £250 if the contract was successful. One-quarter of new business came from such suggestions.

## *Other Terms and Conditions of Employment*

Although details of global practices are rarely reported, workers within the EU are entitled to four weeks' paid holiday, while pensions are highly variable among member states. In Spain employees retiring at 65 usually receive three months' salary (subject to a minimum of 15 years' service). Provincial and company agreements also provide incentives to retire early for longer-serving employees, e.g. an extra eight months' pay at 60.

Evidence suggests that some hospitality businesses, mainly small firms, had to increase workers' basic holiday entitlement and introduce holiday pay to meet the requirements of the WTR. Some of the larger hotel companies now give between 21 and 30 days per annum related to service. Meals, drinks and uniforms, which may be free or subject to a small charge, and discounts are among the most commonly provided fringe benefits.

**Table: Non-pay Terms and Conditions in Context and by Size of Workplace (%)**

| | *AIS* | *PSS* | *HI* | *<25* | *25-49* | *50-99* | *100+* |
|---|---|---|---|---|---|---|---|
| Employer pension scheme | 65 | 55 | 36* | 43 | 20 | 30 | 34 |
| Company car/ allowance | 15 | 15 | 0* | 0 | 0 | 1 | 5 |
| Private health insurance | 15 | 20 | 9*** | 3 | 19 | 17 | 18 |
| 4 weeks+ paid leave (excl. public holidays) | 83 | 78 | 67** | 71 | 53 | 69 | 72 |
| Sick pay in excess of statutory requirements | 64 | 61 | 43* | 43 | 36 | 51 | 48 |
| None of these | 11 | 14 | 30* | 29 | 43 | 18 | 26 |

***Notes:*** *All weighted cases. *Significantly different at the 5% level from AIS and the PSS. **Significantly different at the 5% level from AIS. ***Significantly different at the 5% level from PSS.*

**Table: Non-pay Terms and Conditions by Sub-sector (%)**

| | *Hotels* | *Campsites* | *Restaurants* | *Bars* | *Canteens* |
|---|---|---|---|---|---|
| Employer pension scheme | 35 | 78 | 37 | 27 | 81 |
| Company car/ allowance | 2 | 0 | 0 | 0 | 0 |
| Private health insurance | 19 | 0 | 10 | 0 | 19 |
| 4 weeks+ paid leave (excl. public holidays) | 84 | 78 | 70 | 50 | 93 |
| Sick pay in excess of statutory requirements | 49 | 78 | 40 | 32 | 89 |
| None of these | 12 | 22 | 27 | 48 | 7 |

*Note: All weighted cases*

These indicate just how badly HI employers fare compared to counterparts in AIS and the PSS, especially in bars.

### *Performance Appraisal*

Performance appraisal, one facet of performance management, has a number of different purposes beyond providing the basis for reviewing pay.

### *Case Study: Performance Appraisal in US Hotels*

Performance appraisal is conducted annually for all staff. Most managers use more than one type of appraisal, and appraisals have more than one purpose. Half the managers use a management-by-objectives approach. However not all managers use follow-up sessions to feedback the results. The most frequent application of performance appraisals is for compensation decisions, followed by assessing whether objectives have been met, establishing training needs and determining promotions. A majority considered that appraisals were important to their business.

Annual or six-monthly appraisal in Australia and Singapore forms part of employee development, with management by objectives being almost universal. While systems distinguish between managerial and operative staff in both countries, appraisal is more commonly used to determine pay in Singapore than in Australia where award rates of payment, rather than individual contracts, govern pay rates. Managers have more scope to vary pay in Singapore because of workplace collective agreements.

Within Britain appraisals are regarded as an essential business tool by HR managers to improve company and individual performance. Performance appraisal goals focusing on quality goals, behaviour critical to achieving those goals and use of customer-driven data are more compatible with improving SQ. The identification of training and development needs and evaluating individual performance are the main reasons performance appraisals are used in the private sector in Britain, with most large organizations appraising all employees.

From WERS the four main purposes of appraisal in the HI, which also apply in AIS and the PSS, are to give feedback on an employee's performance, to set/evaluate training and development needs, to give employees a chance to discuss future career moves, and to review and set objectives. Performance appraisal is more likely to be used to determine a pay increase in the HI (half the sub-sample) than in AIS and the PSS. However, performance appraisal is not directly linked to reviews or changes in individual employees' pay in almost all of those cases, the exceptions being found only in large workplaces.

WERS shows that in Britain managers and administrative staffs in the HI are significantly more likely to be appraised formally than their counterparts in AIS and the PSS. Conversely professional, technical and scientific, and clerical and secretarial staff are significantly less likely to be have formal appraisals. A minority of workplaces in AIS and the PSS (one-quarter) and 18 per cent of HI workplaces do not formally appraise any of the specified occupational groups. Further details about appraisals from WERS are given for non-managerial employees only.

Formal performance appraisal schemes covering all or almost all staff have been observed in a large hotels and designer restaurants. WERS shows that performance appraisal of non-managerial employees is less likely to occur in the HI (56 per cent of all cases), and where it applies coverage is slightly less comprehensive. Most private sector schemes operate a formalized process with an annual interview between manager and subordinate, typically of between one and two hours' duration. Within hospitality and leisure Sodexho and David Lloyd Leisure carry out regular reviews outside the appraisal process, in the latter case informally as a precursor that could lead to formal disciplinary action.

WERS shows that where appraisal is used, all employees are included in the scheme in half of HI workplaces compared to 65 per cent in AIS and 73 per cent in PSS. The HI is significantly less likely to operate annual appraisals and significantly more likely to have appraisals that do not conform to a fixed pattern. In all groupings appraisal is most likely to be conducted by the employee's immediate superior, with the wider involvement of another manager occurring in a large minority of cases, especially in restaurants.

Employees are often suspicious of appraisals which, when conducted badly, can side-step crucial issues and lead to one party unleashing pent-up frustrations, leading ultimately to a deterioration in the employment relationship. Dickens (1998) argues that impression management rather than good performance may count for more in obtaining a good rating. Appraisers are usually men who may use proxy measures for measuring commitment, such as visible hours at work and working beyond contract which penalize women.

Chapter 4

# Development and Fair Treatment

## RECRUITMENT AND SELECTION

The philosophy is if you create spaces where people like to spend time, they will spend money. So it's very much a design-driven experience. And although the restaurants were designed for the local market, hotel guests must be treated as "preferred local customers, if they come in without a reservation. Hotel guests must be offered reservations upon check in. Also, as the hotel itself has ample meeting and ballroom space, the restaurants were designed with significant private dining components to capture the dollars of group guests, as well.

High levels of recruitment activity can be attributed to specific conflicting pressures. On the one hand the HI worldwide reports skill shortages and fails to fill current vacancies, inferring a quality problem. Employers may not be targeting appropriate groups of people or national training frameworks may be inadequately geared to the industry's needs. Considering only locals as a source of labour may be outdated in a global economy.

Technological advances facilitate the finding of required labour by targeting recruitment in developing countries, where there are high rates of unemployment among skilled workers, e.g. in Bangladesh 40 per cent of people with a Master's degree are unemployed or under-employed. The increasing presence of MNCs in tourism, in countries such as India, may not necessarily be met by an adequate supply of skilled workers. Skills shortages in Florida are overcome by recruiting from Puerto Rico.

On the other hand the consequences of employment flows, which management may seek to perpetuate, and cost-minimization policies encourage recruitment systems that are highly responsive, flexible and ad hoc. Given high leaver rates noted, it is not surprising to find a high rate of recruitment in Britain.

HI workplaces are significantly more likely to have workforces with 50 per cent or more new employees, and this is three times greater than in AIS. Large workplaces have the lowest rates of recruitment activity.

In the twelve months prior to WERS HI workplaces were most likely to have vacancies for unskilled and sales staff. HI workplaces were significantly more likely to have vacancies for personal service, sales staff and routine unskilled manual workers, and significantly less likely to have vacancies for professional, technical and scientific, clerical and secretarial and operative and assembly workers.

Half the workplaces in AIS, PSS and the HI had no difficulty filling vacancies, while skilled and unskilled job were most problematic in a small minority of HI workplaces. Considerable variations within sub-sectors reflect the different skill bases within them.

A different set of pressures is observed in post-Communist Russia, where bringing in new staff to respond to new demands is difficult to achieve. Overstaffing is rife because of low pay, problems making people redundant and the social responsibility to keep staff in jobs. Consequently staff becomes bored and lazy.

**Table: Recruitment in Last 12 Months in Context and by Size of Workplace**

| | *AIS* | *PSS* | *HI* | *<25* | *25-49* | *50-99* | *100+* |
|---|---|---|---|---|---|---|---|
| *Total recruits* | | | | | | | |
| Mean number | 13 | 14 | 20 | 10 | 25 | 42 | 53 |
| As % of total employees 1 year ago | 27 | 34 | 63* | 62 | 72 | 64 | 33 |
| *New permanent* | | | | | | | |
| Yes (%) | 91 | 93 | 93 | 93 | 89 | 100 | 100 |

***Notes:*** *All weighted cases where there have been recruits (AIS, N = 2,142, PSS, N = 1,331 and HI, N = 154). Means are rounded. *Significantly different at the 5% level from AIS and PSS.*

**Table: Recruitment in Last 12 Months by Sub-sector**

| | *Hotels* | *Campsites* | *Restaurants* | *Bars* | *Canteens* |
|---|---|---|---|---|---|
| *Total recruits* | | | | | |
| Mean number | 29 | 2 | 21 | 15 | 10 |
| As % of total employees 1 year ago | 59 | 5 | 66 | 71 | 24 |
| *New permanent* | | | | | |
| Yes (%) | 97 | 100 | 97 | 88 | 100 |

***Notes:*** *All weighted cases where there have been recruits. Means are rounded.*

## Approaches to Recruitment

Recruitment and selection are an important part of managerial work and workplace life. To proponents of the quality-enhancing employment approach 'employee selection is an important issue. Investing in techniques and skills which improve the selection decision is essential for organisational success'. Good recruitment and selection is based on an assessment of work values, personality, interpersonal skills and problem-solving ability. Testing potential employees can be used to control 'type' and help mould organizational culture.

On the other hand those pursuing a cost-minimization approach may have little incentive or will to deploy other than the most basic of methods, and may respond in an ad hoc way. Using casual staff as ports of entry not only maintains control over staffing levels but also over behaviour and discipline, as casuals can be more easily dismissed. Ease of dismissal may act as a barrier to the adoption of more systematic recruitment and selection, especially where there is a plentiful supply of labour. Lack of job security is likely to undermine the achievement of SQ, and may also reflect the low status of the personnel function or its absence.

The 'employment decision', when the vacancy is filled by an appropriate candidate, is a mutual and voluntary decision, based on employers' and candidates' freedom to withdraw from the process at any time. The process involves chance and risk. Managers have considerable discretion but are never in complete control. Managers' own ways of maximizing cost-effectiveness have different meanings within firms' own employment standards and different labour market conditions.

Studies consistently report high levels of informality, including 'word of mouth' recruitment. Most British students gain employment by initiating contact themselves or through friends and family, which is even more common in Bulgaria, Hungary and Slovakia. Greater formality may be found in larger hotel firms, but is by no means comprehensive. Larger hotel companies looking overseas for staff are providing more accommodation as a first temporary step in the first two months of employment.

A large majority of British HI workplaces in WERS are significantly more likely to treat internal and external candidates equally than in AIS and PSS. Consequently they are also less likely to give preference to internal candidates over external candidates except in medium and large workplaces (one-third favour internal candidates). This is mirrored in slightly lower levels of internal recruitment in the HI. Goss-Turner (1999) notes that multi-unit managers are normally recruited internally on the basis of perceived task and people orientation, without any systematic selection procedures.

*Recruitment Criteria*

We noted how in customer-service work recruitment is more likely to be based on people's personal and aesthetic skills than technical skills, while the preceding discussion suggests availability is also important. Dickens argues that attitudes, behaviour and personality tend to interact with gender and racial stereotypes, which may lead to discrimination in recruitment. Managers' preference for recruitment is made on the basis of personality. Aesthetically employers can signal the type of labour required by using terms such as 'smart young person' in an advertisement, or requiring the enclosure of a photograph with applications. By presenting themselves in person young people enable employers to screen for aesthetic skills. Hence recruitment (and training) is on the basis of customer focus, interpersonal skills, emotional control and empathy. Training in grooming and deportment may follow.

The 'personality' criterion is to an extent confirmed by WERS, which shows that the four most important recruitment criteria in the HI are motivation, references, skills and availability; each is used in three-quarters or more workplaces. The three most important criteria in AIS of experience, skills and motivation apply in 86 per cent or more workplaces. Availability, experience and personal recommendation are significantly more important in the HI than in AIS and PSS. Qualifications are more important in AIS and PSS. Availability is of major importance to restaurants, while age is more important in bars than in any other sub-sector.

We know that a combination of volatile demand, age-related factors, and worker attributes makes young workers, particularly students, a valuable commodity within the HI. Yet firms have not fallen to the temptation of employing more young workers on officially sanctioned lower rates of pay under the NMW. This fits with their pay structures, policies on employing particular age groups for particular jobs or periods of time, or legal restrictions on the serving of alcohol and the operation of dangerous machinery.

### *Selection Methods and Tests*

The interview remains popular with managers and candidates alike, as it is simple, quick and cheap, in spite of reliability and validity concerns. It fulfils a social function, enabling social and aesthetic aspects that are so integral to customer-service work to be addressed, however inadequately. Behavioural interviewing, where standard questions address how the candidate dealt with past situations that are likely to arise in their new job, provides better quality information and encourages a more reciprocal approach to employment decision-making. Like other simulated group exercises its limitations are assumptions that actual behaviour will be in line with intentions, and that a snapshot view is representative of general behaviour. Competency-based interviewing has produced exceptional performers and reduced turnover levels at the Buckhead Beef Company.

Paraskevas suggests that HI managerial selection techniques should be aimed at the application of skills, rather than their possession. Personality is an important consideration, and HI selectors are as likely to accept the validity and usefulness of sophisticated selection techniques as their counterparts in other sectors. Hotels do not use them because of cost and reliability concerns.

According to WERS personality and attitude tests have limited use in general, more so in the HI than in AIS and PSS. They are more likely to be used in HI firms employing 25 or more employees. While performance or competency tests are used by half of AIS firms significantly fewer HI workplaces (one-quarter) use them. They are most likely to be used in the largest HI workplaces but are rarely used in bars. One view is that tests are best suited to jobs involving special knowledge and abilities. Hence such tests have limited application among a largely unskilled workforce.

*Appointment*

Terms and conditions of employment (pay, hours, sick leave, grievance procedures, training opportunities and holiday) are made available in writing in most HI workplaces. However 13 per cent do not convey any of these details in writing, over twice the proportion in AIS and PSS. Restaurants are the worst offenders (one-quarter). Three-quarters of AIS, PSS and HI workplaces have standard employment contracts for their largest occupational group (LOG), although one-fifth of bars do not give their LOG contracts.

*Retention*

The recruitment and retention of managers and skilled workers is a global HCT sector problem. While Redman and Mathews (1998) contend that effective retention programmes will achieve higher levels of SQ, there is a view that the most talented people leave the sector, while the less competent stay for fear of becoming unemployed. In spite of the increase in hospitality management programmes and more hospitality graduates, there are poor graduate transfer rates and demand outstrips supply.

Part of the problem may lie in unsystematic graduate recruitment and selection that relies upon impressions and subjective judgements of character, and pays little regard to academic achievement and performance and supporting evidence from tutors. Poor impressions created by work placements may prompt hospitality graduates to seek careers elsewhere.

A number of the larger hotel companies have adopted training initiatives to improve retention in a tight UK labour market. The Thistle Tower Hotel introduced Modern Apprenticeships in-house, while employees at Harrington Hall were given the chance to study National Vocational Qualifications. The London Heathrow Marriott offers a wide range of courses including Modern Apprenticeships, graduate training schemes, NVQ programmes and English lessons for non-English speaking staff, while Accor also offers NVQs and

Modern Apprenticeships. Rowley and Purcell (2001) note how leading edge employers' retention policies include anything, short of raising pay.

## Training and Development

The state has a vested interest in VET in seeking to develop a more highly skilled labour force to improve economic performance and competitiveness. National systems vary considerably in general and in their specificity towards hospitality and tourism, with many developing countries not yet providing sufficient state support. In India the framework of tourism education is inadequate to a growing tourism sector where increasing professionalism, particularly at managerial levels, is required. Russia may have a highly literate and well-educated workforce, but this presents challenges to bringing managerial staff to the requisite level of skills and competencies where cultural attitudes are non-western.

The training culture of the US can be described as voluntarist and largely uncoordinated, and places emphasis on individual effort and individual payment - a 'protean' career. Germany, France and Sweden have directed and more centralized systems. In Spain many employees (43 per cent) have no school-leaving certificate. A state-funded scheme entitles employers to financial aid on presentation of an annual training plan.

Employees are eligible to up to 150 hours training on full pay. In Australia McDonald's offers employees access to an approved fast food accredited traineeship of 12 months' duration in return for a government subsidy. These arrangements have been incorporated into sectoral agreements. The British system is voluntarist, and not particularly industry-oriented since the demise of the industry training boards in the 1980s.

Hospitality and tourism management education is provided in many countries, but not in Denmark, Sweden or Japan. The corpus of knowledge for hospitality management is the preserve of the HCIMA, which represents 24,000 managers in 106 countries. Baum and Nickson press the case for a stronger pedagogical base in the learning experience of HRM in higher education, arguing that responding to industry demands may perpetuate existing (poor) HRM practice and make little or no contribution to change. Even major chains do not have any involvement with leading UK and US Business Schools.

In response to the 1997 National Targets for Education and Training for the UK, the HI's target for 2000 for the proportion of employers offering NVQs and SVQs was 50 per cent from a base of less than 1 per cent in the mid-1990s. The target for employees to have job-related qualifications increased to 60 per cent from 30 per cent. Such highly ambitious targets, even if met, would still leave major gaps in training provision.

**Case Study: National Vocational, Educational and Training Frameworks for Hospitality and Tourism**

*France*

A highly centralized system of public provision is based on nationally recognized qualifications at staged levels from the craft Certificat de l'Aptitude Professionelle to the management-orientated Brevet de Technicien Supérieur. Higher education tends to be private, often with the cooperation of the local Chamber of Commerce.

*Italy*

Training is highly fragmented, with no industry-level training body. Secondary education is available in Hotel and Catering Schools and Schools of Tourism. Placements in hotels last only one or two weeks and are ineffective. Tourism is a recent innovation in higher education, but there is no provision for hospitality.

*Spain*

Escuelas de Hosteleria provide craft training, while Escuelas de Turismo provide more general training leading to hotel reception, travel agency or tourist guide work. A degree has recently been developed for both industries but is criticized by employers for its lack of practical skill development.

### *Netherlands*

Training is well regulated and well developed. All adults are entitled to three days' training per annum. Apprenticeships involve four days' working and one day's study a week. Three higher-level state-run hotel schools offer degrees and 11 middle-level schools offer diplomas. In both cases there is a one-year industrial placement and qualifications are recognized internationally. Diploma courses are rigorous, including international law, languages and personnel management.

### *Germany*

There is a highly regulated system based on apprenticeships, including two languages, which are subject to national practical and theoretical examinations. Two-year post-apprenticeship training is undertaken at a Fachschule. Most hotel general managers have taken this route. Most college graduates have a related degree.

### *UK*

NVQs are a workplace competency-based assessment of tasks a worker can perform. There is no training requirement, and many workers do not complete enough modules to gain a qualification. There is no external examination. Over 300 colleges and universities provide courses ranging from craft-level NVQs to Masters degrees.

Registrations for NVQs/SVQs have risen and the most popular is food preparation and cooking. Work-based training Modern Apprenticeships have high uptakes but also high drop-out rates. Enrolment on General (G)NVQ, further and higher education courses has been falling. A new network of SSCs replaced NTOs in 2002. Most college graduates have industry-related qualifications.

## *US*

Vocational preparation is rare, and apprenticeships are very rare. Alternatively hotels have formal relationships with colleges for students, which are more formal where hospitality programmes are taught. Twenty per cent of food and beverage operatives are full-time students. There are no national hotel skill standards. A few high-profile universities provide qualifications recognized by the leading international and national hotel companies.

Fifteen per cent of people working in the HI do not have qualifications of any kind, while 17 per cent have a qualification below General Certificate of Education (GCSE) grades A-C or equivalent, which could be an NVQ/SVQ. The majority has a qualification at or above this level.

Baum et al. suggest that the NVQ/GNVQ framework developed in the UK in the early 1990s was done without specific sectoral consideration or recognition of the hospitality and tourism industries' policy priorities, leading to a skills gap. Hales et al. (1996) contend that NVQs have considerable potential in small hospitality firms, as they give a sharper focus to training activities and improve candidates' perceived job satisfaction, morale and career prospects. However the system is seen as weak in the absence of external examination. Other government initiatives such as Modern Apprenticeships and New Deal may be viewed negatively by HI employers, and those that have experience of them may be unwilling to use them again.

Recent employer-led initiatives in Britain include the BHA's Excellence Through People, which identifies and disseminates 'best practice' in recruitment and selection, development, recognition and reward, and communications.

However, only 0.6 per cent of all HI establishments had been certified. Hospitality Assured, developed by the HCIMA and promoted by the BHA, deals with 'best practice' from a customer perspective, enabling those holding an award to benchmark their customer service against the best in the industry.

### *Approaches to Training*

Training can be formal or informal, applied selectively to particular workers, on-or off-job, accredited or non-accredited, occur over variable periods of time, and be provided by the firm or an outside body. Firms' ability and willingness to train depends on the available resources of time, money and staff. An unstable workforce base built upon volatile demand also constrains firms' ability to provide training. Where organizations appear to support external training, they are not prepared to pay high fees, even for managers.

Where demand is more volatile, and jobs involve more numerous tasks, training becomes more difficult. Full-time students with career aspirations elsewhere cannot or are unwilling to participate in formal training even if available. Where demand is steady, employers can subdivide jobs and closely monitor defined tasks. Hence formalized training is likely to be found where there is a clearly defined skills base, usually in food preparation.

Storey regards training and development as the 'litmus test' of HRM. Redman and Mathews (1998) suggest the extent of quality-related training in 'soft' areas such as team working processes and interpersonal skills are positively related to increased SQ. IiP brings benefits in terms of workforce development and improved business efficiency, and can reduce turnover and absenteeism where it is part of an SQ philosophy. However failure will result where training budgets are low and needs assessments are poorly executed. In Singapore the use of guests' comments and employee consultation to inform training needs is regarded as strength.

### Case Study: Training and Development in UK Designer Restaurants

A training manager coordinates, supports and executes training throughout the group. All new recruits attend induction training in the first two weeks. Staff use training manuals to conduct on-job training for kitchen and restaurant staff. Chefs learn through job rotation. Waiting staff are provided with lists of menu ingredients, and are expected to attend periodic tastings, especially when the menu changes. Chefs are encouraged to experiment with new dishes, and an exchange scheme was being piloted with a restaurant in California. Day release is available for achieving NVQs, with several managers working towards NVQ assessor awards to carry out in-house accredited training.

**Case Study: The San Francisco Hotels Partnership Project**

A consortium of 12 hotels and the four largest union locals found a collective solution to skill development and career progression. The collective agreement included joint problem-solving groups and a state-subsidized training programme. All workers were offered 100 hours of training in team building, technical skills and English as a foreign language. This released the potential capability of room attendants with degrees to advance to higher positions. Cross-training enabled them to gain experience as food servers during periods of holiday cover.

Training and development supported by performance appraisal is a primary tool of culture change and communication strategy. People-focused organizations like BA, Singapore Airlines, Marriott and Ritz Carlton do engage in systematic training and development programmes. Case study 4.3 illustrates how trade unions have made a positive contribution to training in the US.

Limitations to managerial training and development feature widely in the literature. The bringing together of all hotel managers at the company's training centre in pairs is lauded as enabling international managers to network and thereby develop a better understanding of global aspects and company philosophy. Perceptions of limited promotion opportunities are not justified in major airlines, international hotel groups and theme parks.

In McDonald's management training is replaced by an operation and training manual, which contains all facets of owning and operating a store. There is an interesting slant to management development. Most line managers start as casual or part-time crew members, and may internalize the leadership or managerial style of the owner or franchisee. This is important in terms of how careers are defined and how future franchises are created.

India, Indonesia and Thailand may have plentiful labour pools, but major investment in training and development is necessary to overcome the lack of cultural and communications skills of front-line employees. Hence training needs in developing countries and other countries with an international market centre on the 'soft' competencies of generic service skills, including the ability to anticipate guests' verbal and non-verbal communication styles.

Small HI firms with informal HRM relying on casual, part-time and seasonal labour are likely to make a poor investment in training. Rather they rely on buying in skills from the external labour market or, if they train, a regular churn of statutory and skills training is needed to service staff turnover. Because career progression is dependent upon moving to another employer, there is a reluctance to invest in training that will benefit a competitor. Recession in post-Communist Bulgaria has curtailed investment in training and development in hotels.

### *Induction and Training*

The first day at work is critical in shaping an employee's attitude to the company, influencing performance, satisfaction, commitment or intention to leave. Within Britain standard induction for the LOG is widespread in the HI, the PSS and AIS (three-quarters of workplaces), but is most likely to be used in workplaces employing 25 or more employees. However, over one-quarter of hotels have no such programme, which may be linked to high turnover. Short induction programmes of one day or less are more common in HI workplaces (four in ten) than in the PSS and AIS (one-third), and these are more likely to be found in medium and large workplaces (over half).

Supervision, job descriptions, induction/initial training and ongoing training are the main methods used to make employees aware of their job responsibilities in all groupings, and these apply in three-quarters or more of HI workplaces. Individual objectives and targets are least used in the HI (30 per cent), with team targets and competency standards (both 31 per cent) also featuring relatively less often. There are variations by size and sector, with most continual reinforcement of job responsibilities occurring in large workplaces.

Many studies find that worker training is basic, and that the unskilled nature of the work enables workers to reach experienced worker standard within a few weeks. There is normally a statutory requirement to provide general training in respect of food hygiene, health and safety and fire regulations. More specific skills training is related to subsectors with a defined skills base, e.g. silver service and wine waiting in restaurants. While some firms may pay a lower training or starter rate to reflect the trainee's lower contribution, there appears to be little uptake among HI firms for two reasons. The duration of training is short and training occurs while the worker is actually working, so lower pay cannot be justified. There has been little use of the development rate of the NMW for adult trainees.

New starters in the LOG in the HI are able to do their job as well as experienced employees significantly more quickly than is the case in the PSS and AIS, which is symptomatic of the low skills base. Within one month new starters would be up to experienced worker standard in over half of HI workplaces compared to only one-third of the PSS and AIS workplaces. Very few HI workplaces have any employees who take more than six months to become experienced, which is significantly different from AIS and the PSS. One-third of HI workplaces offered no off-the-job training compared to one-quarter in AIS and the PSS, and overall HI employees are less likely to have received off-job training.

Limited training (below 20 per cent of the LOG) is most often found in very small workplaces (two-thirds) and restaurants (eight in ten). Even so, those HI employees who do benefit from off-job training received similar amounts of time in training as their counterparts in the PSS and AIS. One-quarter of HI employees benefiting from off-the-job training received less than one day. Off-the-job training of five days or more affects almost one-third of HI workplaces and is more likely to be found in restaurants and small workplaces.

HI workplaces are significantly more likely to give off-the-job training in health and safety (89 per cent), customer service/liaison (85 per cent) and quality control procedures (67 per cent) and significantly less likely to provide training in computing skills (19 per cent) than in the PSS and AIS. Quality control is particularly important in small workplaces and restaurants (over eight in ten).

Reliability and working to deadlines is significantly more important in the HI than in AIS. Team working, operation of new equipment, and improving communications affect 50 per cent or more HI workplaces. The different needs of firms in AIS and the PSS make for a more diverse pattern of matters covered by off-the-job training. Although these workplaces provide off-the-job training in the matters noted above, these tend to happen in a sizeable minority of workplaces, and it may be the case that they are covered in on-the-job training.

In one-third of AIS, PSS and HI workplaces around half or more of the workforce in the LOG has been formally trained to do jobs other than their own. High levels of workers who are functionally flexible are most likely to be found in HI workplaces employing between 25 and 49 employees, and are least likely to be found in the very small workplaces and restaurants.

### *Fair Treatment at Work*

The origins of equal opportunities lie in the social and political agenda of the 1960s and 1970s, in which the US civil rights movement was a powerful driving force for social justice. Perhaps surprisingly, given the free enterprise culture and deregulated American approach to employment relations noted, the US is at the forefront of legal compliance in the form of anti-discrimination legislation in relation to gender, race, age and disability.

The Equal Employment Opportunity Commission (EEOC) deals with all complaints of discrimination on grounds of sex, race, national origin, religion, retaliation and disability, aids complainants, undertakes research and produces publications with a view to removing barriers. Historically Europe's agenda has been more restricted, focusing largely on gender equality, but is now changing. There is no monitoring body independent of government in France.

**Case Study: Peculiar Discrimination at Joe's Stone Crabs**

The EEOC brought a case of sex discrimination against this Miami restaurant, although no individual had claimed discrimination. The EEOC decided that Joe's had a reputation for hiring men only, and therefore women would have been discouraged from applying. The employers were required to review their HR practices, analyse their workforce, and re-examine their recruitment and selection criteria.

***Sex and Race***

Within Europe only Britain deals with race discrimination in a similar way to sex discrimination for persons seeking employment and those in employment. The Sex Discrimination Act 1975(sex and marital status) and the Race Relations Act 1976 (race, colour, nationality, ethnic and national origin) are designed to prevent three types of discrimination - direct, indirect and victimization, which can include harassment. Customers are within the scope of sex discrimination law because it is unlawful for an employer to discriminate on sex grounds in the provision of goods, facilities or services as part of a business, such as service in a restaurant or the letting of rooms. If race (or sex) is a genuine occupational qualification, then an employer can lawfully discriminate in favour of a person from a particular racial group.

If an employer refuses to train a woman simply because she is a married, that is directly discriminatory. The imposition of an age requirement for a post might be indirectly discriminatory where the effect is that a significantly smaller proportion of men, women or married persons are able to comply with it compared to persons of the opposite sex or single persons. Both Acts cover selection, promotion, transfer, training and other benefits, but pay and pensions are within scope of equal pay legislation. Two separate bodies, the EOC and the CRE, exercise specific responsibilities for this legislation.

There is no maximum limit on the amount of compensation that employment tribunals may award to a successful claimant. Although only a very small proportion of total cases reach tribunal (most are settled or disposed of by other means or withdrawn), in 2000/1 compensation of £3.75 million was awarded in sex discrimination cases. The highest award was £1,414,620 and the median award £5,000. However the number of claims dropped sharply from 17,200 to 10,092, and those that are made are becoming increasingly complex. Victims of race discrimination fare less well, with total compensation standing at £0.75 million, the highest award £66,086 and the median award £5,263.

In critique of the effectiveness of extant British anti-discrimination law, Dickens notes that the emphasis is to desist from doing negative things. There is no legal requirement to do anything positive to promote equality such as workforce monitoring or attempting to increase the proportion of under-represented groups in the workplace. Positive discrimination such as preferential hiring quotas is unlawful. Equal opportunities policies are voluntary, and depend on a business case argument rather than being based on a social case.

Business arguments are contingent, resulting in selective and partial action in which employers prioritize gender over race. Putting equal opportunities policies into practice is impeded by men's resistance to sex equality. There are circumstances when women can break through the 'glass ceiling' and achieve senior management positions. An organization-based approach is no use to women in highly feminized employment who remain stuck to a 'sticky floor' because it does not lead to 'a transformation in access to power and the nature of it'. Hence the economic benefits of equal opportunities need to be articulated at a level beyond the organization, but may not produce desirable outcomes.

Dickens also argues that HRM concepts and policies perpetuate rather than challenge gender inequality. The reality of work intensification, increased surveillance and managerial control, and the shifting of risk to employees revealed in more critical empirical reviews of HRM have a disproportionate effect on women and other disadvantaged groups. In pursuit of flexibility, cost-cutting 'hard' HRM has utilized and underpinned existing sex segregation, with the core being defined partly by reference to masculine attributes.

Perceptions of women's (lower) commitment also shape the core-periphery, determining who is hired, trained and developed. Assessment in selection, appraisal and reward needs to be understood in terms of power-based relations. Increasing reliance on attitudinal characteristics exacerbates the problem because attitude, behaviour and personality tend to interact with gender and racial stereotypes and lead to discrimination in selection. Working as cabin crew is defined as women's work by employers, customers and employees. Emotional labour is not gender neutral as work containing significant amounts is dominated by women.

Harassment is unwanted behaviour of a sexual nature including physical, verbal and non-verbal behaviour. In the US the company is responsible for a manager's persistent harassment. The issue of what constitutes a hostile environment has proved difficult to define and sexual harassment need not be so severe as to cause psychological damage. Employers cannot seek a judgement to dismiss charges unless they have a properly implemented policy. Where there is no policy, employers will be liable for the hostile environment created by supervisors.

Harassment is a pervasive and frequent occurrence. Managers and customers can be the perpetrators of sexual harassment. It mainly affects women, reflecting the gendered division of work and existing power differentials. Customer harassment is one of the least rewarding aspects of the interpersonal relationship, and is exacerbated where service staff is encouraged to sell sexuality or to flirt. The more authentic the performance, the more difficult it is for the customer to recognize there is no promise of associated consequences, which may be exacerbated by alcohol. Individual employee re/action may make things worse, as most managerial harassment comes from an immediate superior or more senior manager.

The extent of harassment is likely to be under-reported, unless there is a strong policy and effective channels for challenging such behaviour that by-pass superiors. Consequently individuals sustain stress and poor working relationships, and may quit.

### *Case Study: Women in Hotels*

Italy has a stronger legal framework supporting women, but job opportunities are limited and favourable maternity rights appear to be damaging women's employment prospects. Women returners are considered out of touch, and they are offered chambermaids' jobs. Family-friendly policies are unknown, even to large hotel groups. The pay gap is smaller because all sectors are regulated by legally binding collective agreements. Some employers pay above the minimum in cash to avoid higher tax and social insurance costs.

In the UK increased opportunities are in numerically flexible jobs which are vulnerable to economic fluctuations. As in Italy, restaurant and bar jobs are contingently gendered, as employers seek cheap labour of either sex. Women are largely excluded from kitchen work, but not from nightwork, the reverse of what is observed in Italy. Company economic performance is the most important factor in setting pay. There is greater awareness of gender issues.

### *Disability*

The European approach to disability has generally been based on compulsory employment quota systems, e.g. France, Germany and Spain, and extensive state intervention in contrast to the US model of civil rights and strong anti-discrimination measures. The US model is based on the premise that discrimination owes more to society's attitude and structural barriers than personal limitations caused by impairment or disability. The Rehabilitation Act 1973 provides for affirmative action, which could include the achievement of preferential quotas, while the Americans with Disabilities Act 1992 recognizes disabled people as a group whose relative lack of power has prevented them from achieving fair or equal treatment in the face of societal prejudice. Case study illustrates some early court decisions on disability and acquired immune deficiency syndrome (AIDS), which have become more difficult to document due to HI organizations settling out of court to avoid expensive litigation and adverse publicity. Such cases may arise from the misconception that AIDS can be transmitted by casual contact, e.g. food handling, with the implication that companies need to maintain ongoing employee educational programmes in the context of strong policies.

### Case Study: Disability and AIDS

A New York City hotel was ordered to pay its former accountant, who was sacked less than two weeks after confiding to colleagues that he had AIDS, $13,546 for disability, plus medical bills and $1,000 compensation for pain and suffering. Sheraton stated that termination was for excessive absences. The accountant had been voted Employee of the Year two months earlier.

A waiter in a Texas lodge with AIDS was awarded $60,000 by a jury for disability discrimination, rejecting the company's claim that he was dismissed for excessive tardiness.

Britain diverged from the general European model with the Disability Discrimination Act 1995, which defines disability, covers direct discrimination and victimization, but not indirect discrimination, and places a duty on employers to make positive adjustments to the workplace to accommodate disabled people. The DRC exercises responsibility for the legislation. Even so, almost all British workplaces, including those in the HI, do not employ disabled workers. In 2000/1 employment tribunals awarded £1.5 million compensation to successful claimants, with a maximum figure of £215,000 and a median of £6,019 in the small proportion of cases that proceeded to tribunal.

The US has the longest experience of age discrimination legislation with the Age Discrimination in Employment Act 1967. Canada, France, Ireland and Australia are examples of other countries with legislation, with New Zealand having recently followed suit. In the US the law only protects those aged 40 and over (no upper age limit), and employers cannot make employment decisions on hiring, firing, training or grading on the basis of age.

In 1997 age complaints accounted for 20 per cent of all complaints received by the EEOC. Australia and New Zealand's legislation was a response to the 'demographic timebomb' - a shortage of young people entering a labour market increasingly dominated by older age groups. New Zealand legislation embodies an assertion that age per se does not determine a person's ability or productivity, and should not be used as a criterion in any part of the employment cycle. Reliance should be placed on the person's ability to perform the task required.

Hence Qu and Yee Cheng report how the hotel industry in Hong Kong targeted workers aged 55 and over to alleviate labour shortages. Their favourable attributes, including being hard-working, responsible and cooperative, are perceived to outweigh their weaknesses, including lower productivity and higher employment cost. Conversely in Britain high reliance on young labour, coupled with a given set of managerial attitudes and prejudices, serves to disadvantage 'mature' workers who may be as young as 30.

Britain introduced a Code of Practice on Age Diversity in Employment in 1999, which seeks to introduce good practice into employers' policies on recruitment, selection, promotion, redundancy and retention. Loretto et al. (2000) suggest the Code's impact is likely to be small because its non-statutory basis has more drawbacks than merits. As Sargeant notes, the Code will not outlaw a provision contained within an advertisement for stewards/stewardesses to work on Eurostar that states 'we want to hear from you if you are aged 20-35'.

### *Current and Future Developments*

The legal framework within Europe is changing following the adoption in 2000 of the EU Directive on equal treatment in areas other than sex or race legislation, and anti-discrimination legislation will be extended to other areas including age and disability after extensive consultation. Many aspects of the race and disability proposals are already covered by extant UK legislation, but changes are already taking place:

- New regulations in 2003 change the definition of indirect discrimination in race cases, introduce a definition of racial harassment, and shift the burden of proof in direct discrimination to the employer, in keeping with sex discrimination.
- New regulations in 2003 outlaw discrimination on grounds of sexual orientation and religion. Both are based closely on the principles of the Race Relations Act 1976. The regulations cover orientation towards the same sex, opposite sex or both. Religion covers grounds of religion or belief (religious belief or similar philosophical belief). Religion is not defined, and there is a genuine occupational qualification exemption.
- New anti-discrimination regulations in 2004 widen the definition of disability discrimination, outlaw harassment as a form of discrimination, and remove the small employer exemption (below 15 employees). Further legislation arising from an internal review is expected to widen the scope of the definition of

disability, possibly to include human immunodeficiency virus (HIV) and cancer.

- Age legislation must be in place by 2006, and is unlikely to be earlier, so the continued survival of compulsory retirement age will remain unresolved until then. However some relaxation is necessary to allow future generations to defer their pensions and work longer to enhance their 'pension' provision in a longer living population.

### *Managing Diversity*

In the last 40 years there has been a shift in emphasis from providing equal opportunities in employment to managing diversity of employment. Managing diversity has emerged as an alternative approach to managing the individual, and positively values differences. It takes account not only of race, sex and disability but also other factors, including culture, work experience, personality and workstyle. Maxwell et al. identify two factors that differentiate managing diversity from equal opportunities. First, there is emphasis on the positive perspective of difference among staff in contrast to a negative perspective of disadvantage and discrimination against staff. Second, diversity factors beyond those covered by law are embraced.

A motivating force for addressing diversity polices arises from widespread demographic changes in the US and Europe producing a gradually ageing workforce. Changes in the ethnic mix of the labour force are occurring. In the US most growth in the non-white workforce will come from Asians and Hispanics who together will comprise 20 per cent in 2020, while the black population will only account for 11 per cent. These groups are generally clustered in lower-level occupations in the HI. Sixty per cent of line-level personnel in US restaurants are from an ethnic minority, where diversity needs to be acknowledged through cross-cultural training. Conversely there were only 35 black general managers in 45,000 US hotels. Companies are advised to use mentors and to take more affirmative action.

The extent to which diversity policies complement or supplement equal opportunities approaches is debatable. Maxwell et al. (2001) argue that equal opportunities are outdated in a changed social and political climate where employers need to embrace diversity as a strategic issue for economic and competitive success. As noted above Dickens finds the business case unconvincing, and argues that only regulatory changes at the macro level will lead the greater equality. Studies of diversity programmes in practice have noted ill-defined goals. For example in American chain restaurants the programmes rarely do more than improve employees' awareness, and do not seek to work towards organizational change. Case study also illustrates the limited nature of diversity programmes. Alternatively Iverson identifies a model based on the concerns of a diverse group of employees, but acknowledges that strong and committed leadership from the top is needed to make this work effectively.

**Case Study: Managing Diversity in San Francisco Hotels**

The labour mix in an international hotel chain reflects a diverse labour market. The chain demonstrates a reactive diversification approach. Discrimination and bias are discouraged but affirmative action is not taken. High quit and fire rates may have reflected managers' inability to manage diversity. Employees are expected to assimilate to the organization rather than the organization adapt to them. Trade unions have a positive impact on the hotels and in helping them move towards diversity management, but managers need to move forward and value diversity to become more multicultural.

### *Opportunities and Diversity*

From WERS, while most workplaces have written policies on equal opportunities and managing diversity, and these are slightly more widespread in the HI, there is less likelihood that the effects of these policies will be measured. While a majority of medium workplaces and hotels do not have policies, those that do are more likely to measure their effects. The forms of equality of treatment and discrimination that these policies address are similar in AIS, the PSS and the HI. Ethnic minority or racial groups are most likely to be included, with sex/gender and disability following.

Although this suggests that legislation in these areas may have promoted most workplaces to include them, the same does not apply in the case of union membership, which is least likely to be included. Religion, sexual orientation and age, where anti-discrimination legislation does not yet apply, have more widespread application than trade union membership, which is included in only a large minority of workplaces.

Most workplaces in AIS, the PSS and the HI use the staff handbook to inform their employees about these policies. The letter of appointment is rarely used in the HI and, as with grievance and discipline procedures, is significantly different from AIS and the PSS. Where there is no formal written policy, the main reason in all groupings is because it is deemed unnecessary, a reason that is especially marked in restaurants and very small workplaces.

The second and third reasons are that there is a policy, but it is not written down or the firm aims to be an equal opportunities employer. Given that most workplaces do not measure the effects of equal opportunities policies either, there is a clear indication that the management of equality and diversity is not taken very seriously. By contrast the management of sales, costs, profits and labour costs where there is extensive monitoring is afforded very high priority.

**Table: Equal Opportunities Policy in Context, by Size of Workplace and Sub-sector (%)**

| | *AIS* | *PSS* | *HI* | *<25* | *25-49* | *50-99* | *100+* |
|---|---|---|---|---|---|---|---|
| Equal opportunities or diversity policy | 67 | 62 | 70 | 75 | 67 | 48 | 78 |
| Any attempt to measure effects++ | 16 | 9 | 9 | 8 | 6 | 23 | 7 |

| | *Hotels* | *Campsites* | *Restaurants* | *Bars* | *Canteens* |
|---|---|---|---|---|---|
| Equal opportunities or diversity policy | 45 | 100 | 69 | 78 | 86 |
| Any attempt to measure effects++ | 10 | 0 | 3 | 2 | 56 |

***Notes:*** *All weighted cases. ++Where policy exists.*

Slightly more HI workplaces (six of ten) do not apply practical proactive equal opportunities measures. Hence recording, measuring, monitoring and reviewing specific practices or making adjustments for disabled employees are not at all common.

### *Family-friendly Measures*

In the US the Family and Medical Leave Act 1993, applicable only to companies employing 50 or more people, gives employees the right to take 12 weeks' leave per 12-month period without pay for specific family and medical purposes. These include the birth or adoption of a child, a personal medical condition, and caring for ill close relatives.

However the lodging industry lags behind other industries in the provision of parental leave. Here practices are more open to managerial discretion, but have not affected business effectiveness as being too onerous or costly.

Although WERS took place prior to some important legal changes being implemented, UK workplaces are also not very family-friendly.

HI workplaces demonstrate a significantly different approach to employees needing a day off at short notice. Employees are more likely to be required to take unpaid leave than to benefit from paid arrangements, and there is quite a bit of sub-sectoral variation.

Although a minority of AIS, PSS and HI workplaces make no arrangements for males to take time off when a child is born, significantly fewer HI workplaces have a written policy giving entitlement to special leave for male employees.

**Table: Time off at Short Notice in Context and by Size of Workplace (%) hh**

| | *AIS* | *PSS* | *HI* | *<25* | *25-49* | *50-99* | *100+* |
|---|---|---|---|---|---|---|---|
| Make up time later | 19 | 23 | 20 | 18 | 31 | 13 | 31 |
| As leave without pay | 18 | 20 | 48* | 51 | 52 | 42 | 18 |
| As sick leave | 5 | 5 | 5 | 6 | 2 | 4 | 7 |
| As special paid leave | 24 | 18 | 6* | 8 | 0 | 6 | 8 |
| As annual leave | 24 | 24 | 12* | 7 | 7 | 32 | 32 |

***Notes:*** *All weighted cases. hh Five most frequently mentioned responses.* **Significantly different at the 5% level from AIS and the PSS.*

**Table: Time off at Short Notice by Sub-sector (%) hh**

| | *Hotels* | *Campsites* | *Restaurants* | *Bars* | *Canteens* |
|---|---|---|---|---|---|
| Make up time later | 41 | 4 | 23 | 6 | 29 |
| As leave without pay | 22 | 18 | 44 | 74 | 17 |
| As sick leave | 2 | 0 | 13 | 2 | 2 |
| As special paid leave | 9 | 6 | 14 | 0 | 1 |
| As annual leave | 22 | 72 | 3 | 2 | 50 |

***Notes:*** *All weighted cases. hh Five most frequently mentioned responses.*

**Table: Family-friendly Work Practices in Context and by Size of Workplace (%) hh**

| | *AIS* | *PSS* | *HI* | *<25* | *25-49* | *50-99* | *100+* |
|---|---|---|---|---|---|---|---|
| Parental leave | 34 | 27 | 20** | 24 | 11 | 15 | 18 |
| Working at/from home | 13 | 10 | 5** | 6 | 1 | 5 | 5 |
| Term-only contracts | 16 | 10 | 19 | 13 | 38 | 25 | 14 |
| Switch from full-time to part-time | 46 | 43 | 54 | 47 | 62 | 76 | 55 |
| Job sharing | 26 | 19 | 20 | 18 | 30 | 11 | 30 |
| None of these | 38 | 42 | 36 | 41 | 33 | 20 | 33 |

***Notes:*** *All weighted cases. hh Five most frequently mentioned responses to multi-response question.*

***Significantly different at the 5% level from AIS.*

**Table: Family-friendly Work Practices by Sub-sector (%) hh**

| | *Hotels* | *Campsites* | *Restaurants* | *Bars* | *Canteens* |
|---|---|---|---|---|---|
| Parental leave | 9 | 6 | 33 | 21 | 9 |
| Working at/from home | 2 | 0 | 14 | 0 | 7 |
| Term-only contracts | 17 | 0 | 32 | 17 | 2 |
| Switch from full-time to part-time | 43 | 18 | 62 | 53 | 71 |
| Job sharing | 15 | 0 | 21 | 17 | 53 |
| None of these | 54 | 72 | 34 | 28 | 23 |

***Notes:*** *All weighted cases. hh Five most frequently mentioned responses.*

One or more family-friendly practices can be found in the majority of workplaces, but a comprehensive range of measures is still quite a long way from being widespread in AIS, the PSS and the HI. The significant differences noted are likely to be related to the high proportion of employees without dependent children, and because most HI work cannot be carried out at or from home. There is some variation by size of workplace and sub-sector. Workplace nurseries and financial help towards childcare are almost non-existent in AIS, the PSS and the HI.

## *Recent UK Legal Changes*

The Employment Relations Act 1999 simplified and extended maternity rights, and introduced unpaid parental and urgent family need leave, providing a more coherent, potentially fair and effective legal regime:

- All employees are entitled to take reasonable unpaid time off work to attend to the needs of a dependant (i.e. spouse, parent, child or person relying on employee). This is limited to 'emergencies', including illness, death and disruption of care arrangements, and does not extend to personal needs, e.g. dentist.

  The Employment Act 2002 introduces an equal pay questionnaire in employment tribunal cases, and makes some important additional improvements to family-friendly policies. The actual periods of leave for the purpose of childcare are extended from April 2003. The period of leave, which is payable at the rate of Statutory Maternity Pay (£100 per week or 90 per cent of weekly earnings if this is less than £100), has also been increased. The Maternity and Parental Leave Regulations 2002 and the Paternity and Adoption Leave Regulations 2002 contain the following main provisions:

- Women are entitled to take up to 26 weeks' paid ordinary maternity leave (OML) and 26 weeks' unpaid additional maternity leave (AML). There are increased notification periods for a woman's start and early return dates from maternity leave. Maternity leave is not transferable between partners, but this may be changed after the current review of anti-discrimination legislation.
- Men are entitled to 13 weeks' unpaid parental leave and two weeks' paid paternity leave. A father cannot take both paternity leave and adoption leave. Women who are same-sex partners or one of an adopting couple not taking adoption leave are entitled to paternity leave.
- One adoptive parent is entitled to the same periods of paid and unpaid leave that apply to mothers. The person must have 26 weeks' continuous service by the time they are matched with the child for adoptive purposes. The other parent will be entitled to take two weeks' paid leave (equivalent to paternity leave), if so eligible. Both adoptive parents will, in addition, also be entitled to take 13 weeks' unpaid parental leave.

There is no service requirement for OML. In cases of AML and paternity leave the person must be an employee with at least 26 weeks' continuous service by the fifteenth week before the expected week of childbirth. Thus working mothers require only 40 weeks' service to benefit from the enhanced maternity arrangements in full. There is reimbursement of maternity, paternity and adoption payments, with a full 100 per cent recoverable by small employers and a further compensation payment on top.

The Employment Act 2002 also places a duty on employers to give serious consideration to requests from parents of young children to work flexibly, which has been effected by two sets of Flexible Working Regulations 2002. Employees must have 26 weeks' service, not have made such a request in the previous 12 months, and be the parent responsible for child. The child must be under six (or 18 if disabled), and the request must be for the purposes of caring for that child. Flexibility is not just part-time, but could include variation in daily hours or place of work.

The employer must convene a meeting within 28 days, at which the employee must address specific details, including how the employer may deal with any effects arising from the proposed change, and may be accompanied by a fellow employee or worker. There are 14 days to reach agreement. Employers can refuse requests on one of eight grounds, including cost, the inability to reorganize or find suitable alternative staff and, where this would have a detrimental effect on customers, quality and performance. There is a right of appeal within 14 days, with a further 28 days for the procedure to be exhausted, after which the employee may complain to a tribunal. Tribunals can award only a statutory maximum of eight weeks' pay, and it is possible that complainants may also allege indirect sex discrimination.

These provisions, which apply to men and women, are likely to be used widely, particularly by returning mothers. Hospitality firms experiencing recruitment and retention difficulties are recommended to adopt a flexible approach towards all employees, as this also helps employees address work-life balance. New mothers may opt for different modes of flexibility (subject to the 12-month rule), seeking different arrangements, such as term-time working, once the child is of school age.

Hardy and Adnett argue that the Parental Leave Directive, which has driven recent changes, has not led to the creation of an adequate or consistent framework to enable parents to achieve a desirable work-life balance. Low take-up by fathers effectively reinforces gender inequalities in the labour market. Taylor argues that the word balance is inappropriate, as it implies a settled equilibrium.

Rather, the current issue is about a continual need to reconcile the conflicting pressures of home and workplace for everyone in work, not just working parents. There is also little indication that employers are going beyond the minimum legal requirements for family-friendly work and adopting good practice.

### *Health and Safety*

The issue of health and safety as a discrete topic rarely features in employment relations or HRM texts. Rather it emerges as an underlying theme in discussions about absence, working time, representation, consultation and involvement. Its low-key status is all the more surprising, because nationally a larger proportion of working days are lost from relatively long spells of absence compared to industrial disputes. LFS statistics show that 2.2 million days were lost through sickness in the autumn quarter alone compared to 525,000 working days lost through industrial disputes in the whole of 2001.

There are also legal, commercial and ethical reasons why healthy and safe workplaces serve the interests of employers, workers and customers. Such workplaces are considered more likely to make a positive contribution to company economic performance, while helping achieve fair treatment, well-being and job satisfaction among employees. More efforts are being directed at raising awareness of health and safety issues in small firms.

Boyd challenges the assumption that people-centred management automatically leads to first-class health and safety management, using the case of airlines, where standard EU and UK health and safety legislation does not apply.

Sanctimonious HRM mission statements belie cost-minimization and productivity maximizing strategies. These have a derogative effect on health and safety standards by creating a worse working environment, more stressful work and more intensive work patterns.

Taking a constructive approach to employee welfare is also integral to creating an effective work-life balance. Hence good employers are recommended to offer counselling for stress, work issues, domestic issues, health and disability, and drug and alcohol problems, in addition to assistance with childcare.

### *Case Study: Work Intensification for Airline Cabin Crew*

The use of computer programming was used to manipulate shift patterns within legal limits. This resulted in extended working hours and combined day and night working in the same week. Short period turnarounds gave very little time for meal and rest breaks. Crew numbers were reduced to the absolute legal minimum.

Untrained junior staff were required to stand in for more senior staff. Occupational health was afforded low priority, with only major illness and injury recorded. Crew members frequently complained about faulty equipment and poor air quality.

### *Injury and Illness*

An estimated two million people believe they suffer ill health caused by work, resulting in 18 million days lost and costing society £10 billion per annum. Disabled workers tend to be those suffering long-term health problems. Echoing government and TUC calls for more measures on rehabilitation at work, they advocate better job retention and return-to-work measures based on a 'case management' approach.

WERS enables us to make a closer examination of injuries and work-related illness in the HI. Although the mean number of employees injured per workplace is small, HI employees are more likely to sustain injuries than their counterparts in

AIS and the PSS, especially in very small workplaces, and in restaurants where food preparation is a major activity. In terms of areas of significant difference, burns account for most of the HI workplace injuries (56 per cent), while fewer HI workplaces (37 per cent) reported no injuries in the last 12 months.

Although the incidence is relatively small, there is an above-average level of injury from physical assault at work in bars. There were 100+ injuries per 1,000 employees in half of HI workplaces compared to one-quarter in AIS and under one-third in the PSS.

Work-related illness is less widespread in the HI, but is well above average in very small workplaces and restaurants. A skin problem is the condition most likely to have been exacerbated by work in the previous 12 months in the HI (13 per cent of workplaces). Stress is the most frequently mentioned recent work-related condition in one-quarter of AIS workplaces but stress, like limb disorders, is significantly rarer in the HI. In the last 12 months, there was a rate

**Table: Employees Injured at Work in Last 12 Months in Context and by Size of Workplace and Sub-sector of Work-related Illness of 100+ per 1,000 Employees in One-fifth of AIS, PSS and HI Workplaces.**

| | *AIS* | *PSS* | *HI* | *<25* | *25-49* | *50-99* | *100+* |
|---|---|---|---|---|---|---|---|
| Mean number of injuries per 1,000 employees | 98 | 127 | 198** | 284 | 117 | 96 | 47 |
| Mean number injured | 4 | 4 | 5 | 5 | 4 | 6 | 7 |

| | *Hotels* | *Campsites* | *Restaurants* | *Bars* | *Canteens* |
|---|---|---|---|---|---|
| Mean number of injuries per 1,000 employees | 64 | 42 | 409 | 112 | 335 |
| Mean number injured | 4 | 6 | 11 | 2 | 7 |

***Notes:*** *All weighted cases. **Significantly different at the 5% level from AIS.*

**Table: Work-related Illness and Absence in Last 12 Months in Context and by Size of Workplace and Sub-sector**

| | *AIS* | *PSS* | *HI* | *<25* | *25-49* | *50-99* | *100+* |
|---|---|---|---|---|---|---|---|
| Work-related illness per 1,000 employees | 73 | 66 | 57 | 97 | 28 | 26 | 13 |
| Mean number absent | 3 | 2 | 1** | 1 | 1 | 2 | 2 |

| | *Hotels* | *Campsites* | *Restaurants* | *Bars* | *Canteens* |
|---|---|---|---|---|---|
| Work-related illness per 1,000 employees | 22 | 71 | 96 | 78 | 27 |
| Mean number absent | 1 | 20 | 2 | 1 | 1 |

***Notes:*** *All weighted cases of numbers absent where absence occurred. Figures have been rounded to nearest whole number.*

***Significantly different at the 5% level from AIS.*

### *Stress*

Stress can play a positive role in creating alertness at work, but becomes counter-productive once excessive levels of unresolved physical and psychological discomfort begin to affect the health, safety and well-being of the workforce. Stress has a negative effect on workers' motivation, commitment and performance, as well as being a major contributor to sickness and absence. Smith estimates that five million workers - 20 per cent of the British workforce - may experience very high stress levels, and that 91.5 million days are lost every year from stress-related illness. There is little evidence of progressive health and safety policies, with organizations providing only a limited counselling service.

Within the HI Law et al. attribute the principal causes of stress to management (poor work organization) and managerial behaviour (lack of communications/involvement). Stress also arises from long hours and work intensification, financial insecurity, the lack of opportunity for advancement, pressure to perform well and outside work factors.

Although undue stress is not occupation-specific, it is more likely to affect customer-service workers, because they are subject to competing, contradictory and conflicting demands from managers and customers. Poor service poses a serious threat to performance, especially where it leads to lost customers. There are circumstances when service workers may also find customer relationships rewarding.

As we noted earlier, workers can develop coping mechanisms where stress is within their personal capacity to manage. Otherwise prolonged job stress can lead to burn-out or breakdown, which is more likely to affect women than men.

### *Recruitment and selection*

- Why does the HI perpetuate an approach towards recruitment and selection that undermines the 'high road' that many managers claim they seek?
- Can this be excused?
- What implications does this have for workforce diversity and SQ?

### *Training*

- Discuss the allegation that the 'any hands will do' approach has any foundation by way of a summary of the HI's approach to training.
- Can you suggest and justify circumstances where organizations might afford differential treatment to particular occupational groups?
- Assess the importance of VETs and suggest how they can be made more effective.

## Chapter 5

# Participation and Involvement

## COLLECTIVE BARGAINING

In the complex area of people management paradigms, the terms Empowerment, Participation and Involvement are frequently used within the literature but often interpreted quite differently depending on the perspective of the reader and / or writer. This offer an insight into these terms and to posit them respectively within the context of unitary and pluralist people management perspectives. Firstly it is necessary to distinguish between Participation and Involvement, and then to examine where Empowerment fits within these perspectives.

Hotel Chains represent the intelligence behind the Global Councils whose representatives are specialists in the fields of Human Resources, E-Distribution, Safety and Security, Legal, Marketing, etc. Critical issues are dealt with both from a "bottom up" as well as "top down" basis. Restaurant Chains represent the intelligence behind the Global Councils whose representatives are specialists in the fields of Human Resources, Food Safety, Nutrition, Hygiene and other Foodservice issues. Employee involvement is 'a range of processes designed to engage the support, understanding and optimum contribution of all employees in an organisation and their commitment to its objectives'.

Employee participation is defined as 'a process of employee involvement designed to provide employees with the opportunity to influence and where appropriate, take part in decision making on matters which affect them'. It is clear then that there are differences between employee participation and employee involvement. The literature suggests that employee participation is a pluralist/collective approach with a continuum from 'no involvement' to 'employee control'.Employee involvement, in contrast, is more individualistic and unitarist. It aims to harness commitment to organisational objectives and relies on the maintenance of management control. Collective bargaining is a rule-making process for contract-making and contractchanging.

Having identified employee involvement, where empowerment sits within these approaches is perhaps more complex and hinges on interpretations of 'power' and how 'empowered' workers actually are where such schemes are implemented. Terms and conditions of employment are determined and regulated through the formal process of negotiation between representatives of management and employees. The outcome is a binding agreement for those employees within the bargaining unit, e.g. at national, enterprise or workplace level.

It is based on management's legitimization of employee involvement and influence over aspects of decision-making, and involves a power relationship in which employee representatives may regulate managerial authority. Acknowledgement of the right to strike is embodied within this process. Variations in the scope and coverage of collective bargaining are a reflection of different regulatory regimes across the world.

## International Arrangements

The coverage of workers' and employers' organizations in the HCTS and the scope of collective bargaining vary by country and region. Trade unions may cover a number of sectors, which may include the HCTS, or cover particular occupational groups that are found in other sectors, e.g. workers in services in France. Employers' organizations are more cohesive, and largely cover hotels and restaurants.

The International Hotel and Restaurant Association is the largest employers' organization representing over 750,000 establishments in 150 countries. The largest workers' organization, the IUF, has 326 affiliated organizations representing 10 million workers in 118 countries, including the ECF.

There is only one known case of international trade union recognition between the IUF and the French Accor Group. International awareness has been facilitated through the use of websites for publicity. A dispute in a Seoul hotel came to an end in 2000 after trade unions elsewhere made representations to the Korean diplomatic mission.

There are two federations of employers' organizations in Europe: The Confederation of National Associations of Hotels, Restaurants, Cafes and Similar Establishments in the European Union and European Economic Area (HOTREC) and the European Federation of Contract Catering Organizations (FERCO). For workers there is a special European Trade Union Liaison Committee on Tourism (ETLC). Social dialogue, launched by the ECF-IUF and HOTREC, takes place four times a year under the auspices of the European Commission (EC). Various joint declarations have been adopted including the 1999 Joint Declaration for the promotion of employment in hotels and restaurants, designed to reduce taxes and non-wage costs, and to improve training and certification.

The development of collective and social partnership is hampered by the reluctance among employers to promote partnership with trade unions. The challenges of global competition have caused employers to restructure and adopt new methods. Traditional occupational boundaries are breaking down, as jobs become more flexible. Hence issues on the collective bargaining agenda include the prevention of wage deterioration resulting from unclear definitions in new work patterns, and maintaining continuity of working and employment conditions where there is a change in ownership. The latter is more difficult where the instigating party is an MNC based outside the host country.

### *Variations in Global Practice*

The structure and scope of collective bargaining varies according to legal and national practice. Twelve African countries have collective agreements in existence since the 1970s, and almost all explicitly mention union rights. While enterprise bargaining is more normative in North America, Asia and Africa, in Europe sectoral or sub-sectoral bargaining at national or regional level is more common. In France sub-sectoral bargaining is a function of the way employers are organized, and was for some time restricted to hotel and restaurant chains.

More recently most independent firms adopted this procedure, even though workers are not unionized. Complete coverage is secured by extending the collective agreement to workers in all workplaces by government decree. In Australia trade unions have an almost exclusive right to represent HI employees and to make particular awards.

Trade union membership is not particularly high. There is no law on trade union recognition ballots as in North America and the UK, and trade unions are not especially active. Although the Shop Distributive and Allied Employees' Union (SDA) has almost exclusive rights in fast food in all states, employers are reluctant to engage in enterprise bargaining. They will negotiate with unions where a state industrial award is perceived as too costly. Agreements would incorporate conditions from other agreements that may offset the higher conditions under the award.

Hungry Jack's (a Burger King franchise) and the SDA have reached a multi-state standard agreement, which the unions regard as easier to enforce and maintain. Some successful enterprise agreements have addressed 'low road' practices, building in value-added features such as job rotation, training and performance management, and multiskilling. New Zealand used to have an employment relations system similar to the Australian system. Case study given below shows how in a more deregulated environment collectivism may be enduring on the surface, but is highly symbolic.

## Case Study: Deregulation of Employment Relations in Large Hotels in New Zealand

The Employment Contracts Act 1991 replaced mandated collective bargaining and extensive trade union protection with a new regime allowing employers to engage in individualistic employment relations or innovative cooperative relations with unionized workforces. Union density within the Service Workers Union (SWU) was traditionally low in the hotel industry. The New Zealand (With Exceptions) Major Accommodation Hotel Industry Award expired in 1992.

- Collective contracts persisted but most employers abandoned traditional bargaining and moved to almost exclusively management determined 'consultation'.
- Managers espoused a more limited role for unions, including officials, although all hotels still credited union subscriptions.
- Non-union collective voice mechanisms were developed. Trade union representatives were subject to the same election procedure as their peers.
- All innovations initiated and developed by management were not consistent with high commitment strategies.

Labour-management bargaining priorities in the US have changed post-11 September, with new considerations including job security for airline employees, and employers seeking to add provisions for 'acts of war'. There is also increased video surveillance, bio-terrorism policies, employee background checks and onsite searches of employees' belongings. Current law makes virtually all changes in workplace privacy and security rules the topic of mandatory collective bargaining.

HI employees and, notably, employers, through bodies such as the BHA and BII, have traditionally not associated for collective bargaining purposes. The main trade unions representing HI workers are the TGWU, GMB, USDAW and

NALHM. Historically membership levels have been very low, regardless of the regulatory framework in force. The LFS (2001) indicates that only 9 per cent of HI employees are covered by collective agreements, which drops to 6 per cent if public sector workplaces are excluded. Trade union recognition for collective bargaining is rare, and restricted mainly to the large groups, e.g. USDAW and Compass services, the GMB and Road Chef and Jarvis Hotels.

The legal framework governing the rights, actions, duties, responsibilities and behaviours of employers and trade unions in Britain was seriously weakened in the 1980s and 1990s. The proportion of employees who were members of trade unions declined from 53 per cent in 1979 to 28 per cent in 1999. Consequently similar 'hollow shell' collective agreements to those found in New Zealand have developed in Britain. The Employment Relations Act 1999 contained measures to facilitate trade union organization, including the statutory recognition procedures, although there has been no weakening of the constraints on industrial action.

### *Social Partnership*

Social partnership is a form of collective bargaining that places more emphasis on mutual cooperation and joint problem-solving, often extending into areas such as training, skills, flexibility, career development and quality of working life, which have not been the domain of traditional collective bargaining. It is best viewed on two levels - a relationship between the summit employer and trade union bodies, and at the workplace.

Many, including the trade unions, would regard social partnership as a complementary process to collective bargaining and vehicle for union renewal, while others see it as marginalizing trade unionism as an autonomous force, undermining workplace unionism and weakening the trade union movement.

Partnership is expected to emerge from a common response to the challenges of global competition. In the

Caribbean where tourism is by far the most important economic sector, active steps to improve social partnership can be observed. One major concern of trade unions is the practices of sub-contracting and franchising, which are believed to create divisions among those working in the same workplaces. At international level there is a social dialogue relationship between the partners in the HCTS, but it is at an early stage of development.

The development of trade unions as facilitators of cooperative collective relationships, often through consultative arrangements, is a key dimension of EU social policy. In 1999 agreement between the Union of Industrial and Employers' Confederations of Europe (UNICE) and the ETUC provides a forum for social dialogue leading to agreements. These provide the framework for national governments to introduce appropriate legislation, e.g. non-discrimination for workers on fixed-term contracts in respect of hours of work and holidays. Other consultative arrangements relating to redundancies, proposed business transfers, health and safety, European Works Councils (EWCs), and the forthcoming information and consultation directive, which may involve union and non-union representatives.

Reflecting the new Labour government's espousal of partnership, a Partnership at Work fund has been created to encourage employers, employees and their representatives to build trust, share information and work together to solve business problems. Since 1997 the TUC has deliberately attempted to rebuild relationships with employers by promoting a new role for trade unions based on partnership strategy, additional to collective bargaining.

**Case Study: Partnership with the GMB at Gardner Merchant**

This contract catering company, part of the French conglomerate Sodexho, recognizes the GMB in the UK. Previously each site negotiated their own interpretations of the standard ACAS recognition agreement, with emphasis on negative dispute resolution procedures. A new HR Director in 1994 spurred a reappraisal of Gardner Merchant's way of working in light of the positive collaborative experience gained from Sodexho's EWC. There was a shared desire to formulate a UK national agreement along the same lines.

The new agreement signed in 1998 recognized the legitimacy of each parties' role, a joint commitment to open discussion and improving trust, providing training opportunities and enhancing the company's reputation. It also contained a detailed disputes avoidance procedure, with strike action permissible only after all other avenues are exhausted. Joint policy statements have been issued on best practice in TUPE and the EU's Acquired Rights Directive.

Improved communication and consultation provides both sides with an early warning call about problems and potential areas of conflict. Training in consultation and planning for change was provided for local managers. There are twice-yearly Board level meetings and in early 2000 the company was seeking a national works council.

Nationally the trade unions believe they can play an essential role in helping to determine policy on training, jobs, investment and Europe, while at the level of the enterprise and workplace partnership agreements will help improve organizational performance and quality of working life. The joint problem-solving social partnership approach underpins the work of ACAS and the LPC, both bodies comprising equal numbers of CBI and TUC nominees plus independent members. The Information and Participation Association (IPA) shares similar ideals to the TUC on social partnership.

### Case Study: Partnership in San Francisco's Hotels

San Francisco's major hotels and the Hotel Employees and Restaurant Employees International Union embarked on a new partnership oriented approach in 1994. The 'living contract' provided a mechanism for making work-rule changes by mutual agreement during the term of the contract. Joint study teams examined issues underlying problems that would otherwise have led to a dispute. Joint solutions avoided expensive, often pointless arbitration. Rules were redesigned to make the hotels' restaurants competitive with non-union hotels. The living agreement was renewed in 1999.

### *International Comparisons*

HCT workers across the world are less likely to be organized in trade unions than workers in other sectors, and trade union density may be as little as 10 per cent or less in industrialized countries.

Even where trade unions have been afforded exclusive rights, such as in Australia and New Zealand, actual membership levels have tended to be low. Figures are difficult to come by, but selected examples of density levels in the HI are given. In many cases they indicate density levels below a level at which the 'virtuous circle between union growth and union recognition could begin'.

In her survey of the HI in New Zealand, Ryan found that two-thirds of workplaces had no union members, 18 per cent had up to 50 per cent and 4 per cent had more than half. Only 10 per cent had seen any attempt at union recognition.

National figures disguise differences within sub-sectors. In large hotels, where membership is generally highest, levels of 80 per cent have been achieved in the Canadian cities of Vancouver, Toronto and Montreal. Conversely in Auckland, New Zealand membership can vary from 5 to 20 to 32 per cent. Although density levels were never very high, they dropped in the 1990s following the deregulation of employment relations, remaining higher where trade unions maintained an active role.

In McDonald's in Germany trade union membership in the NGG becomes well established and rises rapidly to around 50 per cent or more after a works council has been created. Conversely the fast food industry in Canada and the US is almost entirely non-union.

**Table: Trade Union Membership in the HI by Country**

| *Country* | *Year* | *Level (%)* |
|---|---|---|
| US | 1993 | <2 |
| Canada | 1998 | 9 |
| Australia | 1997 | 18/13.1 |
| Finland | 1995 | 65 |
| Austria | 1995 | 40 |
| Italy | 1995 | 25 |
| Ireland | 1995 | 20 |
| Netherlands | 1997 | 10 |
| UK | 1995 | 8 |
| France | 1995 | 5 |

**Notes:** *Where two figures are shown, they relate to full-time and part-time workers respectively. The most recent HI figure from the LFS shows 5% union density.*

Even where union density is relatively high, as in Singapore hotels, conservative and accommodative trade unions and the institutionalization of employer- employee relations mean there is little activity or conflict. As the service provided by hospitality businesses cannot be stockpiled like goods produced in a factory, industrial action is potentially more damaging and effective.

As noted, union membership in the HI in the UK is among the lowest in Europe, and may be in decline. Arguably NALHM has been the most successful union within the HI but as Case study indicates, membership has dropped by two-thirds. Trade unions have had a chequered history in attempting to secure recognition in larger hotels. There have been isolated cases of strike action in support of recognition, including the Savoy, London and Torquay. USDAW's approach to McDonald's in the UK for 'talks about talks' was flatly rejected by the company, nor has there been any attempt by the three HI unions to make a coordinated approach to the company.

However the GMB has been actively recruiting in McDonald's and Little Chef. Recognition is pretty rare, and most likely to be found in large companies, GMB and Roadchef and GMB and Jarvis Hotels. Since the Employment Relations Act 1999 there have been no known recognition claims in the HI, although a number of recognition claims have been made in airlines and casinos.

## Case Study: Neutrality Agreements and Organizing Tactics in New US Hotels

In the 1990s most hotels were organized on the basis of HERE approaching hotel companies several months before a new hotel was due to open seeking a neutrality agreement. Under this agreement employers give up their right to contest union organization and the right of employees to vote in a secret ballot election supervised by the National Labour Relations Board to determine whether they wish to be represented by HERE.

By signing the employer virtually guarantees the union will be recognized as the exclusive bargaining agent. Such agreements include a card-check provision which represents a much cheaper and more effective organizing technique than the secret ballot method, which normally goes against the unions. Labour-peace and living wage ordinances coupled with the threat of sanctions from the building-trades unions to disrupt the hotel's construction, have made it easier to union organizers to obtain employers' consent to remain neutral.

## Case Study: The Decline of the National Association of Licensed House Managers

In 1997 NALHM ended 30 years of independence by joining the TGWU as an autonomous section. Membership, restricted to pubs managed by salaried managers of a brewery, as opposed to managers of free houses or tenants, peaked at 18,000 in 1982, but had declined to 6,000 by 1997.

The union's demise is attributed to a combination of local conditions specific to the sector, including the major restructuring following the Mergers and Monopolies Commission Report in 1989. The subsequent Beer Orders changed the role for many pubs and the nature of their managers who became more professional and entrepreneurial.

There have been other recent examples of strike action, for reasons other than recognition. In Norway the first strike for 11 years in 1996 forced the closure of ten leading hotels, at a daily cost of £2.4 million for three of them. A strike by bar workers in Dublin in 1994 closed 70 per cent of pubs during the World Cup.

BA sustained a number of strikes among cabin crew over the 1990s. In 1997 nearly 2000 BA staff went on sick leave rather than participating in the official strike, as they feared disciplinary action. Taking turns to go sick caused considerable disruption to flights. Recent strike action in the British HI is virtually non-existent.

*Recent Experience*

From WERS the state of trade membership can be ascertained in two main ways, by measuring union density and by measuring the percentage of workplaces where there are or have been trade union members in the recent past. The HI continues to sustain significantly lower trade union density in comparison with AIS and the PSS.

Although the picture is slightly more encouraging in larger workplaces, trade union incursion into the heart of the HI is, at best, highly marginal. Recent LFS figures indicate that 5 per cent of HI employees are union members (8 per cent full-time and 3 per cent part-time), and the figure drops to 4 per cent if public sector workplaces are excluded.

In three-quarters of the small caucus of HI workplaces with union members, membership is most likely to be among managers/administrative staff. Union membership is extremely rare among other occupational groups, especially white-collar groups who are most likely to be union members in AIS and the PSS.

**Table: Trade Union Density in Context and by Size of Workplace (%)**

| | *AIS* | *PSS* | *HI* | <25 | *25-49* | *50-99* | *100+* |
|---|---|---|---|---|---|---|---|
| Aggregate density | 34 | 15 | 2* | 2 | 0 | 0 | 5 |
| Actual density No members | 54 | 73 | 92* | 92 | 94 | 94 | 73 |
| 1-59% | 26 | 19 | 8* | 7 | 6 | 6 | 27 |
| 60-100% | 20 | 7 | 1* | 1 | 0 | 0 | 0 |

***Notes:*** *All weighted cases. Column percentages do not sum accurately due to rounding. *Significantly different at the 5% level from AIS and the PSS.*

**Table: Trade Union Density by Sub-sector (%)**

| | *Hotels* | *Campsites* | *Restaurants* | *Bars* | *Canteens* |
|---|---|---|---|---|---|
| Aggregate density | 0 | 9 | 1 | 1 | 15 |
| Actual density No members | 94 | 18 | 100 | 90 | 82 |
| 1-59% | 6 | 82 | 0 | 10 | 9 |
| 60-100% | 0 | 0 | 0 | 0 | 10 |

***Notes:*** *All weighted cases. Column percentages do not sum accurately due to rounding.*

First, there is no de-recognition or absolute decline in union membership in the HI because none of the workplaces without unions had any members five years ago. Second, unions have been slightly more active in attempting to recruit members in the HI, but have touched only a minority of workplaces and their attempts do not appear to have proved successful.

**Table: Trade Union Membership in Context and by Size of Workplace (%)**

| | *AIS* | *PSS* | *HI* | <25 | *25-49* | *50-99* | *100+* |
|---|---|---|---|---|---|---|---|
| Any union members now | 47 | 27 | 8* | 8 | 6 | 6 | 27 |
| Any union members 5 years ago s | 5 | 4 | 0* | 0 | 0 | 0 | 0 |

| | | | | | | | |
|---|---|---|---|---|---|---|---|
| Any recruitment attempts in last 5 years r | 5 | 5 | 12 | 13 | 20 | 2 | 5 |
| Any recognition requests in last 5 years t | 7 | 7 | 0* | 0 | 0 | 0 | 0 |
| Management's attitude towards unions w | | | | | | | |
| In favour | 27 | 13 | 6* | 6 | 7 | 3 | 4 |
| Not in favour | 17 | 22 | 22 | 18 | 28 | 25 | 28 |
| Neutral | 54 | 63 | 72** | 76 | 65 | 67 | 69 |

***Notes:*** *Yes responses to all weighted cases unless otherwise stated. *Significantly different at the 5% level from AIS and the PSS. **Significantly different at the 5% level from AIS. s Where no union members and establishment is five years or older. r Where no union members. t Where union members now or five years ago. w Excludes not an issue and non-codeable responses.*

**Table: Trade Union Membership by Sub-sector (%)**

| | *Hotels* | *Campsites* | *Restaurants* | *Bars* | *Canteens* |
|---|---|---|---|---|---|
| Any union members now | 6 | 82 | 0 | 10 | 18 |
| Any union members 5 years ago s | 0 | 0 | 0 | 0 | 0 |
| Any recruitment attempts in last 5 years r | 2 | 0 | 14 | 19 | 0 |
| Any recognition requests in last 5 years t | 0 | 0 | 0 | 0 | 0 |
| Management's attitude towards unions w | | | | | |
| In favour | 2 | 0 | 0 | 11 | 10 |
| Not in favour | 23 | 0 | 20 | 26 | 7 |
| Neutral | 76 | 100 | 78 | 64 | 83 |

***Notes:*** *Yes responses to all weighted cases unless otherwise stated. s Where no union members and establishment is five years or older. r Where no union members. t Where union members now or five years ago. w Excludes not an issue and non-codeable responses.*

**Table: Non-union Representatives' Role in Employment Relations (%)**

| | *AIS* | *PSS* | *HI* | | | | | | | | | |
|---|---|---|---|---|---|---|---|---|---|---|---|---|
| | *Nego-tiates* | *Consults* | *Informs* | *None* | *Nego-tiates* | *Consults* | *Informs* | *None* | *Nego-tiates* | *Consults* | *Informs* | *None* |
| Pay and conditions | - | - | - | 28 | - | - | 35 | - | - | 66 | - | - |
| Recruitment and selection | - | - | - | 39 | - | 34 | - | - | 56* | - | - | - |
| Training | - | 45 | - | - | - | 49 | - | - | - | - | 66** | - |
| Payment systems | - | - | - | 39 | - | - | 48 | - | - | - | 60 | - |
| Grievances | - | 43 | - | - | - | 42 | - | - | 60* | - | - | - |
| Staffing/ manpower planning | - | 37 | - | - | - | 43 | - | - | - | 75 | - | - |
| Equal opportunities | - | 41 | - | - | - | 38 | - | - | - | - | - | 65 |
| Health and safety | - | 58 | - | - | - | 62 | - | - | - | - | 66* | - |
| Performance appraisals | - | 45 | - | - | - | 50 | - | - | 60* | - | - | - |

**Notes:** Workplaces where there are non-union representatives or representatives of non-recognized unions (AIS N=213, PSS N=121 and the HI N=10). The table shows the most frequently used method for each employment issue. *Significantly different at the 5% level from AIS and PSS. **Significantly different at the 5% level from AIS.

Third, there have been no recognition requests in the last five years. Finally HI managers are significantly less likely to be in favour of trade unions. One should also caution against assuming too much from the neutral responses because Cully et al. suggested that managers who declare themselves neutral might actually hold negative views about trade unions. We can usefully consider the neutrality responses with an earlier observation that managers have an even higher level of preference for consulting directly with employees than with a union. While a majority of AIS and PSS managers do hold negative views about unions, there is a clear indication that HI managers hold even more negative views about unions than their counterparts in AIS and the PSS.

This final observation suggests that non-union representation is unlikely to be much of a force anywhere. This is borne out by the fact that fewer than 10 per cent of workplaces have present non-union representatives or representatives of non-recognized unions, affecting one in 11 workplaces in AIS, one in 12 in PSS and one in 16 the HI. These representatives are more likely to be found in unionized workplaces, and are rarely found in non-union workplaces, suggesting that they are complementary to union representation rather than substitutes for it. Thus most HI workplaces (93 per cent) have no worker representatives of any kind compared to 70 per cent in AIS and 85 per cent in the PSS.

In the HI non-union representatives are most likely to be volunteers, whereas in AIS and the PSS the most common selection method is election by employees. In most cases these representatives sit on a consultative committee covering a wide range of issues. Non-union representatives can also deal with or play a part in employment issues such as pay, recruitment, training, pay systems, grievances, staff planning, equal opportunities, health and safety, and performance appraisal. Their involvement varies from full (negotiation), partial (consultation), token (informed) or none. Although care should be taken in drawing too much from such a small number of cases, there are still some striking differences between AIS, the PSS and the HI.

### *The Consequences of Working without Unions*

'Non-union representation can provide at best only a partial mechanism for employee involvement and participation in the absence of legal underpinnings', because they have no collective sanctions or any of the protections afforded to union representatives. Such representation has no real power base, as it is merely cooperative, and ultimately, at managerial discretion, often abandoned in times of crisis and change when managers should be at their most open if they are to convince employees of their commitment to participation and of its effectiveness.

Workers in non-union workplaces appear to be penalized in a number of other ways. Collective bargaining appears to facilitate access to and improvement on statutory rights. Unionized workplaces have more alternative voice mechanisms than non-union workplaces, where workers also lose out on family leave and gender equality. Even though trade unions have gained the right to accompany a worker in a grievance or disciplinary hearing, including where the union is not recognized, accompaniment does not imply the right to represent. Most HI employees do not actually know any trade union officials. The absence of union voice mechanisms reinforces managerial prerogative and may weaken employees' chances of resolving a dispute or grievance. In McDonald's in Australia employees raise such concerns through the Personal Action Letter (PAL), which is brought to the attention of management or head office. Few workers are aware of PAL or use it.

The individualized nature of contractual, remuneration and bargaining arrangements provides more limited provision of procedural justice and equity. Workers seek advice and representation outside the traditional labour movement and from voluntary organizations such as the Citizens' Advice Bureau (CAB). The CAB has experienced a steep rise in the number of employment problems brought to them, and is becoming increasingly active in resolving such problems, in the absence of workplace mechanisms. This may change following the introduction of new statutory minimum grievance and disciplinary procedures. On issues such as redundancy, dismissal and the unilateral variation of the terms and conditions of employment, workers also seek the help of ACAS.

### *Forms of Workplace Conflict*

The absence of unions does not indicate an absence of conflict. Rather alternative forms of worker behaviour, other than strike action, are normally deployed. By worker behaviour we mean the ways and means used by workers to cope with or resist managerial control in the everyday conduct of their work, which arise from their lack of power as individuals. These can be individual and collective, including mass and individual absenteeism.

More days are lost from absence than from strikes. 'As with absenteeism, pilfering is arguably more costly than strikes'. Rather than raise a formal grievance about low pay that is likely to be ignored, workers enhance their pay by shortchanging customers. Employee theft may be responsible for one in three business failures, and is especially prevalent in food service, with employees' own estimates three times higher than their managers'. Ultimately workers may leave the organization voluntarily or involuntarily, and may seek resolution of the dispute outside the workplace, notably at employment tribunal.

Lucas identifies how students use their tacit skills to resist managers and customers. In customer-service work flight attendants' response to work intensification is to slow down and smile less broadly. Fuller and Smith (1991) report how the use of mystery shoppers so incensed hotel workers that they also conducted a 'smile strike'.

Law notes an interesting instance of customer protest in one of the most luxurious hotels in Hong Kong, which illustrates the effectiveness of mass action in response to the perceived inequitable treatment of a customer breast-feeding in a public area, who was asked to go somewhere more private. Eighteen women 'protested' by breast-feeding in the same area, and the hotel staff did nothing.

Three sets of circumstances are relevant to low levels of unionization:

- Do the structural characteristics of workplaces and workforces provide an environment in which it is possible to conceive effective levels of unionization?
- Do workers have an interest or motivation to join trade unions?
- What role do employers and trade unions play?

### *Structural Factors*

The substantial presence of small workplaces and their wide geographical dispersion pose considerable challenges to trade union recruitment and organizing strategies. The ideology of a 'family culture' is a significant barrier to organizing in SMEs.

## Case Study: Resisting Managers and Customers in Hospitality Work

### *Getting by*

One student worked four eight-hour shifts per week for a 'pittance' of £3.00 an hour managing the leisure centre of a city centre hotel. She used the extensive amount of working time spent on her own to complete all her college work. Others read books or collected data for their assignments or dissertation. None claimed they were actually skiving.

Another student stated they all stuck together with difficult customers. Where the customer gave them a £20 or £50 note, they would shout out the amount to the other person in the bar to have a witness should the customer claim the note was for a different value.

## *Getting Back*

A change in managers led to a change in management style from no procedures to enforcing the rules. Staff responded by giving customers free drinks and helping themselves.

A student serving drinks on large trays at a large arena had to step over customers and reported getting 'touched up' by men. If she reported this she knew the customer would claim it was accidental. If she had to return, she would keep the tray between her and the customer so they could not do it again. If customers were particularly horrible she would make a point of treading on their feet, of course smiling and apologizing.

Workplaces under the control of one parent company may be fragmented by sub-contracting and franchising arrangements. In the US and Canada hotel restaurants are frequently leased, becoming part of the non-union restaurant subsector. In Las Vegas where virtually all food beverage operations are leased HERE represents 900 workers, whereas the figure would be 2,700 if they were not leased. Although trade unions are opposed to sub-contracting a priority is to negotiate protection against a deterioration of terms and conditions of employment in these circumstances. Franchised units have the legal status of an independent employer, which places them outside scope of company-wide representative bodies based on a minimum headcount. Thus agreements may only apply to a minority of a company's workplaces in a particular country, as Royle demonstrates in the case of McDonald's.

Additionally work is structured and organized around highly flexible patterns to match stochastic demand, so gaining access to a critical mass of employees is very difficult for trade union organizers to achieve. The fast food production system offers protection against trade unions through a casual and youthful labour force, which is difficult to organize, and which reduces the likelihood of union pressure for higher wages and potential interruptions through strikes.

### *Employees*

Many, if not most, employees work in different departments or at different times on different contracts, which keeps communications and group identity low among workers, especially in larger workplaces. This, heightened by departmental rivalry and fuelled by high labour turnover, militates against the establishment any collective ethos. High turnover causes membership attrition, although this could be attenuated if check-off was available within large organizations with fluid internal mobility, e.g. breweries. Individualized contracts lead to a sense of individual identity and also sharpen competition among individuals. Individual employees doing different jobs, each with its own set of benefits, prefer to negotiate for themselves, believing strongly that they can influence their own working environment. The notion of service may instil a sense of submission, and there is little collective kudos to be gained from excellent service.

A young workforce, and to a lesser extent part-time working, is strongly correlated to lower levels of density, especially in the UK. The GMB's strategy to recruit students on a 10p a week subscription achieved only a small level of membership. Part-time workers are one of the least committed work groups and therefore less likely to be interested in trade unions, although some display strong support for the ideals and protection afforded by unions. Workers with less than two years' service, temporary and zero hours workers, and sales and customer service staff sustain substantially lower trade union density.

The issue of gender is more ambiguous, as density levels of men and women in Britain have converged towards similar levels of around 30 per cent since the early 1990s. Women with higher education qualifications have the highest density levels, and are more than twice more likely to be union members than women with no qualifications or qualifications at A-level or below. This is consistent with Lowery and Beadles' (1996) observation that industrial and craft workers are less likely to choose union representation than professional workers.

Weaker affiliation to union membership among females may be attributed to their disproportionate representation in part-time and casual work, and to their irregular hours. Women often feel neglected by trade unions or are dissatisfied with their experience of them. This creates a negative perception of trade unions, as in the case of an Asian woman who found her white, male trade union official 'dismissive' and sought advice instead from the CAB.

### *Employers and Unions*

The role of employers is also crucial. In the US employers cannot be compelled to grant union organizers access to their employees where other reasonable means are available, e.g. shopping malls and entrances to hotels.

### Case Study: Anti-union Tactics in the German Fast Food Industry

Anglo-Saxon-based MNCs, including McDonald's, Pizza Hut and Burger King, are more likely to adopt anti-union policies. Employment relations in most German-owned firms appear to be less antagonistic. Maredo and Churrasco enjoyed good relations with the NGG while under German ownership, but these have become more difficult since the takeover by the UK Whitbread group. A subsidiary of the UK Compass Group 'Eurest' works cooperatively with unions.

McDonald's has sought to root out or inhibit union membership by sending 'flying squads' of senior managers to trouble spots, making 'troublemakers'' job duties more unpleasant, actual or threatened dismissal, or paying people to leave.

Where employers are unwilling to recognize trade unions, workers have less reason to join and may even fear repercussions. Positive views of trade unions are unlikely to convert into action as employees are thwarted by a sense of fatalism about the likely success of a union dealing with a hostile employer. Or it may well be the case that workers, instilled with a sense self-reliance and in the knowledge that work is temporary or readily available elsewhere, are simply not dissatisfied enough to seek trade union protection and representation.

Given the difficulties HERE has had in organizing HI workers, Lcwery and Beadles (1996) suggest that unions' past patterns of organizing need to be altered, as they may be targeting the 'wrong' workers. In spite of the TUC's positive attempts to encourage the trade union movement to target women, ethnic minorities and part-time workers sex and race inequality remains institutionalized within trade unions. If unions in Britain are to stem union decline, they must overcome their traditional antipathy towards non-standard workers based on the fear that recruiting them would undercut full-time jobs. Such workers, including low-wage service workers, need to be the target of union recruitment and retention efforts. Fundamentally 'rebranding' towards non-standard workers is difficult, time-consuming and costly, even if unions change their organizing structure to facilitate their increased participation.

This is not to say that hospitality and tourism workers are 'unique'. Rather, their orientations to work and their role within the capitalist relations of production do not differentiate them from production workers. But there is a complex mix of factors that clearly contribute to an explanation of why trade unions, even where they enjoy strong institutional support, have made few incursions into large swathes of the HCTS.

### *Workforce Participation*

Participation provides employees with the opportunity to influence and take part in organizational decision-making and is, therefore, mainly pluralist. It is based on collective representation, which may be union or union-union, and is often referred to as indirect participation. Where worker representatives are elected, trade unions are generally involved. Non-elected participation tends to be ad hoc. Effective participation is dependent upon an equitable power balance.

Participation normally extends to areas outside the focus of traditional collective bargaining, i.e. the effort-reward bargain. Hence social partnership dealing with issues such as training and skills can be regarded as a variant of participation. Initiatives for participation normally emanate from the state, trade unions or employees. Examples discussed below include transnational EWCs, the forthcoming national-level information and consultation directive, works councils and joint consultative committees.

Involvement is closely associated with 'soft' and 'best practice' HRM and is management driven. As it seeks to enhance employee support and commitment to the objectives and values of the organization, it is mainly unitarist. As any increase in employee control and decision-making is limited to the job and work operation only, involvement is sometimes called task-based or direct participation. Involvement practices addressed below include briefing groups, suggestion schemes, problem-solving groups, teamworking and empowerment.

Worker representation at employers' initiative rarely addresses fundamental issues of pay and working time. Rather, it has more to do with improving management and workforce communications, and with improving day-to-day business issues and training. In one Accor hotel, while two-thirds of the staff attended meetings, only half of them participated actively. The remaining third did not bother to attend. Employee support and enthusiasm for meetings may be patchy, particularly where management determines the 'consultation' agenda.

Since the 1980s successive WIRS/WERS have shown an increase in direct participation and a decline in indirect participation and collective bargaining in Britain. Hence involvement 'may be desirable to enhance the status, opportunity and work satisfaction of the individual it may reduce the capacity of employees to challenge and influence managerial decisions by undermining collectivism and the representational role and power of trade unions'. Involvement and participation are not discrete or mutually exclusive practices and can be depicted on a continuum. Ultimately participation hinges upon the extent to which managers control workers and the degree of control afforded to workers within the organization or in their work.

### *IndirectPparticipation*

EWCs came into being as a result of the EWC Directive (1994), and are crossborder meetings between worker representatives and managers of companies with businesses in more than one country. Every enterprise with at least 150 employees in each of at least two countries and a total of at least 1,000 employees in the European Economic Area (EEA) is required to have an EWC. The procedure for consultation is if at least 150 employees from at least two countries require it. The meetings are for information and consultation purposes, not collective bargaining, as employee representatives have no powers to block management decisions.

A number of MNCs operating in the EU established EWCs by 'voluntary agreement' ahead of the legally required implementation date of 1996. This enabled companies to appoint employee representatives instead of those determined by national law or practice. By August 2000 there were 14 EWCs, only two of which were set up after the deadline for voluntary agreements.

### Case Study: Positive Outcomes from European Works Councils

- Club Mediterranee consulted and came to an agreement on closing operations and restructuring processes.
- Accor concluded an agreement with the IUF on trade union rights.
- Compass extended equal opportunities policies to all subsidiaries and promised training for all employees. Compass committed itself to becoming the 'Preferred Employer', linking customer satisfaction to employee satisfaction.

## Case Study: Pizza Express Forum

A structure for feedback and consultation for more than 250 British restaurants was established in 2000. This was developed by a working party of volunteers, with a former waiter recruited to act as full-time coordinator. Each restaurant has its own staff representative, who feeds into one of 27 Area Forums (each covers around nine restaurants). Each Area Forum elects a representative for one of three Regional Forums.

Issues raised by representatives have included a new menu and a service charge. At the National Forum representatives have brought up questions about training, pay slips and recycling. Most of Pizza Express's 6,000 staff are in the UK, and the aim is to ensure that the Forum complies with rules on EWCs. Although some staff are union members, the initiative will have failed if staff see joining unions as an alternative to the Forum.

Examples of those agreements signed jointly with trade unions are European and include Accor (French), Bass plc and Compass (UK) and Scandic Hotels (Swedish). By contrast agreements affecting EWCs in American MNCs, such as McDonald's, Tricon Global Restaurants and the tour operator American Express, were not signed by trade unions. McDonald's was able to negotiate the kind of EWC it wanted, which applies only to one-third of their workers because franchised stores are excluded. Britain was excluded from coverage of the Directive until the new Labour government opted into the Social in 1998. Transition arrangements meant that British-based MNCs had until 1999 to make voluntary agreements, as the UK regulations to comply with the Directive did not come into force until 2000.

### *Other Driven Consultation*

Other EU directives have required the UK to legislate for consultation with representatives in circumstances of collective redundancies, transfers of undertakings and health and safety. In keeping with EWCs, representatives do not have to be union representatives, and in health and safety employers may consult directly with employees or their representatives. However a number of factors limit their practical effect in the HI. Redundancy consultation with workers' representatives is required only when 20 or more employees at an establishment are to be made redundant within 90 days.

Many workplaces will not qualify because they are too small, and the use of atypical labour, high labour turnover and dismissal to regulate headcount means the HI sustains relatively few redundancies. Because redundancies and transfers are sporadic, often situation-specific events, standing structures for such purposes are rare anywhere in Britain. There may be little real consultation as employers may use such procedures to legitimize their decisions or to reassure workers.

As James (1994) has observed, the ongoing nature of health and safety may assure some continuity of management-employee dialogue. Health and safety is the one domain where there is some form of representative structure in non-union workplaces. Workers in non-union workplaces face difficulties in gaining access to health and safety representation.

Our WERS analysis shows, in the absence of any consultative committee or a committee that deals with health and safety matters, HI workplaces are significantly less likely to have joint committee to deal with health and safety matters. Such committees are most likely to deal with health and safety matters only. HI representatives are most likely to have been volunteers, whereas slightly more democratic methods are used in AIS and the PSS.

Adding the number of workplaces with health and safety committees to the number of workplaces with a JCC that discusses health and safety conveys a more complete picture of health and safety consultation. Even on this measure only one- fifth of HI workplaces consult formally on health and safety issues, significantly below AIS (48 per cent) and the PSS (37 per cent).

**Table: Health and Safety Arrangements in Context, by Size of Workplace and Sub-sector (%)**

| | *AIS* | *PSS* | *HI* | *<25* | *25-49* | *50-99* | *100+* |
|---|---|---|---|---|---|---|---|
| Joint committee | 27 | 21 | 10* | 0 | 13 | 33 | 61 |
| Any representatives where no committee | 37 | 29 | 14* | 4 | 45 | 15 | 33 |

| | *Hotels* | *Campsites* | *Restaurants* | *Bars* | *Canteens* |
|---|---|---|---|---|---|
| Joint committee | 23 | 24 | 13 | 0 | 13 |
| Any representatives where no committee | 23 | 0 | 12 | 11 | 4 |

***Notes:*** *All weighted cases. *Significantly different at the 5% level from AIS and PSS.*

Where there is no consultative committee that deals with health and safety issues, HI workplaces are significantly less likely to have representatives that deal with management over health and safety matters. The Directive on information and consultation adopted in 2002 is to be phased in from 2005, following consultation arising from the discussion paper High Performance Workplaces: The Role of Employee Involvement in a Modern Economy.

It will also apply a size of firm threshold. Initially it may apply only to companies with 150 or more employees, and by 2008 it will still only affect businesses with more than 50 employees. The Directive will extend consultation beyond the issues discussed above. Employees have the right to be:

- Informed about the business's economic situation;
- Informed and consulted about employment prospects;
- Informed and consulted about decisions likely to lead to substantial changes in work organization or contractual relations, including redundancies and transfers.

Information must be given in time to allow employee representatives to examine and prepare for consultation. The government is likely to encourage voluntary agreements within social partnership, imposing a statutory minimum framework where this is not possible. As with EWCs, there will be some impact among larger, but not most, HI businesses.

### *Works Councils*

Many European countries have highly formal institutional arrangements providing for works councils with written constitutions covering inter alia the election of representatives, frequency of meetings, and terms of reference. The German system of co-determination is often heralded as the 'best practice' model. Two-level worker participation comprises a works council in the workplace, and worker representatives on the supervisory board of the enterprise.

While McDonald's theoretically has a works council in every store, very few have been established because of company interference to delay and discourage any attempts to elect one.

Tactics have included transferring the store into different ownership, buying out the instigators of a works council and nominating management candidates to provide a management-based agenda.

Employee acquiescence and inadequate legislation have enabled McDonald's to stick to its American-style approach to participation, which is more in keeping with employee involvement, and to circumvent requirements for works councils in many other European countries. Similar avoidance strategies are deployed by other Anglo-Saxon-based MNCs in the German fast food industry.

### *JointCconsultative Committees*

One covers similar terrain to works councils (integrative participation), another allows employees to influence decisions before they are taken (classical consultation), while a third is largely symbolic, entailing downward communication only (pseudo participation). JCCs may be upgraded to marginalize collective bargaining and downgraded to deal with trivia.

**Table: Consultation and Communication in Context and by Size of Workplace (%)**

| | *AIS* | *PSS* | *HI* | *<25* | *25-49* | *50-99* | *100+* |
|---|---|---|---|---|---|---|---|
| System of briefings | 83 | 82 | 84 | 79 | 91 | 96 | 91 |
| Consultative committee | 23 | 18 | 11*** | 0 | 25 | 21 | 53 |
| Problem solving or quality groups | 33 | 28 | 16* | 9 | 17 | 35 | 48 |
| Formal opinion survey p | 39 | 36 | 43 | 36 | 46 | 56 | 58 |
| Other dd Entire workforce meetings | 42 | 42 | 47 | 55 | 40 | 27 | 36 |
| Management chain/ cascade | 54 | 47 | 37*** | 28 | 47 | 54 | 71 |
| Suggestion schemes | 24 | 25 | 25 | 21 | 36 | 24 | 29 |
| Newsletter | 43 | 39 | 42 | 41 | 48 | 42 | 39 |
| Disclosure of information bb Internal investment plans | 50 | 46 | 55 | 52 | 56 | 64 | 70 |
| Financial position of establishment | 63 | 58 | 69 | 69 | 68 | 67 | 73 |
| Financial position of organization m | 66 | 67 | 78 | 92 | 67 | 44 | 57 |
| Staffing plans | 63 | 59 | 53 | 50 | 59 | 55 | [illegible] |

**Notes:** *Yes responses to all weighted cases unless otherwise stated five years for establishments five years or older. dd Four most mentioned other ways in which management consults or comm employees (multi-response). bb Regularly given by managemer or their representatives. m Where part of a larger organiza establishment. *Significantly different at the 5% level fr ***Significantly different at the 5% level from AIS.*

WERS tells us that management consultation, rather than negotiation, are si the HI, although they are only present in of AIS workplaces. While the likelihoo increases with workplace size they ar sub-sectors. Committees are very workplace and most common in large workplaces. None of the smaller HI workplaces without committees had had one during the previous five years. However, one-quarter of the large workplaces no longer had a committee (all hotels), although the reasons for its disappearance are unknown.

Where committees function in the HI, health and safety is most likely to be discussed, followed by training, working practices and welfare services and facilities. Pay and government regulations are the least frequently discussed issues. HI committees are significantly less likely to discuss employment and pay issues. There is a different emphasis on the range of issues discussed in AIS and the PSS, making for a fuller, more rounded agenda. Even so the vast majority of committees discuss a range of issues rather than a single topic, with the exception of restaurants where most discuss a single topic.

**Table: Consultation and Communication by Sub-sector (%)**

| | *Hotels* | *Campsites* | *Restaurants* | *Bars* | *Canteens* |
|---|---|---|---|---|---|
| System of briefings | 97 | 94 | 91 | 73 | 81 |
| Consultative committee | 22 | 28 | 5 | 9 | 3 |
| Problem-solving or quality groups | 25 | 0 | 17 | 4 | 49 |
| Formal opinion survey p | 36 | 78 | 50 | 39 | 62 |
| Other dd | | | | | |
| ntire workforce eetings | 22 | 6 | 59 | 61 | 18 |
| anagement chain/ cade | 52 | 100 | 37 | 30 | 20 |
| gestion schemes | 20 | 24 | 39 | 22 | 12 |
| sletter | 29 | 24 | 36 | 51 | 66 |
| sure of ation bb | | | | | |
| investment | 71 | 100 | 34 | 55 | 77 |

| | | | | | |
|---|---|---|---|---|---|
| Financial position of establishment | 76 | 96 | 49 | 74 | 88 |
| Financial position of organization m | 64 | 72 | 76 | 89 | 71 |
| Staffing plans | 65 | 78 | 68 | 34 | 62 |

**Notes:** *Yes responses to all weighted cases unless otherwise stated. p In last five years for establishments five years or older. dd Four most frequently mentioned other ways in which management consults or communicates with employees (multi-response). bb Regularly given by management to employees or their representatives. m Where part of a larger organization or sole UK establishment.*

In the very few HI workplaces where a consultative committee deals with a range of issues (N = 13, all of which employ 50 or more workers), employee representatives are significantly more likely to be elected and not to be appointed by management than in AIS and the PSS. In AIS there are proportionately more workplaces where committees deal with a range of issues (N = 441), but representatives are less likely to be elected, and appointment by management features in one-quarter of workplaces. These committee meetings occur slightly more frequently in AIS and the PSS. HI managers were significantly more likely than their AIS and PSS counterparts to consider these committees as fairly influential or not very influential.

### Direct Participation

Marchington and Wilkinson identify a fourfold schema of involvement, all of which embrace empowerment to differing degrees. Whether involvement schemes benefit all or are wholly exploitative, benefiting only employers depends on the context and the processes, and employees can simultaneously experience greater job discretion and increased satisfaction and increased work demands. Workers will always resist so it is 'unrealistic to expect these sorts of schemes to remove problems from work, given that the employment relationship in any organization is built upon both conflict and co-operation'.

The use of employee involvement practices to foster an open, supportive and participatory employment relations climate will be positively linked to improving SQ. Communication systems, based on the 'involvement' model of indirect participation are an important prerequisite to culture change. Guest and Conway see a parallel between managing organizational culture and the psychological contract, as both embody people-building and high trust relationships. The process is complex and, if left to chance, will lead to poor relations with employees.

Communication is most effective at entry and on-job, while communicating down the organization is the most difficult aspect. The problem for managers in attempting to communicate full and accurate information is that simple explanations may distort reality.

Most of the literature on employee involvement in the HI is concerned with empowerment and team working. After discussing these we focus on other involvement mechanisms drawn mainly from WERS.

### *Empowerment*

Empowerment is a central component of SQ management and, like team working, is managerially led. It is wider than delegation, as power and authority are devolved, giving employees greater responsibility to solve problems, akin to Friedman's (1977) 'responsible autonomy'. Rather than providing greater autonomy or self-

### *A four-fold schema of Involvement*

Downward communication is the most diluted, and includes written documentation, face-to-face meetings, house journals and team briefing. Its purpose is to convey information, reinforce managerial prerogative and shape employee expectations. Upward problem solving taps into employees' knowledge and ideas, and includes suggestion schemes and ad hoc problem-solving groups or quality circles, where small groups meet voluntarily on a regular basis to identify, analyse and solve quality-related work problems.

These practices are part of 'best practice' HRM. Like downward communication it is essentially unitarist and 'bolted' onto the work process.

Task-based participation is integral to the job and part of everyday working life, and includes quality of working life programmes. It may entail performing more tasks at the same level or at a higher level, or some managerial/supervisory responsibility. Teamworking and self-management (one of Pfeffer's (1998) seven key HRM practices) allows employees to take responsibility for the task, work without direct supervision, to have discretion over work methods and time, to multi-skill and to recruit team members. Managerial control is at its most subversive and effective when employees take on responsibility for peer surveillance management, empowerment may lead to greater work intensification and increased stress, and may represent a form of control. Lashley (1997) identifies four meanings of empowerment through:

- Participation (autonomous work groups, job enrichment);
- Involvement (quality circles, team briefings);
- Commitment (share ownership, profit-sharing);
- Delayering (job redesign, job enrichment).

Claims for empowerment need to take account of the way managers use these different definitions and meanings, as different forms of empowerment lead to different working arrangements and boundaries for what employees can and cannot do. Empowerment as participation is observed in Marriott Hotels where employees have to identify and satisfy customer needs. In Harvester Restaurants where delayering requires staff to make decisions about work organization or scheduling, the culture is still largely control-oriented. Empowerment as involvement is practised in Hilton Hotels (team briefing), McDonald's (suggestion schemes) and Accor (quality circles).

The challenge for international companies is how to balance the consistency and certainty demanded by customers with elements of employee discretion necessary to add the nebulous quality factor to social interactions in variety of cultural contexts. Jones et al. (1997) report how one American hotel company encourages employees to 'share' and 'celebrate' employment stories, including access to a worldwide empowerment hotline. This helps reinforce a level of commitment perceived as necessary to go 'beyond contract'.

Managers find themselves caught between the contradictory impulses of standardization and customization, and cannot abandon either. Legge (1995a) identifies a similar contradiction within quality management, which seems to argue for delegation and control simultaneously.

Marriott Corporation and Harvester Restaurants use empowerment to produce greater efficiency, improve employee commitment, and ultimately increase customer satisfaction. At Harvester Restaurants the removal of a layer of management and the formation of employees into self-managing teams succeeded because of low turnover, the commitment of the team manager and the active support of senior managers. The greater autonomy and discretion afforded by team working may be accompanied by work intensification and increased surveillance, e.g. management, peers, customer feedback and 'mystery shoppers'. 'Quick fix' empowerment will rarely succeed.

**Case Study: From Empowerment to Control in a Canadian Nightclub**

Employees had developed an articulate and sophisticated culture with an elaborate customer-service hierarchy and system of reward and punishment, based on high-tipping customers. The main product was status not alcohol. There was low staff turnover and high flexibility, and core values were instilled in informal after-work gatherings, where employees shared stories, thereby training each other. There was high group cohesion although staff developed their own highly personalized styles of service to suit their particular customers.

The change was designed to generalize service to as wide a market as possible, with a new manager exercising control from the top. Job training was to manipulate employees' perception of their role. All intermediate supervisory posts were removed, so grievances had to be taken to the top. Employees' behaviour was monitored by 'spotters'. Superficial agreeability, a form of industrial sabotage, replaced authoritative emotional exchange. Employees were deskilled because they engaged in more limited social interaction and lost income because they had to serve different customers. After-work gatherings reduced and workers became stressed. Customers went elsewhere, sales fell, morale declined and employees lost any respect they had had for the manager.

The key to success is communication that builds a shared understanding of what empowerment means, surrounded by commitment, ownership, skills and competencies, leadership and sustainability.

Hales and Kildas claim that 'The notion of empowerment is beset by conceptual ambiguities, contradictions and a lack of compelling supporting evidence.' Their study of five-star hotels in Amsterdam found little evidence of empowerment in spite of management rhetoric. What there was amounted to increased employee responsibility rather than greater choice over how work is done or more voice in organizational decisions. Support systems of recruitment, training and remuneration were mostly absent.

The critical issue of how to balance control and autonomy in securing both compliance and cooperation is also addressed by others. As Lashley points out, 'Employers are concerned with both employee control and commitment. Employers are merely shifting the locus of control from one imposed externally on employees, to one which generates increased self-control in each employee.' At best worker power in enhanced but in highly controlled circumstances.

Sosteric's ethnographic account of a nightclub provides a case of empowerment in reverse, as a management sought to impose direct control in a workplace where work organization was based on responsible autonomy.

### *Teamworking*

Service industry characteristics and customer orientation are conducive to teamworking, which is one of the three key principles of SQ management. Claims that teamworking is used in two-thirds of British workplaces are rather hollow as only 5 per cent actually had autonomous work groups.

Rees examined the nature and extent of employee involvement through teamworking in hotels, including the methods used and the levels of responsibility and autonomy afforded to teams. Two approaches were used. Task-based teams were created to make workers functionally flexible, e.g. within food and beverage operations across the bar, restaurant and room service.

Problem-solving teams met to discuss improving customer service when management signalled a problem. Actual levels of discretion and responsibility were low because managers deployed various mechanisms to limit empowerment. Although the employees reported a strong sense of teamwork, they felt it should allow them to have more input into problem-solving and decision-making. Rees defines constrained responsible autonomy as 'reorganized control', as the increased level of employee involvement is within increasingly defined and measured limits.

WERS shows that HI workplaces are significantly less likely to have most of the LOG working in formally designated teams. Higher levels of teamworking occur in large HI workplaces, where three-quarters of workplaces have half or more workers so involved. The HI is also significantly more likely to have just a few or no workplaces using teamworking, especially in very small workplaces. The lack of teamworking is interesting given that it is one of Redman and Mathews' eight key HRM practices necessary to make a positive contribution to SQ.

## *Workforce Briefing*

WERS tells us that a large majority of workplaces in AIS, the PSS and the HI operate a system of briefings for one or more sections of the workforce. Nine in ten HI workplaces employing 25 or more workers operate a system of briefings. An all-inclusive approach involving the whole workforce is especially marked in very small workplaces. A more selective or tiered approach of departmental or work group/section/team briefing occurs as workplace size increases, and is most common in hotels.

Briefing occurs less frequently in the HI than in AIS and the PSS, with six in ten HI workplaces briefing on a monthly or less frequent basis compared to half in AIS. Infrequency of briefing is particularly marked in very small HI workplaces and bars, with more frequent briefing occurring in large workplaces and hotels. HI workplaces give slightly less time at meetings to questions from employees or for employees' views, and the amount of time available decreases with HI workplace size.

Thus nearly two-thirds of large workplaces allocate less than a quarter of time at meetings for this purpose, while six in ten very small workplaces allow one-quarter or more of the meeting for employee feedback. This suggests that employees in very small workplaces do have more opportunity to participate in such meetings although the opportunity for them to do this is less frequent. Conversely briefing in large workplaces is less 'consultative' although it occurs more frequently.

The vast majority of HI workplaces in New Zealand communicate directly with individuals, usually on an 'as and when' basis, although more formal methods such as JCCs are found in larger workplaces. Workplaces are less likely to seek employees' input than to supply information. Newsletters, suggestion schemes and notice boards were common only in hotels and fast food.

### *Problem-solving Groups*

The HI is significantly less likely to have problem-solving groups for specific problems or to discuss aspects of performance or quality than AIS and the PSS. In the HI the probability of a group operating increases with workplace size. Where there is no group and the establishment is five or more years old, groups have been used during the last five years in only a tiny minority of workplaces.

Although such groups are more likely to be permanent in the HI than in AIS and the PSS, the HI is significantly more likely to have groups with a finite life than AIS. In the HI a group's contribution is significantly more likely to be recognized by non-financial reward and is significantly less likely to get nothing at all. Financial rewards are given in around one-third of cases.

Whether or not such groups exist, employees in most workplaces in AIS, the PSS and the HI can make suggestions for improving working methods through other channels, most commonly through their managers.

### *Opinion Surveys*

A significant minority of workplaces in AIS, the PSS and the HI has used formal surveys to elicit employees' views or opinion during the last five years. In the HI this is more likely to happen in workplaces employing 50 or more workers than in workplaces employing fewer than 50 employees. The results are most likely to be made available in written form to all employees than not made fully available.

However, full disclosure is more likely not to take place at all in very small HI workplaces. Chung (1997) suggests that opinion surveys enable employees to provide valuable information about guests' characteristics, appropriate people to hire and the training they need, and how best to reward employees. The results may be used to adjust HR practices in support of SQ.

### *Communication and Consultation*

The HI is most likely to communicate or consult using regular meetings with the whole workforce, while the management chain and cascading information are most likely to be used in AIS and the PSS. In addition to these two methods, regular newsletters distributed to all employees and suggestion schemes constitute the four most often used methods in AIS and the HI. Even, so one-fifth of HI workplaces (16 per cent in AIS) offers no other forms of communication and consultation.

Disclosure of information relating to plans about organizational and establishment financial performance and internal investment and staff plans is a majority practice in AIS, PSS and HI workplaces. Regular information about the financial position of the whole organization (where part of larger organization or sole UK establishment) is the issue most likely to be disclosed to employees or their representatives. Looking at all HI workplaces, financial information about the establishment is more likely to be disclosed than information about internal investment plans and staffing plans.

It appears through pluralist, democratic processes i.e. an employee participation paradigm with collectivized relations that share decision making and power; 'empowerment' as currently applied within many organizations inside and outside of the hospitality and tourism industries, appears largely to be of the unitarist / HRM variety which seeks to gain commitment through an employee involvement paradigm.

These sources investigate in depth, the complex concept of empowerment as it is applied across a number of hospitality organisations. It recognises a broad spectrum of interpretations of 'empowerment' including 'participatory' approaches, however the main foci are on forms of empowerment centred on 'employee involvement'.

Chapter 6

# Reflections on the Significance

## INTEGRATING PERSPECTIVES

A hotel is an establishment that provides paid lodging, usually on a short-term basis. Hotels often provide a number of additional guest services such as a restaurant, a swimming pool or childcare. Some hotels have conference services and meeting rooms and encourage groups to hold conventions and meetings at their location.

Hotels differ from motels in that most motels have drive-up, exterior entrances to the rooms, while hotels tend to have interior entrances to the rooms, which may increase guests' safety and present a more upmarket image. A comfortable room, good food, and a helpful staff can make being away from home an enjoyable experience for both vacationing families and business travellers. While most lodging managers work in traditional hotels and motels, some work in other lodging establishments, such as camps, inns, boardinghouses, dude ranches, and recreational resorts.

In full-service hotels, lodging managers help their guests have a pleasant stay by providing many of the comforts of home, including cable television, fitness equipment, and voice mail, as well as specialized services such as health spas. For business travellers, lodging managers often schedule available meeting rooms and electronic equipment, including slide projectors and fax machines.

Lodging managers are responsible for keeping their establishments efficient and profitable. In a small establishment with a limited staff, the manager may oversee all aspects of operations. However, large hotels may employ hundreds of workers, and the general manager usually is aided by a number of assistant managers assigned to the various departments of the operation. In hotels of every size, managerial duties vary significantly by job title.

It is an honour to provide a commentary to the JIBS 2005 Decade Award-winning article 'Revisiting Multinational Firms' Tolerance for Joint Ventures: A Trust-Based Approach' by Anoop Madhok, a truly international scholar by background, training, spirit and vocation, and a prolific author who has enriched the field of international business (IB).

Madhok's trust-based approach shifted the attention from ownership as a means for multinational companies to control their international ventures to trust as a source of long-term resilience of the partnership. By building a bridge between Stopford and Wells (1972) and Franko's (1971) mainstream IB theories of ownership and the literature on trust, including earlier work on international joint ventures (IJVs) by Beamish (1985) and Parkhe (1993) among other insights, Madhok changed the discourse in the field of IB.

Furthermore, his award-winning article is a manifestation of a fruitful cross-disciplinary exchange: on the one hand, it brought into IB insights from disciplines such as sociology and anthropology, and on the other hand, it successfully exported IB contributions to other domains, through the universal appeal of the proposed framework. A decade after the article's publication, both the questions it poses and its integrative approach appear remarkably contemporary. The issue of what makes alliances persistently popular despite the challenges in achieving resilience and success continues to draw attention and re-kindle vigorous debates in the field.

This provides some reflections on the significance and implications of Madhok's (1995) article. It is structured as follows. First, I review a number of aspects of the original paper, high-lighting their contribution to the field of IB. Second, I trace the diffusion of some of the article's core ideas in subsequent scholarly publications in IB and other related domains. Lastly, revisiting Madhok's claim that trust matters, I pose some questions for further research.

Albeit Madhok's award-wining article is full of insights, I have chosen to focus on two main contributions: first, the shift in perspective from ownership to relationship, suggesting that trust matters in making IJVs resilient and successful; and, second, the integration rather than substitution of perspectives, using the relationship-centred approach in conjunction with the ownership-based approach in order to better understand the tolerance of multinational firms for IJVs with local partners.

The gist of Madhok's (1995) article is that trust is critical for cooperation. That trust-centred perspective focused attention on those aspects of the relationship that have been overlooked in the mainstream structural concern with control through ownership. In elaborating the framework for a trust-based approach, Madhok distinguished two mutually reinforcing components of trust, a 'yin and yang' of a kind, which he labelled 'structural' and 'social' trust.

The so-called structural component captured the synergic complementarities of the partners' resources and capabilities and, hence, their potential to create more value together than separately. The social component of trust, which Madhok himself has labelled 'social glue', kept the parties together, allowing the value-creating potential of their collaboration to be realised. In that sense, Madhok's trust-based approach appears to me to be concerned not so much with the multinational firm's tolerance for JVs but, rather, with its ability to create and capture value by paying attention to the social aspects of its partnerships.

This distinction between value-attainment potential and value realisation has been further elaborated by Madhok and Tallman (1998), who defined the inter-firm relationship as a productive resource in need of specific expenditures.

In addition to value, another essential element of Madhok's trust-based approach is the notion of trust-building expenses, which the parties of the IJV incur over time. Drawing on extant studies, Madhok posited that the building of a trusting relationship is a lengthy process demanding relational investment and 'various forms of hard and soft commitments'. In his framework, he argued that this investment was more likely to be made by partners in a relationship characterised by both strong structural and social components of trust — that is, a relationship that counts with strategically complementary resource bundles and with willingness to operate jointly in an efficient and flexible manner.

In addition, Madhok arteculated that investment requirements for trust-building depended on the life cycle of the relationship, with larger investment expected in the beginning, so that shared commitment can be established. Once there is a sound shared foundation, he hypothesised, maintaining the relationship usually becomes less investment-intensive. In the application of his trust-based framework to the case of multinational firms engaged in collaboration with local partners, Madhok argued that the investment in trust-building would differ depending on the strategy and structure chosen by the multinational firms. Madhok sustained that above-normal return would give a multinational firm the slack resources necessary for making what he called 'trust-building gestures' to its local partners. In my interpretation, this view of trust-building investment is rather instrumental and associates trust with payoff.

A related contribution is Madhok's attempt to elaborate on and clarify the dynamic nature of trust. Trust needs time to emerge. In addition, it requires repeated successful interactions as well as ongoing perception of equity. The nature and pattern of these interactions, Madhok posited, are influenced by the combination of structural and social trust. The stickiness of the relationship through the investment in trust allows for conflicts to be addressed and transitory states of inequity endured.

This dynamic assumes that the increased flexibility of the relationship resulting from its relational quality will in turn enable greater adaptability to changes in the environment, and will ultimately lead to improved performance of the alliance. Yet, this is but an assumption, and a recent study by Carson et al. (2003) reveals that the performance of trust-based governance is contingent on the ability of partners to read each other's behaviour in the process.

Madhok did not position his trust-based view as an alternative to the ownership-centred perspective. Rather, he argued that the two approaches were compatible and complementary, and demanded an integration of insights that could advance the understanding of IJVs' success and resilience. Such integration was possible because the two approaches had a common objective of achieving flexibility and efficiency in the way a relationship operates. In addition, they had different orientations, which allowed different aspects of the joint venture to be revealed.

For the ownership-centred perspective, flexibility and efficiency are achieved through hierarchical relations, that is, through control based on ownership. For the trust- or relationship-centred approach, they are attained through the management of the social relationship. By investigating cooperative phenomena, such as JVs, within a structural framework, the ownership-centred approach is outcome-oriented and relatively static. It fails to address the critical role of social context in inter-organisational relationships.

The so-called relationship- or trust-based approach is dynamic, process-oriented and concerned with issues such as reciprocity, commitment and forbearance, rather than control. Another distinction is that the ownership-centred perspective is a macro-approach, which connects strategy-structure-ownership levels of the MNCs with JV's tolerance. The relationship-centred approach is a micro-approach in that it pays attention to the dynamic processes underlying a relationship. Taken together, the two approaches overcome their respective limitations and provide a more balanced and refined understanding of what makes IJVs tick.

One final distinction is that, in addition to flexibility and efficiency, a trust-based approach is attentive to the coordination aspects of the partnership and the need for resolution of conflicts triggered by differential contribution and/or learning by the partners, temporary inequity, as well as exogenous events that can change the partners' strategic priorities.

Beyond its direct contribution to a field, a published piece of scholarly work gains a life of its own in those studies that build on its ideas and the articles that cite it in their theoretical and empirical developments. In this, seek to identify some of the influences of Madhok's article upon studies of IB and the related domain of interorganisational relationships. Also, I trace the article's diffusion to other fields and scholarly discourses.

A decade since its coming into print, Madhok's (1995) article in JIBS is alive and oft-cited. It has served as a building block or inspiration for studies on international JVs and cross-cultural collaboration, as well on strategic alliances in general. Moreover, its ideas have travelled to fields such as marketing, supply chain management, engineering, psychology and law, thus proving their universal appeal and usefulness.

There are two main areas in which Madhok's ideas have been most visible and have exercised the most significant impact – international JVs and strategic alliances. In the first theme – IJVs – scholars who have delved into the issues of control and collaboration with particular interest in trust have found Madhok's framework relevant. Their work has centred on the effectiveness of the JVs, the processes of trust-building, the multi-levelled nature and meaning of trust or the partnering skills needed for success.

The second theme, that of strategic alliances, represents a phenomenon much broader than the original scope of Madhok's framework, centred on IJVs of multinational companies with local partners. Beyond that, Madhok's trust-based framework has become part of a fruitful stream of research into alliances. Scholars dealing with issues of inter-firm relationships have taken on Madhok's ideas when examining formation of strategic alliances or their co-evolution, establishment of commitment through bonding and trust, sources of alliance success or failure, or the link between trust and risk.

Understandably, the biggest diffusion and impact of Madhok's (1995) article has taken place on the pages of JIBS, with numerous scholars drawing inspiration from it. However, the seeds of Madhok's (1995) framework have been planted in a wealth of other journals in the field of strategy, management == and organisation, which place the issues of alliances, relational advantage and inter-organisational relationships at the heart of their editorial agendas.

Thus, the article has been referenced in publications in the following journals (listed alphabetically) including: Academy of Management Review; Accounting, Organization, and Society; Group and Organization Management; International Journal of Management Reviews; Journal of Business Research; Journal of Management; Journal of Management Studies; Journal of Organizational Change Management; Journal of World Business; Long Range Planning; Organizational Science; Organizational Studies; Research Policy; Strategic Management Society.

Furthermore, scholars from various fields and domains have built upon Madhok's ideas. Some examples of diffusion, infrequent in academic circles that tend to operate as silos, include Batt's (2003) article on supply chain performance, Farrelly and Quester's (2005) work on relationship quality in sponsorship exchanges, Robson and Dunk's (1999) article on co-marketing alliances, Salbu's (1997) contribution to business law with work on contracts as device for flexible coordination and control, and Tjosvold's (1998) work in psychology, with focus on cooperative and competitive approach to conflict.

Hence, it is not surprising that journals from other disciplinary domains have also published articles that acknowledged Madhok's (1995) original ideas, including: American Business Law Journal; Applied Psychology – An International Review; Industrial Marketing Management; International Marketing Review; Journal of Engineering and Technology Management; Journal of International Marketing; Journal of the Academy of Marketing Science; and Supply Chain Management – An International Journal. This diffusion of IB ideas to fields of strategy, management and organisation, as well as to other, not necessarily adjacent, areas and disciplines, signals with optimism that IB research is capable of inspiring and informing scholarly conversations in other domains.

**Future Research**

Madhok (1995) suggested broadening the scope of his trust-based approach beyond the particular case of a multinational firm and its local partners. Madhok proposed a potential extension in the direction of partnerships between two multinational companies, in which the geographical, product and activity scope of the partnership is much broader and the dynamics much more complex. In my view, another fruitful avenue for further exploration, for which the JIBS 2004 Decade Award-winning article by Oviatt and McDougall (1994) has paved the way, is the perspective of the entrepreneurial firms forming the alliance and the dynamics of the partnerships these international new ventures form.

They are distinctive types of player in the IB arena and lack the resources that multinational companies possess to invest in trust-building gestures. In addition, as a variety of new alliance forms have come into being in the decade following the publication of Madhok's award-winning article, the nature of their dynamics is also worthy of further investigation. In that sense, thinking in network rather than dyadic terms can be insightful and informative.

Madhok (1995) employed trust, relationship and cooperation as interchangeable descriptors of his trust-based perspective. Upon reviewing the developments in the trust literature and the cumulative contribution to the field of alliances in the last decade, in my interpretation these three terms are not interchangeable, as they evoke different emphases in understanding the stability of interfirm partnerships. For example, cooperation is not necessarily sustained by trust, and a relationship can be glued by shared social norms and sanctions instead of trust as a 'social lubricant'.

Hence, there is a risk of trust becoming 'a residual term for the complex socio-psychological processes necessary for social action to occur'. Special issues of the Academy of Management Journal (1998), Organization Studies (2000) and Organization Science (2003) have furthered knowledge of the levels, types and effects of trust. Despite their collective contributions, however, trust continues to be an unresolved concern and a rather fragmented and diverse theme.

Doubts continue to be raised 'about the universality of the effect of trust on business transactions'. In this sense, the focus and, in some cases, over-reliance on trust in the alliance literature has obscured a more general treatment of the nature and role of enforcement mechanisms. It may have also confounded the most interesting sources of variation in safeguarding inter-firm relationships and their stability.

Concluding his 1995 JIBS article, Madhok admitted that '[i]t would be naive to overemphasize trust'. In subsequent articles, he continuously and vigorously sought to clarify or deepen understanding of certain aspects and terminology of his trust-based framework. For example, he and Tallman proposed 'a nontrust explanation of why firms might knowingly forgo opportunities to take advantage of their partners'. Recently, Carson et al. (forth-coming) raised doubts on whether social sanctions suffice in stopping opportunism in situations of high ambiguity.

They sought to clarify the contingency nature of formal and relational contracting in conditions of volatility and uncertainty. Furthermore, they went beyond merely assuming opportunism to directly testing its relationship with uncertainty. All these efforts enriched and expanded the scholarly conversation on alliances. Yet, they also signalled the need to consider approaches that provide alternative, integrative and more nuanced explanations of why inter-firm relationships continue experiencing high rates of both foundings and failures, and how their stability can be enhanced.

Svejenova et al. (2005) argue that, in order to improve understanding of the issue of stability in international alliances, attention should be paid to enforcement. Enforcement ensures that behaviours are enacted or that individuals would act in a particular way. Enforcement mechanisms differ from deterrence mechanisms in that the latter rely on avoidance and preclusion of particular types of behaviour, whereas the former enable collaboration and ensure partners' actions are consistent with expectations. They are also likely to evolve with the strategic intent of partners. The sources and certainty of enforcement remain a relatively little explored theme. There is a lack of agreement in the literature on when trust is the enforcement mechanism and when other mechanisms create an enforcement environment that results in trust-like outcomes.

Svejenova et al. (2005) proposed a framework of enforcement. (1) With it they seek to clarify the role of trust in safeguarding inter-firm collaboration and identify other mechanisms that could generate trust-like outcomes of the kind of reliability or predictability of partners' cooperative behaviour. In elaborating their enforcement perspective, they do not allege that trust is unwarranted or unlikely to emerge in a process of productive cooperation; only that its many roles may have been overstated.

The theoretical perspective advanced by Svejenova et al. (2005) defines an enforcement space that takes shape along ownership, legal and social dimensions. Legal enforcement is manifested in the existence of a reliable legal system, with its codification and transparency of laws (e.g., property, contract and commercial law), and a realistic expectation for fair and relatively speedy legal adjudication in the courts. The agreement can be formal, informal, written, oral or just plain 'taken-for-granted'.

The creative complexity and variety of alliance forms has outpaced the legal arena and the analytical tools used by antitrust enforcement agencies to assess their legality. Hence, mechanisms other than contracts have been used as complements to or substitutes for legal enforcement. Social embeddedness has been considered another source of enforcement of cooperation through mechanisms such as friendship (enforcement by the strength of the interpersonal relationship), reputation (enforcement by an open network of third parties) and social norms and sanctions (enforcement by a closed, cohesive network such as kinship relations).

A third source of enforcement is the ownership dimension. To its traditional depiction, understood and conceptualised in terms of financial equity, Svejenova et al. (2005) added two other ownership-related mechanisms: revenue-sharing and brand equity. Revenue-sharing agreements do not involve equity participation of the partners in their respective companies or in their joint venture.

Brand equity is another enforcement mechanism, particularly relevant in franchising and licensing relationships and especially in those cases in which the intellectual property of technology included as the basis of the alliance is proprietary and difficult to imitate. For example, Contractor and Kundu (1998) found that, in the hotel business, registered brand names are a potent source of control, and the threat of withdrawing permission to use the brand moderates the opportunistic behaviour of the firm's international partners.

Taking into account mechanisms with different nature, the framework advanced by Svejenova et al. (2005) seeks to identify when trust is a requisite for the alliance and when it may not be essential. This is especially useful in the cases of cross-border alliances, when local partners can occupy enforcement spaces different from those of the multinational company that seeks to partner with them. While each of the three dimensions – legal, social and ownership enforcement – has important individual implications for the enforcement of a partnership, they may act as complements rather than substitutes.

There is a range of intermediary cases shaped by different combinations of the three enforcement mechanisms. For example, within this framework, trust is a requisite enforcement mechanism in the case of friends who cooperate on the basis of a handshake or an oral agreement and share revenues. Trust is dispensable when there is some kind of assurance, that is,

> *"expectations of benign behaviour from an exchange partner based on knowledge of an incentive structure that encourages such behaviour rather than exploitation. Mechanisms that provide assurance include legal or normative authorities that impose sanctions for violations of agreements or failure to fulfil one's obligations, guarantees such as collateral that protect against loss, warranties that assure certain standards of quality, and so forth."*

For example, assurance rather than trust can enforce cooperation in the case of a partnership embedded in a closed, cohesive network, based on a detailed contract and exchange of financial equity.

Further understanding of, and empirical work on when trust matters remains to be done. Future research should consider a broader range of dimensions for the enforcement of stability in a partnership. It should seek to identify what factors may influence the parties in an alliance to seek certain types of enforcement. In his analysis of the smaller economies of Pacific Asia and their business systems, Redding (2005) described how their social and legal embeddedness differs owing to differences in culture, religion, legacies of the former colonial powers (the English, Dutch or the French), etc. Using the enforcement framework, Svejenova et al. (2005) hypothesise that firms that have been historically and spatially embedded in cultures where institutions are weak or underdeveloped will tend to favour relations, as opposed to contracts, in safeguarding the exchange.

In the case of China, for example, 'Personal networks are ... particularly significant modes of economic transacting in China because of the weak institutional sanctions against reneging on commitments'. However, those personal networks can be of little use to a foreign company without access to these networks or previous history of collaboration, when considering a partnership with a Chinese firm.

In that sense, a focus on the dynamics of nation-institutional configurations rather than on culture may be more meaningful in capturing differences along the enforcement dimensions. Importing and integrating insights from political-institutional approaches to sociology into the field of IB could contribute to a more comprehensive view of inter-firm collaborations. How do adjustments in nation-state institutional arrangements affect inter-firm relationships and choices of alliance partners?

How are differences in institutional contexts imprinted on management decisions about initiating and maintaining international alliances? There is a need for studies into alliances being established in developing countries, not only from the perspective of the foreign organisation but also from the point of view of the local partners, which has been largely unaccounted for.

A better understanding is needed of the role played by interlocked business and state elites in purporting their impact on alliances not only as a source of reputation but also as matchmakers. A range of well-known Italian, French and Asian cases illustrate the importance of powerful, well-connected individuals in the business and political elite in triggering and guaranteeing inter-organisational collaboration. Bank managers are in a position to identify from among the portfolio of their clients potential partners whose interests could match theirs. Further attention is needed to the strategies that firms pursue not only to safeguard a partnership by securing partners who behave according to expectations but also to convey an image of a reliable partner. This is especially true for entrepreneurial firms in need of a partner with incumbents to enhance their legitimacy and reputation.

In addition, given that alliances usually have proponents and detractors in the partnering organisations, more studies on the role of organisational politics in developing or detracting from the realisation of the value potential of a partnership over time could enhance understanding and better management of the alliance dynamics.

Expected contribution of comparative sociology to understanding alliance differences across nation-states, along with the accentuated role of political behaviour, individual cognition and attachments in maintaining inter-organisational relationships, raise the issue of the need for multi-level studies and co-evolutionary perspectives. They also suggest that IB literature can benefit from insights coming from other domains, which in turn would allow it to advance knowledge that can be inspirational for scholars from those domains.

Another element in an agenda on inter-firm relationships may encompass their dysfunctional consequences and negative effects. Here, a critical issue that future studies could clarify is the concept of failure in a strategic alliance. Furthermore, research on the dysfunctional outcomes of alliances and networks could help in understanding how and why firms get locked into and sustain unproductive partnerships that could hinder opportunities to collaborate with other viable firms.

International alliances continue to be a vast and vibrant scholarly domain in IB studies in need of further clarification and integration of disparate contributions. In order for future research to result in a better understanding of the enforcement of stability in alliances, studies must incorporate approaches from comparative sociology and economic geography, which can provide a broader and better foundation than merely the culture-based one for understanding alliance differences. In addition, researchers must strive to separate trust from trust-like mechanisms for initiating and maintaining a partnership, which would afford an explanation of how firms who are 'strangers' can initiate a potentially profitable relationship in the absence of a common relational history.

Since its publication, Madhok's award-winning article has enriched and expanded the IB discourse and opened up numerous avenues for theoretical and empirical work on inter-firm relationships. With the extent of its diffusion and influence, it has also revealed that the IB literature could successfully integrate insights from other domains and, in turn, serve as a source of inspiration to scholarship in other disciplines.

By considering the benefits from change in assumptions from opportunism to trust 'till proven otherwise', Madhok (2006) poses yet another challenge to researchers in IB and inter-firm relationships. I am convinced that he will continue planting the seeds of his ideas in numerous forthcoming publications and igniting the imagination of scholars to come.

### *Staffing Policies and Strategic Control*

While the effective management of human resources is increasingly being recognized as a major determinant of success or failure in international business, in practice many organizations are still coming to terms with the human resources issues associated with international operations.

In the international arena, the quality of management seems to be even more critical than in domestic operations. This is primarily because the nature of international business operations involves the complexities of operating in different countries and employing different national categories of workers. Yet, while it is recognized that HRM problems become more complex in the international arena, there is evidence to suggest that many companies underestimate the complexities involved in international operations. The field of international human resource management, however, is only slowly developing as a field of academic study and has been described by one authority as being in the infancy stage. Moreover, there is relatively little empirical research that documents the international HRM strategies and practices of international firm - particularly firms that have their headquarters outside North America.

This reports some of the findings from a recent study of international human resource management in Britain- and Ireland-based international firms. One particular feature of the study was the exclusive focus on "managing managers." Particular attention is given to three key issues in the area of international human resource management: international staffing, international recruitment, and the variety of issues surrounding the problem of shortages of international managers. I will also briefly consider the nature of the human resource management challenges facing companies in the light of the Single European Market.

A study of how companies deal with the international human resource management issues outlined above is particularly appropriate for the reasons enumerated below.

First, the international staffing process is of considerable importance to an international firm: "Virtually any type of international problem, in the final analysis, is either created by people or must be solved by people. Hence, having the right people in the right place at the right time emerges as the key to a company's international growth. If we are successful in solving this problem, I am confident we can cope with all others".

The staffing problems facing international firms are more complex than in domestic firms, and inappropriate staffing policies may lead to difficulties in managing overseas operations. The international literature indicates that expatriate failure is a persistent and recurring problem, particularly for U.S. multinationals. Frequently, the human and financial costs of failure in the international business arena are more severe than in domestic business. In particular, indirect costs such as loss of market share and damage to overseas customer relationships may be considerable.

Second, the shortage of international managers is becoming an increasing problem for international firms. A survey of 440 executives in European firms claimed that a shortage of international managers was the single most important factor constraining corporate efforts to expand abroad. Almost one-third of the executives surveyed had experienced difficulties in finding managers with the necessary international experience and orientation. The findings of the survey suggest that the successful implementation of global strategies depends, to a large extent, on the existence of an adequate supply of internationally experienced managers.

Third, there is little empirical research on the international human resource management issues associated with the management of managers in British and Irish international firms, especially in comparison to the considerable literature on international human resource management in U.S. firms.

Fourth, the advent of the Single European Market and the rapid growth of British direct investment abroad since the early 1980s mean that issues of international staffing, recruitment, and development are increasingly important concerns in a far wider range of organizations than the traditional giant multinationals. International HRM problems are becoming increasingly important for a growing number of smaller and medium-sized companies that have significantly internationalized their operations in recent years.

### *Research Methodology and Sample*

The principal research method was structured interviews with each company's corporate personnel or human resources director, or with a senior corporate HR executive. The majority of interviews were conducted in 1990, the remainder in 1991. The duration of interviews varied from two hours to three and a half hours. During each interview, information was sought on company structure and international operations. The interviewer also asked questions concerning international staffing, expatriate performance, international HRM policies, and international management development.

These questions were adapted from a study by Tung (1981) and through consultation with a number of international HRM practitioners. The purpose of the questions was to provide a structured basis for each interview, and responses to questions were noted by the interviewer since interviewees were not asked to fill in a questionnaire. Additional information was obtained from company reports, company documents such as international personnel policies, and newspaper articles.

Forty-five international companies participated in the study. Forty companies were British-owned and five were Irish-owned international firms. The sample was specifically chosen to include companies from both the manufacturing and the service sectors. Twenty-six companies in the study were primarily manufacturing firms and sixteen were service sector firms. Two oil companies and one mining company also participated.

The size of the companies in this international firm sample ranges from medium to very large, with the total number of employees worldwide ranging from 9,500 to 240,000. The smaller size of the Irish international firms and their relatively recent internationalization were two principal reasons for their inclusion in the study. For the sample as a whole, there was a wide range in the number of countries the companies operated in, and in the length of experience in international operations.

### *International Staffing Policies and Practices*

International firms face three alternatives with respect to the staffing of management positions abroad - namely, the employment of parent-country nationals, host-country nationals, or third-country nationals. Much of the existing research focuses on the advantages and disadvantages of using expatriates as opposed to local managers and it identifies a range of host-country, company, and individual factors as important considerations in international staffing decisions. Most studies are, however, largely inconclusive on the question of when parent-country nationals should be sent abroad.

The findings of the present study on staffing practices in British and Irish international firms reveal that a majority of the companies continued to rely heavily on parent country nationals to run their foreign operations. The research findings showed that, while almost 50 per cent of companies had formal policies favouring the use of host-country managers to run their foreign operations, in practice just over one-third operated with host-country nationals in senior management positions in their foreign operations.

In other words, two-thirds of the companies relied primarily on expatriates to run their foreign operations. Furthermore, the trend has moved in the direction of greater use of expatriates. Half of the companies in the sample (22 out of 45) reported an increase in the use of expatriates over the previous decade and only 20 per cent indicated that they had reduced their use of expatriates. The remainder reported no significant change.

These findings raise serious questions about the ability and commitment of some British multinationals to identify and develop host-country managers effectively in their foreign operations. Therefore, the recruitment, selection, and development of host-country managers emerges as a vital issue for British and Irish multinationals, given the need to develop global teams with a variety of different perspectives and competences.

The findings of the present study on staffing practices in British and Irish firms reveal sharp differences with U.S. experience. Indeed, recent work by Kobrin suggested that the tendency of U.S. multinationals to reduce the numbers of expatriates had gone too far. He argued that U.S. firms have tended to substitute host-country nationals to replace expatriates primarily in response to the difficulties U.S. managers have experienced in adjusting to other cultural environments.

Kobrin recognized that the increased use of host country managers may in part reflect the cost of maintaining expatriates abroad, the greater sensitivity of local managers to local culture, and local market needs and the growing international maturity of some multinationals. It is suggested, however, that expatriate reduction may result in U.S. multinationals facing reduced identification with the worldwide organization and its objectives, difficulties in exercising control, and a lack of opportunities for U.S. managers to gain international experience abroad. The principal concern is that U.S. multinationals could face major strategic management control problems where managers identify with local units rather than with global corporate objectives.

The present study identified a number of principal reasons for employing expatriates. The first was the lack of availability of management and technical skills in some countries. There was a greater tendency for companies to use expatriates in less developed countries due to the weak pool of available local management talent. This was also true for those companies that used host-country managers to run their foreign operations in advanced countries.

The second major reason cited for using expatriates was the objective of control of local operations. Thirty-three out of forty-five firms in the present study identified control as a key reason for their use of expatriates. Expatriates were felt to be more familiar with the corporate culture and the control system of headquarters, and this was felt to result in more effective communication and coordination. Indeed, a key role for senior expatriates was to train local managers to understand corporate financial and control systems.

This point is illustrated by a comment by the human resource director of a financial services company: "The main advantage of using expatriates is that they understand our [corporate] culture and reporting systems and they teach the locals how to relate to the centre. This is vital when you are establishing a new foreign business."

This finding on the importance of control is consistent with previous research on European multinationals which shows control to be an important reason for expatriate transfers. Yet, in previous research, only rarely has control been identified as an important aim of expatriate assignments. This probably reflects the North American origin of much previous research and the tendency of some managers and researchers to view control as a rather disreputable rationale for using expatriates.

A further key reason for using senior expatriates was to maintain trust in key foreign businesses, following large international acquisitions. This finding is particularly interesting because previous research has suggested that the employment of expatriates will be lower in acquisitions by comparison with greenfield sites. The emergence of trust as a major factor is related to the rapid growth in the number and scale of foreign acquisitions by British companies in the 1980s.

For example, in the late 1980s, a U.K. brewing and leisure company emerged as one of the world's leading hotel groups, following a massive [pounds]2 billion acquisition of a global hotel chain. In this example, a major reason given for using expatriates to run the acquisition was "the need to have the peace of mind which comes from having our people running such a large and strategically important investment." There was often an unwillingness to allow newly acquired foreign businesses to be run by the existing host-country national management, primarily because they were not known well enough and their loyalty to the business was not proven.

The research also found that using expatriates for management development purposes was important and was increasing in significance for British multinationals. Thirty-four out of forty-five companies reported that expatriates were used for development purposes, and twenty-five of these firms claimed that use of expatriates for this purpose was becoming more important. This reflects the tendency of British companies to see expatriation as part of the career-development process. In this context, it is interesting to note that, in most cases, the management of expatriates was the responsibility of the corporate human resource function. This was the case even in some highly decentralized organizations (e.g., engineering companies) where the corporate human resource role was rather limited.

One very recent trend identified by the research was the tendency for companies to give younger managers international experience much earlier in their career than previously. Over half of the companies in the sample (26 out of 45 companies) reported significant changes in this respect. This was linked to the growing problems of mobility (spouse's job, children's education, etc.) for older managers. This also reflects the strategy of some companies to broaden the opportunities for international development, and the growing recognition in some quarters that the payback on the investment of a developmental assignment may well be greater with a younger manager.

The performance of foreign subsidiaries also emerged as a significant factor influencing the use of expatriates. There was a greater tendency for the companies in the sample to use senior expatriates where the acquired business had been underperforming before the foreign acquisition. Similarly, poor performance by host-country managers in the post acquisition phase was cited as an important reason for replacing them with expatriates. This finding is well supported in the literature, which has frequently reported that crisis accentuates headquarters control.

This is well illustrated by the case of a major British food and drinks company that made two very large acquisitions in the United States in the late 1980s. The first acquisition was a global drinks business with its headquarters in the United States, and the second was a large U.S. food business. The staffing policy differed sharply in the two acquisitions. In the former case, the existing management team (composed entirely of host-country managers) continued to run the business. "In this case," said a corporate HR executive, "we inherited an excellent management team who were achieving first-class results. Why change a winning team and upset morale by introducing expatriates?" In the second case, by contrast, the entire U.S. management team was replaced by expatriates, "mainly due to poor financial results and weak managerial performance."

Another factor influencing the approach adopted by companies was a strong expectation on the part of major foreign customers (and sometimes foreign governments) that the top managers in their country should be parent-country nationals. Thirteen of the sixteen international firms in the service sector and a minority of manufacturing firms (6 out of 26) said they had taken this into account in deciding their policy. Public relations and marketing were usually the key roles in this context. Previous research has largely ignored this factor because it has concentrated on the very largest multinationals and tended to neglect the service sector.

For example, two Irish banks operating in the United States felt that there were considerable marketing and public relations advantages in using expatriates, given their marketing strategy of targeting the ethnic Irish population. In the banking, insurance, and finance areas, British companies reported that, in many countries, major foreign customers frequently had a strong preference for their senior executives to be British expatriates.

There is also strong evidence from the present research that expatriates are more likely to be used in the early stages of new foreign operations. This is consistent with previous research that shows this practice is common in the early stages of internationalization where a company is setting up a new business, process, or product in another country, and prior experience is considered essential. A majority of firms indicated that control and trust were particularly important in the early stages of internationalization. In the present study, this factor had become more significant due to the rapid growth of international business in the last decade.

Nearly half of the companies (21 out of 45) also cited weaknesses in their training and development of host-country national and third-country national managers to explain their continued use of expatriates, despite a formal policy to replace expatriates with host-country managers after the startup phase. A typical comment in this respect came from a pharmaceutical company: "The training and development of host-country nationals and third-country nationals is a major weakness in achieving our objective of localising management in our operating companies."

### *Shortages of International Managers*

It was argued above that the successful implementation of global strategies depends, to a large extent, on the existence of an adequate supply of internationally experienced mangers. In the present study, two-thirds of the companies (30 out of 45) said that they had experienced shortages of international managers and over 70 per cent indicated that future shortages were anticipated.

While the faster pace of internationalization was cited as the primary reason for shortages by thirty-four of forty-five firms in the sample, the findings suggest that over half the firms (24 out of 45) reported that failures to recruit, retain, and develop host-country managers effectively were another key reason why shortages exist. A number of factors make the recruitment of host-country managers more difficult and costly compared with recruiting in the home country. These include: lack of knowledge of local labour markets; ignorance of the local education system and the status of qualifications; language and cultural problems at interviews and trying to transfer recruitment methods that work well in the United Kingdom to foreign countries.

Many international firms have tended to neglect the training and development needs of their host-country managers and focus virtually all of their managerial development efforts on their parent-country nationals' managers. Twenty-six of the forty-five firms in the sample reported that weaknesses in their training and development in respect of host-country managers had contributed to shortages of international managers. The failure to develop local managers effectively was frequently given by British multinationals as a reason for continuing to use U.K. expatriates in similar management positions rather than using local managers. Alternatively, this could be interpreted as something of an excuse for their preference to use expatriates beyond the development phase of international operations.

The present research highlighted three important lessons for those international firms that are seriously attempting to provide management training and development for host-country nationals and third-country nationals. First is the need to avoid the mistake of simply exporting parent-country training and development programmes to other countries. This point is illustrated by the following comment from the personnel director of a large chemical firm: "We have learned from some tough experiences that training and development programmes for local managers must be culturally adapted to local conditions."

Second, the management development programmes for host-country and third-country nationals need to be linked to the strategic situation in each country, as well as to the overall strategy of the firm. This need to take into account a variety of foreign product-market situations superimposed upon the overall strategic thrust of the firm adds considerably to the complexity of devising appropriate management development programmes.

The third lesson is the need to utilize much further the practice of developing host-country managers through developmental transfers to corporate headquarters. It has been argued that this type of international transfer exposes host-country nationals and third-country nationals to the headquarters' corporate culture and facilitates their developing a corporate perspective, rather than simply reflecting their own local interests.

It has also been argued that this approach to development can be very effective in helping to develop global management teams and is a necessary part of successfully operating a truly global firm. The present research indicated, however, that a majority of British companies still failed to recognize the need to develop high-potential host-country national managers to senior positions that exist outside their own countries, and this exacerbates the problem of attracting and retaining high-potential young managers in the host countries.

### *The Shortages of International Managers*

Nineteen of the forty-five companies had responded to the shortage of international managers by attempting to identify parent country managers of high potential at an earlier stage in their career, and by giving them international experience at a much younger age. Over one-third of the companies reported that they were sending young managers of high potential on international assignments partly for developmental purposes.

This was in sharp contrast to the previous practice when many MNCs relied on developing a cadre of career expatriates who moved from one international position to the next. The trend towards giving younger managers from the parent country the opportunity for international experience earlier in their careers was often part of a more general trend to give international experience to a wider range of managers, and not just to a relatively small group of expatriates. Increasing numbers of international firms were also using short-term developmental assignments in order to develop larger pools of employees with international experience.

Another significant response to the shortage of international managers was the rapid growth in importance of external recruitment to fill management positions abroad. Until a few years ago, the majority of firms had relied almost exclusively on internal recruitment for foreign management positions. British MNCs traditionally had a strong preference for well-known internal managers for expatriate management positions, as they had established track records and their loyalty to the company was proven. Over one-quarter of the firms in the study had, in the past five years, introduced external recruitment to fill management positions abroad, and several others were planning to do so. Financial services companies were a good example of this: some of these companies had rapidly internationalized relatively recently and felt they had to recruit externally at the senior level to establish their foreign operations.

A third response to the shortages of international managers by fourteen of the forty-five companies was to attempt to sell themselves more effectively to graduates through various types of marketing designed to highlight the international nature of their activities (e.g., in graduate recruitment brochures and in national press advertising). This type of marketing highlighted the prospects of early international experience to attract graduates seeking an international career. This can be illustrated by the example of the two textile companies that had a policy of sending young graduates on international assignments within three or six months of joining the firm.

This policy was very effective and was designed specifically to recruit high-potential young graduates who were particularly interested in an international career. The corporate human resources director of one of the textile companies commented: "Textiles is not a particularly fashionable industry. We are competing for the best graduates with companies that enjoy a more glamorous image. The fact that we can offer the opportunity of very early international experience is the main reason we can attract some high potential graduates when the big guns, such as Shell, BP, and ICI, are fishing in the same pool."

A minority of companies were also broadening their sources of graduate recruitment to include some continental European countries, and this reflected their anticipation of a growth in the competition for high-potential graduates following the advent of the Single European Market. Two computer companies had recently introduced Euro-graduate management development programmes.

A feature of these programmes was that graduates were recruited from several European countries for a two-year period of training and development in the United Kingdom. On completion of their training, graduates were transferred to a management position in a third country. The need to develop more flexible succession planning systems to support the development of Euro-graduates was identified as an important issue by both firms operating this type of programme.

There was also growing recognition of the importance of developing effective international management development programmes to help secure an adequate supply of international managers. The majority of firms reported that they were spending more money and more time on international management education, particularly for top and senior management. These firms were using a combination of internal and external international management development programmes. One interesting feature of these programmes was that teachers frequently came from prestigious foreign business schools in Europe and the United States, as well as from internal sources. However, only three of the forty-five firms claimed they had effective systems for evaluating their international management development programmes.

The introduction of language training for top, senior, and middle levels of management by the majority of companies in the study was seen as an important development in light of the acute shortages of international managers with language skills. This suggests that the importance of language training is increasingly being recognized by British multinationals. This finding is in sharp contrast with studies of U.S. MNCs, which found that only a minority of U.S. MNCs felt that knowledge of foreign languages was necessary for conducting business abroad.

Increasingly, it was recognized that language training increased the effectiveness of staff working abroad and helped them relate more easily to a foreign culture. There was also a growing awareness that language training promoted a better image of the MNC in the host country.

There were two areas, however, where the companies were clearly failing to take effective action to ease the acute shortage of international managers. First, there was no evidence that British multinationals were taking serious steps to increase the proportion of women in international management. International management has long been a masculine preserve in Europe and the United States. Adler's study estimates that under 3 per cent of North American expatriates are female.

In the present study, no company claimed to have more than 3 per cent of female expatriates. Indeed, the evidence suggests that women in British multinationals are not making as much progress in international management as women in U.S. multinationals. For example, in the U.S. banking and financial sector, there has been a significant increase in female expatriates.

The under representation of women in international management is illustrated by a quote from a woman HR executive of a U.K. pharmaceutical company: "In the UK, the majority of marketing staff are women. By contrast, in our foreign operations, the vast majority of marketing staff are male. Companies still tend to shy away from using female expatriates because of fears that women will not be accepted in some countries and the major problem of disrupting the career of their partner." The lack of willingness to recruit and develop women as international managers is worrying as recent research suggests that, in many ways, women are well suited to international management.

The second area that impacts on the supply of internationalists is the failure by many companies to adequately address repatriation problems. The repatriation of managers has been identified as a major problem for multinational companies in the United Kingdom and North America. Over 70 per cent of the firms (33 of 45) in the present study said they faced significant problems regarding reentry. Further, it was generally recognized that this may lead to low morale and a higher turnover of expatriates.

For example, only three of the firms claimed that repatriates had no difficulty reintegrating into the U.K. organization. A key problem for the majority of companies was finding suitable posts for repatriates of similar status and responsibility to those they held abroad. For many British MNCs, this problem had become more acute in recent years because, for many of the companies, expansion of overseas operations had taken place at the same time as the rationalization of U.K. operations, thereby reducing the number of senior posts in the United Kingdom.

Other problems associated with reintegrating into the United Kingdom are loss of status, loss of autonomy, loss of career direction, and a feeling that international experience is undervalued by the company. Further, there was growing recognition that where companies are seen to deal unsympathetically with the problems faced by expatriates on reentry, managers will be more reluctant to accept the offer of international assignments.

Research in North America indicates that 20 per cent of all managers who complete foreign assignments wish to leave their company on return. This was a growing problem for British multinationals, particularly when many companies are willing to pay a premium to attract the experienced international manager. Yet, while it is widely accepted that the costs of expatriate turnover are considerable, very few firms had introduced formal repatriation programmes to assist managers and their families with repatriation difficulties.

Similarly, very few companies had introduced mentor systems to check the career progression of the international manager. Many expatriate managers were concerned about losing out on opportunities at home, and, in some companies, this was a constraint on their willingness to go abroad. Clearly, British companies need to give a higher priority to the issue of repatriation in order to encourage international mobility and to help secure an adequate future supply of international managers.

### *Barriers to International Mobility*

This briefly considers the reasons why shortages of international managers are expected to continue. In particular, it examines the growing restrictions on international mobility and their significance for the international capability of the firm.

Over 70 per cent of the firms (34 out of 45) reported that they anticipated shortages of international managers over the next five years. There was a growing concern on the part of many firms that the pace of internationalization would further outstrip the supply of international managers. The growing internationalization of European firms and the advent of the Single European Market in 1993 led firms to expect a more international and competitive market for managers and graduates.

For example, one financial services corporate HR executive expressed the problem like this: "Attracting and retaining high potential graduates and managers with international experience is vital if we are going to implement our corporate objective of achieving a much stronger presence in Europe. The problem is that the pool of available talent is not growing fast enough to meet demand." The same executive commented: "In the short run, we have to ensure that our reward package becomes internationally competitive, but this will not be enough. We need to look at new sources of labour supply such as women, host-country managers, third-country nationals and reduce our dependency on expatriates."

The problem of ensuring an adequate supply of international managers is further exacerbated by growing resistance to international mobility. Indeed, it was suggested by twenty-six of the forty-five firms in the sample that individuals were becoming less internationally mobile just when there was a growing need for international managers because of expansion abroad. The reduction in international mobility was attributed to several factors, including continued rationalization in the United Kingdom, which created uncertainties regarding reentry; the growing unwillingness to disrupt the education of children; the growing importance of quality of life considerations; and finally, continued uncertainty regarding international terrorism and political unrest.

Concerns about dual-career problems and disruption to children's education were seen as major barriers to future international mobility by many companies. In the past, working spouses were less common, generally female, and were prepared to follow their partners' career transfers. More frequently now, however, spouses must also leave a job or career in order to follow their partner to the foreign country. The growing significance of the dual-career problem is well illustrated by a quote from the HR corporate executive of a large oil company: "Nowadays families are less willing to disrupt personal and social lives even where they accept that international experience will enhance the manager's career prospects."

And a banking HR executive described the problem in these words: "More and more women have careers and not just jobs. For many it would be impossible to continue their careers in a foreign country. Increasingly international mobility is limited by the dual-career factor. Also we need to recognise that dual-career problems can seriously affect career development plans for our international managers."

Two further restrictions on international mobility are illustrated by the following quote from an HR executive in a chemical firm: "It's becoming more common for offers of foreign assignments to be rejected because the location does not appeal to the family, and when managers are willing to go abroad, they are much more demanding about all aspects of the remuneration package."

The above discussion would suggest that restrictions on international mobility appear to be growing just at the time when the need for international mobility is becoming vital for the internationalization of U.K. business. Indeed, the problem of international mobility could emerge as a key factor in determining the international capability of a firm.

In the present study, companies were asked to identify the main HRM challenges they faced arising from the advent of the Single European Market. Eighty per cent (36 out of 45) of firms felt that the main challenge was to secure an adequate supply of international managers. A majority of firms said they needed to upgrade management skills and competences in order to compete effectively in Europe, and many companies were concerned about the poaching of graduates and managers by firms based in continental Europe.

Over 70 per cent of companies identified recruitment as a priority area. It was felt that the Single European Market would intensify competition for labour, increase the mobility of labour, and augment pressure on U.K. salaries. While some companies identified a number of positive opportunities presented by 1992 - namely, an increase in opportunity to recruit labour and management from other European countries - the majority of firms felt there would be a net loss of staff to continental Europe.

A small minority of companies were seeking to develop a pan-European approach to recruitment, but they were facing many practical problems such as which journals to advertise in and which qualifications to seek. In addition, there is a problem of the profile of a company abroad, because a company that is well known in the United Kingdom may be much less well known in other countries.

The need to develop a more international top management team to reflect the growing international nature of the business was increasingly recognized as a major challenge because, at the present time, very few British companies can claim to have a truly international top management team. Similarly, a growing concern was the need to assess what new knowledge, skills, and competencies are required to operate effectively in the internal European market.

There was also growing anxiety about the managerial skills and competencies needed to deal with the complex HRM issues and problems associated with the growth of international joint ventures (e.g., the evaluation and promotion of managers and the problem of conflict of loyalty of managers to the joint venture or to the parent companies.

There was also a growing recognition by the companies of the need to understand the importance of cultural differences within Europe. This is particularly interesting in the light of the finding that only a very small minority (3 out of 45) of companies currently use cross-cultural training to help prepare managers for international transfer within Europe. By contrast, it was much more common for firms to provide cultural training for transfers to countries in the Far and Middle East, where the culture gap was seen to be greater. Specialist external courses were often used but not for international transfers within Europe.

The above discussion suggests that the most formidable task facing British companies wishing to operate across Europe is the recruitment and development of a cadre of managers and executives who understand and can operate effectively in the international environment. In practice, the impact of the Single European Market on human resource management strategy varied according to the stage of internationalization and the overall strategy of the firm. Most multinational firms traditionally pass through various stages of internationalization between the evolution from a domestic to a truly global organization.

For some well-established international firms, the Single European Market intensifies and sharpens the focus of problems associated with internationalization, rather than creating new problems. A small number of highly internationalized businesses that regarded themselves as transnationals (companies with the ability to manage across national boundaries, retaining local flexibility while achieving global integration) felt the nature of the HR challenge of 1992 would be marginal rather than central.

Such companies (e.g., the oil companies) tended to see pan-European recruitment and language training initiatives as a response to the single market, but they stressed that fundamental issues such as the supply of managers and management development should be related to the broader international strategy of the business rather than to the Single European Market alone.

The single market did, however, represent a major HR challenge for "new" international firms that had internationalized in the recent past, and for firms that were significantly shifting the focus of their international activities towards Europe. International human resource management strategy, like human resource management strategy generally, must be linked to the strategic evolution of the firm.

This has highlighted some of the HRM issues and challenges that such firms will face as they undergo the internationalization process. It also suggests that, for British international firms, the recruitment and development of international managers will be the key challenge of the 1990s.

**Competitive Advantage**

An impressive body of literature on the management of service companies has emerged since 1977' that services "break free". The unique characteristics of services have received acceptance, while related issues of service design and production, services marketing, and services management have been given an impressive amount of attention in books and leading journals.

Despite this progress, a number of issues mandate continued scrutiny. There is the growing recognition that the boundaries between goods and services have become increasingly blurred and that the majorities of goods contain significant service components and vice versa. For example, some commentators have noted the potential for competitive advantage that is inherent in correctly leveraging the service components of products. This fluidity is perhaps best captured in Shostack's (1977) molecular model, which views all market entities as containing some tangible and intangible elements with services being defined as intangible-dominant entities.

The outcome of this dialogue has been an increase in the number of services management perspectives that are applicable in what were traditionally considered manufacturing domains and, conversely, an increase in the level of attention given to the strategic management of service firms. Central to this debate is the issue of how service companies can attain a sustainable competitive advantage."

Service businesses generally are noted for their high level of mimetic or imitative behaviour. Innovations, such as new types of bank accounts or investment vehicles, are invariably quickly imitated by competitors. Innovative airlines, which sought to use frequent flyer programmes to build switching costs for customers, found that, very quickly, many other major airlines were offering similar incentives. This level of imitation has focused attention on what kinds of resources and capabilities a service firm might leverage in order to gain a competitive advantage.

Gaining positions of competitive strength has become more important in an environment that has become increasingly global and competitive. Competition in industries such as air travel and transportation is inherently more global than in many manufacturing businesses. Deregulation in the likes of financial services has ushered in a new era of global competition and quick competitive reactions. The size and importance of the service sector has grown considerably. This sector accounted for 74 per cent of gross domestic product and about 79 per cent of national employment in the United States in 1992. In addition. almost 60 per cent of total value added in the U.S. economy in 1992 came from private (nongovernment) services.

This responds to these developments by proposing a model of competitive advantage in the international services sector, which is designed to help managers evaluate the potential sources of such advantage. It draws heavily on an existing foundation of literature spanning the disparate fields of services marketing, strategic management, international business, and industrial organization economics. At the intersection of these strands of thought is the resource-based view (RBV), which is the conceptual premise of this paper.

The next outlines the perspectives provided by the RBV for international services firms. Subsequently, a conceptual model is presented, and selected sources of international competitive advantage are outlined. Finally, conclusions are drawn and implications discussed.

Competition in international business: Insights from the resource-based view.

Organizational strategy has long been viewed as the challenge of matching internal resources and strengths with the opportunities existing in the environment. This is perhaps best summarized in the seminal framework of Learned, Christensen, Andrews, and Guth. Thus, the task of strategic management is viewed in terms of the interplay of the personal values of management with the firms' skills and resources, and of how these are matched to environmental opportunities/ threats and broader societal expectations.

Throughout the early 1980s, the broad thrust of strategy research focused on the second quadrant. This research is best demonstrated by the work of Porter (1980, 1981). It posited that a firm's performance was largely a function of the structure of the industry and the firm's position in the industry. However, empirical research toward the end of the decade increasingly began to show greater performance differences among firms in the same industry than across industry boundaries.

Allied to this was a conceptual swing toward the end of the decade back to a forgotten portion of the LCAG framework, namely quadrant 1. Building on earlier work by Penrose (1959) and Nelson and Winter (1982), what has become known as the resource-based view is illustrated by the work of Barney (1986, 1991), Conner (1991), Dierickx and Cool (1989), Grant (1991),

Mahoney and Pandian (1992), and Peteraf (1993), to name but a few.

The resource-based view focuses on heterogeneity among firms in the same industry. It views firms in terms of unique bundles of resources and capabilities that provide the basis upon which a competitive advantage can be pursued. The normative implication of this view is that the firm should base its strategy on its own resources and capabilities. Irrespective of the markets or combination of markets served, firms should seek to leverage the resources best suited to those markets.

This may even lead to a situation where the firm will choose to compete in inherently less structurally attractive markets if it possesses resources that are valuable in serving those markets. Of course, in an international context, there may be other motives for competing in structurally unattractive markets, most notably defensive foreign direct investment or cross-subsidization, where firms try to preempt the strategic moves of international rivals.

### *Conditions Necessary for Competitive Advantage*

The potential to confer a competitive advantage is not inherent in all resources but, rather, in only those that meet a rigorous set of conditions. The first condition is that the resource must be valuable – it must provide the opportunity to exploit some environmental opportunity or neutralize some threat. Resources are considered valuable when they enable a firm to conceive of or implement strategies that improve the firm's efficiency or effectiveness. Some authors construe value in terms of meeting a key buyer need.

In addition, resources must have the characteristic of rareness. If valuable resources are possessed by a large number of competitors or potential competitors, they no longer represent a source of competitive advantage.

This is the key issue of heterogeneity underlying the resource-based view – firms possessing unique bundles of skills and resources can attain a sustainable competitive advantage. Third, there must be the condition of imperfect mobility of resources. Where resources are easily traded between competitors, no competitive advantage can be maintained.

Imperfectly mobile resources include those that are idiosyncratic to the firm, those for which property rights arc not well defined, or those that are co-specialized assets.(2) The imperfect mobility of assets is a critical factor in service businesses as people are the key assets in many cases, and their high mobility frequently results in the loss of accounts and the emergence of new competitive threats as in the case, for example, with personnel employed by advertising agencies and moving to other ones.

Finally, for an advantage to be sustained, resources must be imperfectly imitable or provide some ex-post limits to competition: That is, subsequent to a firm gaining a superior position and earning rents, forces must exist that limit competition for those rents. It was noted above that innovations such as the development of a new type of account by a retail bank or a new advertising style by a creative department frequently results in a host of imitations from competitors.

For a firm to be in a position to exploit a valuable and rare resource, there must be a resource position barrier preventing imitation by other firms. Sustaining a competitive advantage over a period of time requires the presence of isolating mechanisms that prevent imitation. Several such barriers that have been cited in the literature include causal ambiguity and uncertain imitability, where the drivers of success are difficult to identify. Imitation may also be prevented by the process of asset stock accumulation within the firm.

Where these stocks possess the characteristics of time compression diseconomies (accumulation has taken place over a long period of time), asset mass efficiencies (a critical mass of stocks has been developed), and interconnectedness (stocks are interrelated), then imitation is difficult. Indeed, the significance of asset stock accumulation in the services sector has been demonstrated elsewhere, when the "reservoir of organizational and managerial expertise that has been built up over the years can provide branch offices with information at a cost very much lower than a de novo indigenous firm would have to incur" – in other words, an ownership advantage in international competition.

Thus, service firms must seek to identify the skills and resources they possess and that meet the above criteria, and to leverage such resources to attain a competitive advantage. For service firms trading internationally, there is the added dimension of the location of such resources, which may be in the home or host country, or both.

The traditional international-business literature and the more recent global strategic management literature have identified that the success of a multinational firm is likely to be based on some combination of three sets of advantages, namely, firm-specific advantages, country-specific advantages, and internalization advantages. In resource terms, this effectively amounts to the combination of country-specific and firm-specific resources since internalization or coordination can be viewed as a managerial capability and hence a firm-specific resource.

The conceptual lens of the RBV demonstrates important differences between these two sets of resources. Country-specific resources derive from the resource endowments of countries or, in neoclassical economics terms, its comparative advantages. Country-specific resources are available on equal terms to all firms competing in an industry. Therefore, there are no barriers to prevent competing firms from imitating a given firm's portfolio of country-specific advantages. It is recognized, however, that a given firm's ability to gain access to these resources or to preempt their usage may be dependent on firm-specific political competences.

In addition, some authors suggest that country-specific advantages are dynamic and change over time – for example, Japan's move from a low-labour-cost country to a high-labour-cost country. However, firm-specific resources are considered unique to the firm, and, therefore, are likely to possess greater barriers to imitation, which suggests that they will be a more important source of competitive advantage.

### *Resources Versus Capabilities*

Authors have recently sought to distinguish between the potential rent-generating assets of an organization. A variety of distinctions have been suggested, including assets and core competences, resources and capabilities, intellectual assets and nonintellectual assets, tangible and intangible resources, and assets and skills. Despite the range of nomenclature, the issue being addressed by the various authors is similar, namely, that the rent-generating assets of an organization can be broadly classified in terms of two basic types.

On the one hand, there are the organization's resources, which are tangible, can be either inputs or outputs, and possess two key attributes: ownership and value. Ownership can be legal in terms of title deeds to land, property, or equipment, or in intellectual property such as patents, trademarks, licenses, or trade secrets. In addition, the firm may own assets that are not legal in nature, such as reputation with customers, organizational or personal networks, and databases. The most acceptable measure of value from an accounting perspective is exchange value. Thus, resources in the main are viewed as relatively easy to trade between firms.

On the other hand, organizations also possess capabilities or competences – that is, the capacity to deploy resources, usually in combination, in order to effect a desired end. The key characteristics of capabilities are that they are firm-specific and developed over time, but, unlike resources, they are not easily tradable between firms. In general, capabilities are information-based or intellectual assets.

In addition, they tend to be cross-functional or arise from the integration of individual functional capabilities and thus are sometimes referred to as "intermediate goods" in the production process. Therefore, by definition, capabilities meet the requirements of rareness and inimitability and are a strong basis for competitive advantage. The normative implication of this logic is that service-firm capabilities are likely to be the most sustainable source of competitive advantage.

The issue of potential synergies between home- and host-country firm-specific advantages has been a central issue in the vast body of work that broadly falls within the gambit of globalization. The globalization debate began in the early 1980s and has continued with intensity ever since. One of the primary hypotheses of globalization was that markets were converging. Reaching back to the marketing-standardization literature of the 1960s, this meant that companies could be successful by selling standardized products throughout a global market at low prices due to the resulting economies of scale, in effect utilizing only home-country firm-specific advantages.

This was in sharp contrast to the earlier view of the multinational corporation as a collection of autonomous subsidiaries tailoring resource use and strategy to particular local market needs. However, even some of the early proponents of globalization conceded that this hypothesis might be a little simplistic, and began to suggest that standardization was a matter of degree.

From this recognition of complexity emerged the view that, to be successful in the global marketplace. the firm must organize itself to achieve the benefits of global integration, national responsiveness, and learning. In resource terms, this meant that the firm should not rely solely on the resources of the parent company (global integration) or the subsidiary (national responsiveness), but must seek to emphasize both and successfully transfer learning in both directions (i.e., from the home-country headquarters to the subsidiary and vice versa). So, while several authors contend that a company should pursue a global strategy on the basis of the globalization potential of the industry, there is a contrasting view that firms need to combine both global and local dimensions, sometimes known crudely as ""localization".

Stated in resource terms, this "transnational solution" suggests that superior performers in international business will combine both home- and host-country firm-specific resources and capabilities. This suggests that service firms must consider extensive foreign direct investment and create an opportunity for the successful combination of home- and host-country firm-specific resources and capabilities.

However, other "nonequity" forms of organization, with origins largely in the services sector, such as licensing, franchising, and management contracts, equally present an opportunity for the successful integration of home-and host-country resources. Their effectiveness in achieving such integration seems to be greater in consumer services than in industrial or business services.

### *Firm-specific Resources*

Porter (1990) highlighted that many firm-specific resources were rooted in the firm's country of origin. This is illustrated by the strength of German companies in engineering, of U.S. companies in consumer goods and services, and of Italian companies in craft-based industries. Kogut (1991) extended this analysis to show that long cycles of country leadership in international competition can be explained by differences in country capabilities embodied in the firms in these countries.

In addition, many of these capabilities are sticky and diffuse slowly across borders due to four factors: technological opportunities, selection forces, identifiability, and institutional lock-in. In terms of technology, many firms have established relationships with country-specific research centres, trade associations, educational institutions, and skilled individuals. These relationships are built up over a long time and are not easy to replicate in other countries. In many cases, these are the clusters of organizations identified in Porter's "diamond" framework.

Equally, selection pressures are analogous to Porter's concept of domestic rivalry, an essential requirement to the development of globally competitive firms. Identifiability refers to domestic firms having a better understanding of the sources of success of domestic competitors than do international competitors.

This understanding can have numerous reasons and results in a greater propensity to imitate domestic competitors that leads to greater national rather than international diffusion of management capabilities. Institutional lock-in is analagous to the notions of administrative heritage or strategic commitment at a national level where the change and adoption of new techniques are impeded by previous investment, past practices, and perceived wisdom. The immediate implication of this analysis is that the firm-specific advantages underlying service-firm strategy are likely to vary from country to country, reflecting the fact that such advantages derive largely from the country of origin and diffuse slowly across borders.

Kogut (1991), however, noted that long cycles of country leadership are driven not only by technological investments (resources) but also by the efficiency of the dominant organizing principles (capabilities).

Foreign direct investment is the extension of the organizing principles of domestic firms to foreign markets. Organizational types, such as the global firm, provide a vehicle for the diffusion of capabilities across borders due to the high level of integration or coordination of its activities. Close interaction between parents and subsidiaries is also a central aspect of the transnational firm, which has been advocated as the organizational type most suitable, given the current complexity of international business. though not necessarily in every industry.

Most major multinational firms have at various times experimented with increasing the integration of their operations. The learning that has accrued from these integration efforts suggests that the firm-specific advantages underlying the strategy of leading international competitors will not vary from one host country to another, thereby reflecting the diffusion of management capability.

Toward a resource-based model of competitive advantage in international business. The process by which resources and capabilities are translated into a competitive advantage for the multinational firm is outlined, which demonstrates that superior performance is likely to be attained through the adoption of strategies based on a combination of home- and host-country firm-specific resources with host-country location-specific resources.

It highlights that management plays an essential role in leveraging this resource pool in ways that enable the firm to gain advantage. Management must make choices regarding which product markets to compete in, whether to try to attain a position of low-cost leadership or differentiation, or both, and which resources and capabilities to use in order to attain these positions of competitive leadership. Superior performance, which can be measured in the conventional terms of market share leadership or return on investment, accrues to firms achieving a competitive advantage. Sustaining the advantage over time requires reinvestment on the basis of competitive strength.

This model is an extension of the model of competitive advantage that can be found in the strategic-management literature, but it clearly sits very comfortably with the extant international business literature, as well as the "transnational solution" proposed by Bartlett and Ghoshal (1989) to help managers deal with the complexity of international business.

The model presented is designed to assist managers of service firms in building a sustainable competitive advantage on the foundation of the resources and capabilities inherent in the company. It also helps managers identify which skills and resources are most likely to be an important source of advantage and to realize the importance of being able to combine potential advantages from both home- and host-country locations. In specific cases, the actual skills and resources underlying competitive advantage are likely to be contingent on the characteristics of the service itself, the service firm, and the service industry as well as of the country of origin of the firm.

However, sources of advantage in service industries identified elsewhere can be seen to meet the requirements outlined in the model. For example, Stalk, Evans, and Schulman (1992) contend that the growth and subsequent market dominance of WalMart resides in the company's unique logistics capability, which confirms the importance of capabilities as a potential source of competitive advantage. The logistics system known as "cross-docking" ensures that goods are simply moved from one loading dock to another in forty-eight hours or less, resulting in minimal inventories and shaving between 2 per cent and 3 per cent off the cost of sales.

The system is a source of competitive advantage because it meets all of the criteria outlined earlier. It is used in a value-generating way — creating cost savings in a business where tight margins are critical and low costs are a key success factor. It is a rare system, and, because it combines people, delivery vehicles, and communication systems, it is clearly immobile. But it is its inherent barriers to imitation that help to confer a competitive advantage on WalMart. It is extremely difficult to duplicate the required constant communication between suppliers, distribution centres, and sales outlets achieved through the company's investment in a private satellite communications system.

Similarly, Pleval, Nellis, Lane, and Schuler (1994) attribute the success of AT&T's Global Business Communication Systems (GBCS) division to its unique human resource capability. Its human resource strategy is linked to overall business strategy, and review and reward mechanisms are designed to increase personal motivation while simultaneously achieving company goals. The company views its employees as "its only sustainable competitive advantage."

Again, this division of AT&T has been successful because it utilizes a set of resources/capabilities that meet the criteria necessary for competitive advantage. GBCS uses people in a value-generating way by explicitly connecting their efforts with key company goals. such as using a total quality management approach, being a leader in customer-led applications of technology, and being the best value supplier.

People can always leave an organization, so why do many firms contend that their people are their only sustainable advantage? In the ease of GCBS, mobility of personnel is not a major concern, as its success resides not in individuals but rather in a complex set of relationships among individuals reflected in performance management, recognition, compensation practices, and communication programmes. Furthermore, even though individuals who are hired away by competitors are able to describe them, these systems prove difficult to imitate because of the levels of reaming that occur while these "asset stocks" are being accumulated.

The key role of people, as a source of competitive advantage in internationally traded services, is demonstrated by the high level of foreign direct investment by firms in industries like financial and management services in order to maintain control over this resource.

This paper contends that competitive advantage for service firms lies in the unique resources and capabilities possessed by the firm. Not all resources or capabilities are a source of competitive advantage-only those that meet the stringent conditions of value, rareness. The actual sources of competitive advantage are likely to vary depending on the nature of the service, the particular traits of the firm, the nature of the industry, and the country of origin.

The normative implication of this analysis is that service managers conduct a rigorous analysis of internal resources and capabilities. What eve resources and capabilities does the firm have, and which of any of these strengths are unique? What scope is there for making investments to develop unique resources and capabilities that would yield competitive advantages in the future? The analysis also raises the question of control of key sources of competitive advantage.

Foreign direct investment arguably creates the greatest potential not only for control but also for the effective integration of resources across national boundaries. More traditional forms of organization in the services sector, such as licensing, franchising, and management contracts, have been shown to be effective control mechanisms in consumer, though not in business, services. Their effectiveness as a means for integrating resources may represent a fruitful area for further research.

Chapter 7

# The Future of Hotel Organisation

## ORGANIZATION OF A LODGING ESTABLISHMENT

As their facilities grow in size, lodging managers are faced with the need to group certain jobs in order to ensure efficient coordination and control of activities. These job groupings are usually called departments. In general, departments might be grouped as front of the house (those departments in which employees have guest contact, such as front desk), and back of the house (where employees have little guest contact, such as accounting).

However, separating departments by function is the most common method of organizing a hotel or a lodging business. The limited-service hotel, a full-service hotel with under 500 rooms, and a full-service hotel with over 500 rooms. There may be as few as 2 or as many as 50 employees in a particular department. In a very small lodging business, such as a bed-and-breakfast, the owner can supervise each department. However, as the lodging business increases in size (i.e., above 20 rooms), it is most effective to create managerial positions within departments.

Typically, the rooms department (called the front desk department in a limited-service facility) includes reservations, the front office, housekeeping, and telephone or PBX. In smaller full-service hotels, security and engineering might also be included in the rooms department. Responsibilities of the rooms department include reservations, guest reception, room assignment, tracking the status of rooms (available or occupied), prompt forwarding of mail and phone messages, security, housekeeping of guest rooms and public spaces such as lobbies, and answering guests' questions.

To perform these many duties effectively, the rooms department may be divided into a number of specialized subunits. To complicate matters, in many instances these subunits are also referred to as departments. For example, the laundry department. Because of its specialized function, little of the knowledge and skills required to manage a laundry operation is transferable to other areas of hotel operations.

The front office is one of the most important departments in a hotel, as it often offers the only contact between guests and staff. A hotel's front office is where guests are greeted when they arrive, where they are registered and assigned to a room, and where they check out. Usually, the telephone operator, other guest communications functions, and the bell staff or those employees responsible for delivering luggage and messages and attending to special guest requests also fall under the front office umbrella.

The reservations department takes and tracks the hotel's future bookings. The housekeeping department is responsible for cleaning guest rooms and public spaces. Because of their specialized nature, the security and engineering departments are discussed in separate sections. A great deal of interdependence exists among the subunits of the rooms department.

For example, reservations must inform the front office of the number of presold rooms each day to ensure that a current inventory of salable rooms is always available. On the other hand, the front office must let reservations know whenever walk-in guests (those who do not have reservations) register. A similar level of cooperation is required between the front office and housekeeping. When a guest checks out, the front office must inform housekeeping so that the room may be cleaned.

Once a room is cleaned, housekeeping must inform the front office so that the room may be sold. Certain tasks within the rooms department must occur in a specific order. For example, housekeeping cannot properly provision a guest room if the laundry does not supply enough clean towels or bed sheets. Engineering cannot replace a defective light switch in a guest room if housekeeping does not report the problem. Effective management of this busy department calls for standardized plans, procedures, schedules, and deadlines, as well as frequent direct communication between the executives who manage the key operating units of the rooms department.

### *Security*

The hotel and lodging business is vulnerable to security and safety problems. Problems can be created by guests, employees, or intruders. Security breaches can result in embezzlement, theft, arson, robbery, and even terrorism. Depending on the size of a hotel or a lodging establishment, the security function may be handled by a fully staffed department on site, contracted to an outside security company, or assigned to designated staff members or on-premises supervisory personnel in the rooms department. In a larger, full-service hotel, the director of security may report directly to the general manager. In smaller hotels, the security function might become a task of the rooms department.

### *Engineering.*

Typically, the engineering department's responsibilities include preventive maintenance; repair; replacement; improvement and modification to furniture, fixtures, and equipment (FFE); and ensuring uninterrupted provision of utilities (gas, electricity, water). Preventive maintenance involves routine checks and inspection of the key components of all equipment.

Maintenance of recreational facilities may be part of the engineering department's responsibilities. In particular, swimming pools require extensive maintenance to ensure proper filtration and to prevent the accumulation of algae and other conditions unsuitable for swimming.

Prompt repair minimizes loss of productivity in other hotel operating departments and inconvenience to hotel guests. When a particular FFE has reached the end of its useful life and repair is no longer cost-effective, replacement is indicated. Improvement projects enhance the existing operation or reduce operating costs of the facility. Modification projects alter the existing operation to accommodate one or more new functions.

One hotel might have a large engineering staff that includes plumbers, carpenters, painters, electricians, and other technicians. Another might have maintenance personnel who have general knowledge and understanding of the hotel's operations but rely on outside contractors for specialized jobs. In larger, full-service hotels, engineering may be a separate department, with a director who reports directly to the resident manager.

The primary function of the food and beverage department is to provide food and drink to a hotel's guests. In earlier times, when an inn had a single dining room that could hold a limited number of guests, this was a fairly simple task. Today, however, providing food and drink is much more complicated.

A large hotel might well have a coffee shop, a gourmet restaurant, a poolside snack bar, room service, two banquet halls, and ten function rooms where food and beverages are served. It might also have a lounge, a nightclub, and a lobby bar. On a busy day (or night), it's quite likely that functions will be booked in many outlets at the same time. In addition, some outlets may have multiple events scheduled for a single day. As you can see, there is great diversity in the types of activities performed by a food and beverage department, requiring a significant variety of skills on the part of its workers.

## Food Department

Because of the diversity of services provided, the food and beverage department is typically split into subunits. The executive chef, a person of considerable importance and authority in any full-service hotel, runs the food production, or kitchen, department. A variety of culinary specialists who are responsible for different aspects of food preparation report to the executive chef.

The actual serving of food in a large hotel's restaurants is usually the responsibility of a separate department, headed by the assistant food and beverage director. The food service department is composed of the individual restaurant and outlet managers, maitre d's, waiters, waitresses, and bus help. Because of their special duties and concerns, many large hotels have a separate subunit that is responsible only for room service. Because of the high value and profit margins associated with the sale of alcoholic beverages, some hotels have a separate department that assumes responsibility for all outlets where alcoholic beverages are sold. The person responsible for this department is the beverage manager.

Most full-service hotels also do a considerable convention and catering business. The typical convention uses small function rooms for meetings and larger rooms for general sessions, trade shows, exhibits, and banquets. As a hotel or lodging business increases the use of its facilities for conventions and meetings, it may form a separate convention services department.

The convention services department and its personnel are introduced to the client, a meeting planner, or an association executive by the marketing and sales department. The convention services department then handles all of the client's meeting and catering requirements. Individually catered events include parties, wedding receptions, business meetings, and other functions held by groups. To provide for the unique needs of these types of customers, hotels often organize separate catering and convention departments. Depending on the size of the hotel, the job of cleaning the food and beverage outlets themselves as well as of washing pots and pans, dishes, glasses, and utensils is often delegated to a subunit known as the stewarding department.

It is only through continuous cooperation and coordination that a hotel's food service function can be carried out effectively. A guest who is dining in a hotel restaurant requires the joint efforts of the kitchen, food service, beverage, and stewarding departments. A convention banquet cannot be held without the efforts of the convention and catering department along with the food production, beverage, and stewarding departments. The sequence of events and cooperation required among the food and beverage staff is even more important than in the rooms department, thus increasing the importance of communication between managers and employees alike.

Another challenge faced by management is the diversity of the employees in the food and beverage department; the dishwasher in the stewarding department is at a dramatically different level than the sous chef in the kitchen. Coordination is not as important an issue in the marketing and sales department, which is generally much smaller than the food and beverage department. The primary responsibility of the sales managers who make up the marketing and sales department is sales, or the selling of the hotel facilities and services to individuals and groups. Sales managers sell rooms, food, and beverages to potential clients through advertising, attendance at association and conference meetings, and direct contacts.

The marketing and sales department is also removed from most of the day-to-day operational problems faced by other departments. The division of work among the sales managers is based on the type of customers a hotel is attempting to attract. Individual sales managers often specialize in corporate accounts, conventions, or tour and travel markets. Sales managers' accounts are sometimes subdivided along geographical lines into regional or national accounts. The sales staff of the largest full-service hotels usually does not exceed a dozen or so. These sales managers work more or less independently in their particular market segments.

The human resources department serves no customers, books no business, and prepares no meals, yet it plays a vital role in a hotel's efficient operation. The three functions of the human resources department are employee recruitment, benefits administration, and training. The director of human resources is also expected to be an expert on federal and state labour laws and to advise managers in other departments on these topics. The human resources department's major challenge is in its interactions with other hotel departments. Although the human resources department recruits, interviews, and screens prospective employees, the final hiring decision rests within the department in which the potential employee will be working. The same is true of promotion and disciplinary decisions; the human resources department's input is, in most cases, limited to advice and interpretation of legal questions.

The human resources department's effectiveness depends on its manager's ability to form effective working relationships with managers of other departments. In many hotels, the accounting department combines staff functions and line functions, or those functions directly responsible for servicing guests. The accounting department's traditional role is recording financial transactions, preparing and interpreting financial statements, and providing the managers of other departments with timely reports of operating results (line functions). Other responsibilities, carried out by the assistant controller for finance, include payroll preparation, accounts receivable, and accounts payable (staff functions). Another dimension of the accounting department's responsibilities deals with various aspects of hotel operations, cost accounting, and cost control throughout the hotel.

The two areas of central concern to the accounting department are rooms and food and beverage. The accounting department's front office cashier is responsible for tracking all charges to guest accounts. At the close of each business day, which varies by hotel but typically occurs at midnight or after the bulk of guests' transactions have been completed (i.e., check-in, restaurant charges, retail charges, etc.), the night auditor is responsible for reconciling all guest bills with the charges from the various hotel departments.

Although the front office cashier and the night auditor physically work at the front desk and, in the case of the cashier, have direct contact with guests, they are members of the accounting department and report to the assistant controller of operations.

The food and beverage department may be responsible for food preparation and service, but the accounting department is responsible for collecting revenues. The food and beverage controller and the food and beverage cashiers keep track of both the revenues and expenses of the food and beverage department. The food and beverage controller's job is to verify the accuracy and reasonableness of all food and beverage revenues. In addition to tracking and preparing daily reports on the costs of the food and beverages used in the hotel, in many cases the accounting department is also responsible for purchasing and storeroom operations.

Finally, the director of systems is responsible for designing the accounting and control systems used throughout the hotel. As you can see, the accounting department is anything but a passive staff unit contending with routine recordkeeping. The accounting department is also responsible for collecting and reporting most of a hotel's operational and financial statistics, which provide important data for decision making and budget preparation purposes.

The head of the accounting department may report not only to the hotel's general manager but also to the hotel chain's financial vice president or to the hotel's owner. The reason for this dual responsibility and reporting relationship is to afford the hotel corporation an independent verification of the financial and operating results of the hotel. In addition to being in charge of overseeing all of the departments that we have discussed, the hotel's general manager (GM) is responsible for defining and interpreting the policies established by top management.

The general manager serves as a liaison to the hotel's owner or corporate parent, sets (or communicates) the overall strategic course of the hotel, sets hotel-wide goals, coordinates activities between departments, and arbitrates interdepartmental disputes. It is common practice in a large, full-service hotel for a director of public relations to report directly to the GM. The GM also has corporate-level responsibilities, participates on civic boards and committees, and engages in industry-related activities such as serving on the local tourism commission or hotel-motel association.

In addition to possessing a high level of technical skill (i.e., a thorough understanding of each operating department in the hotel), the general manager must also be decisive, analytical, and skilled with both computers and people. He or she must be able to see the big picture and how all of the parts of the hotel fit into the overall organization. An executive may be promoted to relieve the general manager of some operational duties. This is often accomplished by elevating the duties and responsibilities of one particular department head without relieving that person of regular departmental duties.

The title of this position is usually resident manager. It is quite common (and logical) for the general manager to select the manager of the rooms department to be resident manager. Responsibilities of the resident manager include serving as acting GM in the GM's absence, representing the GM on interdepartmental hotel committees, and taking responsibility for important special projects such as major hotel renovations, VIP guests, and operating reports that require in-depth analysis for the regional or corporate offices.

**Patterns of Authority**

The delegation of authority creates a chain of command, the formal channel that defines the lines of authority from the top to the bottom of an organization. The chain of command consists of a series of relationships from the highest position in the organization to the lowest. The chain of command specifies a clear reporting relationship for each person in the organization and should be followed in both downward and upward communication. Following the chain of command enables each new employee, no matter what his or her position, to know exactly for whom and to whom he or she is responsible.

When designing an organizational structure, managers must consider the distribution of authority. Defined simply, authority is the organizationally sanctioned right to make a decision. Authority can be distributed throughout an organization or held in the hands of a few select employees. Decentralization is the process of distributing authority throughout an organization. In a decentralized organization, an organization member has the right to make a decision without obtaining approval from a higher-level manager. Centralization is the retention of decision-making authority by a high-level manager. Traditionally, hotel and lodging management has been very centralized, probably due to its roots in small, owner-operated lodging. In recent years, as the hotel and lodging industry has expanded, decentralization has become a more frequent style of operation.

Decentralization has several advantages. Managers are encouraged to develop decision-making skills, which help them advance in their careers. The autonomy afforded by this style of operation also increases job satisfaction and motivation. When employees are encouraged to perform well, the profitability of the organization increases. Many hotel and lodging organizations have begun to empower employees and supervisors to make decisions that typically have been made by managers.

One example that we have already discussed is the use of the quality circle. For example, if a front desk agent determines that a guest's bill is incorrect, in a decentralized organization the agent has the power to make the correction immediately.

If that same front desk agent determines that a guest's stay has been unsatisfactory, he or she has the power to reduce the guest's bill by an amount previously specified by management.

Additional challenges, control of the process, and quality assessment become part of everyone's job, and each employee is given the authority to take positive actions that will lead to high quality and improved performance.

### Span of Control

Span of control refers to the number of people who report to one manager or supervisor. A wide span of control results in a flat organization— that is, a large number of employees reporting to one supervisor. A narrow span of control results in a tall organization, in which a small number of employees report to a supervisor, necessitating a larger number of supervisors. No formula exists for determining the ideal span of control. The following factors determine the most appropriate span of control: task similarity, training and professionalism, task certainty, frequency of interaction, task integration, and physical dispersion.

When a large number of employees perform similar tasks, the span of control can be increased. When the employees perform very different tasks, the supervisor must give each subordinate more individual attention in order to keep in touch with the different types of tasks; this requires a narrower span of control.

For example, the rooms department manager might easily manage the front desk agents and housekeepers until the brand standards for check-in or checkout of a guest increase in complexity and the standards for the various types of rooms and their cleaning procedure increase in detail. At this time, the rooms department manager's span of control must be narrowed. The better trained and more skilled a subordinate is, the less supervision is required. For example, a front desk agent might require a higher level of training and skill than a room service waiter. Thus, a front desk supervisor can supervise more employees (wider span of control) than the room service supervisor (narrower span of control).

Task certainty refers to the predictability of a task. Routine tasks allow management to devise standard procedures for subordinates to follow, minimizing questions about the job and widening the span of control. On the other hand, close supervision is called for when tasks are ambiguous and uncertainty is great. For example, the task of checking a guest in or out of the hotel can be documented and standard procedures can be created, so the front desk manager can have a relatively wide span of control over the front desk agents.

However, because of the diversity of customers the sales manager encounters, the tasks of a hotel sales manager are less certain. The director of sales is responsible for coaching the sales managers, observing sales calls, and ensuring deal closings; these tasks require a hands-on approach that limits the number of employees the director of sales can handle, narrowing the span of control.

If the supervisor-subordinate relationship requires frequent interaction, the span of control must be narrow. If interaction is infrequent, the span of control can be wide. For example, the hotel controller must review regularly the status of collections and payments with staff.

In contrast, the frequency of interaction between the chief engineer and his or her subordinates is directed by written work orders in most circumstances and thus requires less direct communication, enabling a wider span of control.

If the supervisor must integrate and coordinate the tasks of subordinates, the span of control narrows. For example, in the production of a meal for one table of four guests with different appetizers, salads, and entrées, the chef must have a narrow span of control to ensure that each component of the meal is assembled correctly and delivered to service personnel on a timely basis. The span of control of the executive housekeeper can be much wider because the procedure for cleaning and preparing each guest room is similar, if not exactly the same, for every room.

Physical dispersion refers to the distribution of employees within the lodging establishment. For example, if the executive housekeeper has guest room attendants on 20 floors in two buildings and the front desk manager has all front desk agents located in one place, the span of control would narrow for the executive housekeeper and widen for the front desk manager.

The ideal number of people that one person can supervise depends on a variety of factors. Consistent with trends in organizational structure such as teams, quality circles, and employee empowerment, many hotel and lodging organizations are widening their span of control. The objective behind these trends is to develop a flatter, more responsive organizational structure in which employees can make decisions without going through several levels of management.

**Functional Organisation Design**

The most important strength of a functional organizational design is efficiency. The performance of common tasks allows for work specialization, which increases overall productivity. Workers develop specialized skills and knowledge more rapidly. Training is easier because of the similarity of tasks and the resulting opportunities for inexperienced workers to learn from experienced workers. This helps new employees quickly learn the kinds of behaviour that lead to success and promotion. Coordination of activities within functional departments is easier than in more broadly based organizations.

A functional organization fosters efficiency, teamwork, and coordination of activities within individual units. However, the functional organization's most important strength is also the source of its greatest shortcoming. The success of a hotel as a business is measured by its overall performance and not by the performance of any one department. A hotel with spotless guest rooms will not be successful if guests' front desk experiences are not up to par. Even if guests' dining experiences are superb, the hotel will fall flat on its face if its rooms are dismal.

It is sometimes difficult for each department to fully appreciate its role in the overall success of the organization. It is vital that each department keep in mind the hotel-wide goals of customer service and profitability rather than focus narrowly on its own concerns. Some means must be found to coordinate the activities of functional departments and to set hotel-wide strategies and goals. A hotel's functional organization demands strong leadership.

New initiatives in hotels often require cooperation and coordination between functional departments. New ideas tend to be stillborn if department heads lack a hotel-wide perspective or have difficulty coordinating their activities. The tendency to concentrate on doing things right often overshadows the organization's ability to do the right thing.

The GM, as the chief executive of the hotel, emerges as the single person capable of providing the overall organizational direction, decision making, coordination, and arbitration needed to make a hotel's functional departments work together effectively. A hotel simply cannot run itself from the departmental level. Thus, the GM must be a strong leader to be effective.

## Meetings and Committees

An organizational chart is useful in identifying the formal reporting and authority relationships of a hotel or a lodging enterprise. However, it is not of much help in coordinating administrative units at the department and subdepartment level.

Consider this scenario. If the director of sales increases group bookings without consulting other hotel departments, a disaster is in the making. If the reservations department is not consulted, the sales department might guarantee more rooms to a group than are actually available at a price lower than the reservations department's quarterly goal. If the convention services manager is not consulted, necessary meeting rooms might not be available.

If the food and beverage department is not consulted, the group might be sold a banquet that exceeds the hotel's capabilities. If the accounting department is not consulted, credit terms might be extended that violate the credit manager's policies. If the front office is not consulted, the group might experience lengthy delays at check-in (groups are usually preassigned rooms and keys).

The executive operating committee (EOC) of a hotel, made up of the general manager and senior executives from each department, is designed to increase the level of coordination between departments. There is no standard membership for this committee, but it usually comprises those executives who report directly to the general manager. The EOC is also responsible for a hotel's major budgetary units, such as the food and beverage and housekeeping units. EOC functions depend on how the hotel GM chooses to use the group, the GM's style, and the structure of other management meetings in the hotel.

Typically, the EOC meets weekly, focusing on matters ranging from day-today operational issues (daily function schedules and labour and food cost control) to comparing budgets with actual operating results. Many hotels increase communications through an elaborate structure of additional committees and meetings, including some or all of the following: operations, staff, sales forecast and marketing, departmental, subdepartmental, credit, safety, energy conservation, and employee meetings.

The operations committee comprises the general manager, department heads, front office manager, manager on duty, and representatives from housekeeping, security, engineering, and food and beverage. This committee might meet four or five times per week for 15 to 20 minutes to review upcoming activities and assess the results of previous activities.

The staff committee might include the GM, department heads, and all subdepartment heads who report to the department heads. This committee, which might meet weekly for one or two hours, reviews the prior week's performance, the current week's activities, the next week's plans, and special projects. The staff committee also presents performance awards to employees.

The sales forecast and marketing committee might meet one to four times per month for several hours so the GM and department heads can review room demand for the coming 90 days and devise strategies to increase room nights (and thus bring in more revenue) and to increase average daily rates by up-selling potential guests to higher-rated rooms with perhaps more amenities or services.

The departmental committee consists of the department head and his or her subdepartment heads, managers, and supervisors. Meeting once or twice per month for an hour or so, the group reviews departmental issues. Similarly, subdepartment committees meet monthly for about an hour so the subdepartment head, managers, and supervisors can address issues unique to their subdepartment, such as the selection of a new type of floor cleaner by the housekeeping department or a more energy-efficient light bulb by the engineering department.

The credit committee includes the general manager, the controller, sales, the front office, reservations, catering, and the credit manager. Meeting monthly for an hour, the committee reviews those guests and clients of the hotel who were granted credit but have not settled their account. The safety committee typically comprises representatives from human resources, food and beverage, housekeeping, and engineering. Meeting monthly for an hour or so, the committee reviews safety programmes and safety records, addresses problems, and discusses the implementation of new safety regulations.

In some full-service hotels, an energy conservation committee includes the chief engineer, resident manager, food and beverage staff, human resource representatives, rooms staff, and housekeeping representatives. The committee typically meets monthly for an hour to discuss strategies and programmes for controlling energy costs. Most full-service hotels convene a monthly meeting or at least an annual meeting of all hotel management and employees to review performance and to distribute awards. This event ranges from an hourlong meeting to a company-wide celebration lasting several hours.

## THE FUTURE ORGANIZATION OF HOTELS

As new business practices are evolving as fast as our technologies, resistance to change has become a primary cause of business failure. The future success of a hotel will be driven in large part by the ability to foresee and capitalize on change. As we go through global transitions, the successful hotel will examine the key factors that will not only define success but also the ability to survive in coming years. These key organizational trends must be acknowledged by the successful hotel organization: visionary leadership, globalization, diversity, flexibility, flat structure, customer focus, zero defects, network orientation, and being in the information fast lane.

The organization must be able to respond to increasingly globalized sales, the movement to maintaining sales offices in many countries and hotel properties across the globe, and an increasingly globalized labour market. Intercontinental Hotels Group recently introduced a new organization structure to more efficiently use regional and global resources to drive higher levels of innovation, customer focus, and revenues.

Diversity means the organization must respond to a workforce that is heterogeneous sexually, racially, and chronologically; innovation and conflict/communication issues; and different styles of interaction, dress, presentation, and physical appearance. Flexibility in the modern hotel organization means assuring that systems, processes, and people can respond differently to different situations; fewer detailed rules and procedures; greater autonomy and encouragement of initiative; customizing employment relationships to include telecommuting and job-sharing; and lifetime employability rather than lifetime employment.

The trend toward flatness in hotel organizations means fewer levels of management, workers empowered to make decisions, and fewer differences in responsibility. The organization's employees need to believe in a sense of entrepreneurship that reacts proactively to market diversity. Traditional organizations that follow well-documented rules must give way to leaders who can balance a sense of discipline with one of flexibility.

If the customer is king or queen in the 21st century, hotel organizaions will be best served by focusing less on their hotel assets as measures of success and more on their customers. This involves a fundamental shift from viewing the real estate asset as the wealth creator to seeing the customer as the key to building shareholder wealth. A customer focus must reflect business decisions at all levels of developing and operating a hotel organization. Pursuing such a course will inevitably impact shareholder wealth.

The Japanese concept of zero defects in products and services can yield tremendous benefits for a hotel business organization. In practical terms, the hotel industry finds it extremely difficult to meet the standard of zero defects in service. Hotel services are based primarily on people, not on computers or other equipment. Twenty years ago, a business executive did not expect a consistent and predictable level of service wherever he or she traveled.

Today that is the standard, not the exception, as is the expectation of sophisticated technology in hotel rooms to support business needs. With customer discrimination so acute, it is not surprising that brand loyalty is a diminishing commodity in the hotel industry. Today's hotel organization must recognize the need for visionary leadership. The old command-and-control model of leadership is giving way to a focus on leadership in ideas, information, inspiration, vision, and teamwork. A failing hotel organization is overmanaged and underled.

The networked hotel organization can facilitate direct communication across unit and property boundaries, ignoring the chain of command; cross-unit team structures; outsourcing and downsizing; strategic alliances with competitors and others; customization; and decentralization. Being in the information fast lane is critical. The traditional role of information technology as a back office support for accounting and bookkeeping has clearly moved to front and centre stage. Information technology today influences all aspects of business from corporate strategies to organizational structure.

Technology was once viewed as a way to reduce costs by replacing people. That attitude has been firmly supplanted by the idea of seeking information technology support for the creative work all organizations must pursue. Information technology must enable organizations to react more speedily to market needs and, of course, produce the fulfillment of customer demands both quickly and accurately. To do this it must operate on a decentralized basis. Information technology delivers, but it has to deliver the right information to the right people at the right time.

## The Hotel Staffing System

Staffing, which is one of a hotel's most important management functions, is an ongoing challenge because of the high rate of employee and manager turnover. Full-service hotels can experience annual turnover rates in excess of 100 per cent in certain employee classifications. Some managers consider an annual employee turnover rate of 33 per cent low. (In other words, in a single year, one-third of a hotel's employees must be replaced.) At this rate, the entire hotel must be completely restaffed every three years. The higher the turnover rate, the larger the number of employees who must be replaced. For example, if a hotel with 450 employees has a 75 per cent annual turnover rate, it will be completely restaffed every 16 months.

In an attempt to reduce employee turnover, hotel and lodging businesses are giving increasing attention to job design, seeking to enhance those job characteristics that give the employee the greatest satisfaction and motivation. Good job design must take into account the needs of employees as well as the demands of the job. Well-thought-out job design begins when management conducts a job analysis—that is, a thorough evaluation of the specific tasks performed for a particular job and the time required to perform them. Job analysis is an ongoing process, as many jobs change with improvements in technology and pressure to improve product quality.

The job analysis is the basis for the job description and job specification. A job description includes the job title, pay, a brief statement of duties and procedures, working conditions, and hours. The job specification is an outline of the qualifications necessary for a particular job. In response to the limits of specialization, organizations can redesign jobs to improve coordination, productivity, and product quality while responding to an employee's needs for learning, challenge, variety, increased responsibility, and achievement.

Such job redesign often involves job rotation, the systematic movement of employees from one job to another; job enlargement, an increase in the number of tasks an employee will do in the job; job enrichment, the attempt to give the employee more control over job-related activities; and flextime, a flexible work schedule that permits employee input in establishing work schedules. In team-driven job redesign, a concept similar to job rotation, employees can transfer back and forth among teams that provide different services or products.

Hotels recruit employees from a variety of sources. Newspapers and employee referrals are used to recruit nonskilled hourly employees. Supervisory and management employees generally are recruited through colleges and universities, promotions from within, professional associations, and management recruiters. Hotels that take more time in making their selections are more successful in retaining employees.

Discussions of employee training and development often concentrate on training techniques without giving a full explanation of what a hotel is trying to accomplish. As training and development impart job skills and educate employees, supervisors, and managers, they also improve current and future employee performance, which affects the bottom line. Effective training includes problem solving, problem analysis, quality measurement and feedback, and team building.

Performance evaluation, also called performance appraisal, is the systematic review of the strengths and weaknesses of an employee's performance. The major difficulty in a performance appraisal is quantifying those strengths and weaknesses. The performance of some jobs is easy to quantify, while for others it is more difficult. An important part of the appraisal process is a well-established job description, so that the employee and the supervisor have similar expectations.

Compensation includes the monetary and nonmonetary rewards that managers, supervisors, and employees receive for performing their jobs. In order to set compensation levels, the human resources department must periodically conduct job evaluations, which determine the value of the job to the hotel. Knowledge of the value of the job to the organization and of wage rates for each job classification allows the hotel to establish a fair compensation policy.

If you complete your course of study and graduate with a bachelor of science degree in hotel management, most likely you will enter the business at the managerial level. Along the way you will have learned that a successful manager provides clear direction, encourages open communication, coaches and supports people, provides objective recognition, establishes ongoing controls, follows up and gives subordinates feedback, selects the right people to staff the organization, understands the financial implications of decisions, encourages innovation and new ideas, gives subordinates clear-cut decisions when needed, and consistently demonstrates a high level of integrity.

There are three levels of management careers in the hotel or lodging business: first-line, middle, and top. First-line refers to those who have day-to-day contact with the guests and clients of a lodging business. The first-line manager oversees the work of the supervisors and line employees. In a hotel or lodging business, first-line positions may include assistant manager of housekeeping, assistant front office manager, and assistant restaurant manager.

First-line managers are responsible for a hotel's basic work, such as checking guests in and out, making up the guests' rooms, and preparing and serving the meals. First-line managers are in daily or near-daily contact with line employees. Middle management of most hotel or lodging businesses includes the department manager, general manager, and any position between those levels.

Depending on the size of the hotel, the regional manager (who supervises the general managers of the hotels in his or her region) can also fall into this category. Unlike first-line managers, those in middle management plan, organize, lead, and control other managers' activities and are responsible for the performance of their departments. Top management comprises a small group of managers such as the chief executive officer, president, or vice president.

Top management is responsible for the performance of the entire hotel business as well as for supervision of the middle managers. The top manager is accountable to the owners of the financial resources used by the organization, such as the stockholders or executive board.

As you have already seen, there are numerous attractive careers in the hotel and lodging business. The following is one of the many paths your career might follow:

1. Assistant manager of the reservations department
2. Reservations department manager

3. Rooms department manager
4. Resident manager
5. General manager
6. Regional manager

In a full-service hotel or lodging business, the movement from entry-level position to general manager might encompass 15 years. Career advancement in a limited-service hotel or lodging business can occur more rapidly. A career in a limited-service hotel or lodging establishment might commence at the assistant general manager level, with movement to general manager within three years and to district or regional manager within five to eight years. This accelerated pace is due in large part to the more restricted range of services the manager must master before advancing.

The four basic components of organizational structure include job specialization, departmentalization, patterns of authority, and span of control. Job specialization includes increased worker productivity and efficiency, but it increases the need for managerial control and coordination. Work teams can be used to alleviate the routine caused by job specialization. A similar concept, the quality circle, can also enhance employee productivity.

The departments of a full-service hotel and lodging establishment include rooms, food and beverage, marketing and sales, human resources, and accounting. These departments report directly to the general manager or to a resident manager who is responsible to the general manager. In smaller hotel or lodging businesses, the audit, front desk, housekeeping, maintenance, and sales departments all might report directly to the general manager.

While patterns of authority remain centralized in many hotel or lodging businesses, increasingly employees have become empowered to make decisions that typically have been made by managers. Decentralization is the distribution of authority throughout an organization. Centralization is the retention of decision-making authority by a high-level manager. Span of control refers to the number of people who report to one manager or supervisor. In a narrow span of control, fewer subordinates report to each supervisor, resulting in a tall organization. In a wide span of control, a larger number of subordinates report to each supervisor, resulting in a flat organization.

The level of coordination and communication between departments can be increased by the activities of committees. The executive operating committee includes the general manager and designated department heads. Other committees include operations, staff, sales forecasting and marketing, departmental, subdepartmental, credit, safety, and energy conservation. Larger organizations conduct an annual meeting for all employees of the organization, to discuss company performance and to distribute awards.

Staffing is an ongoing challenge in the hotel and lodging industry because of the high percentage of employee turnover. Successful staffing depends on providing adequate job descriptions, including job specifications, as well as realizing that job descriptions must be flexible. In some cases, it becomes necessary to redesign jobs; this can involve job rotation, job enlargement, job enrichment, and flextime.

Employees must be properly trained; effective training includes problem solving, problem analysis, quality measurement, feedback, and team building. Successful managers enjoy certain common characteristics including providing clear direction, feedback, and recognition; encouraging open communication and innovation; and establishing ongoing controls. The management of a hotel or a lodging business falls into one of three categories: first-line, middle, or top.

# Index

## C



## D



## E